The Survival of Love

For Eileen

The Survival of Love

Memoirs of a Resistance Officer

by
JÓZEF GARLIŃSKI

Basil Blackwell

Copyright © Józef Garliński 1991

First published 1991

Basil Blackwell Ltd
108 Cowley Road, Oxford, OX4 1JF, UK

Basil Blackwell, Inc.
3 Cambridge Center
Cambridge, Massachusetts 02142, USA

British Library Cataloguing in Publication Data

A CIP catalogue record for this book is available from the British Library

Library of Congress Cataloging in Publication Data
Garliński, Józef.
   The survival of love : memoirs of a resistance officer / Józef Garliński.
      p.   cm.
   ISBN 0–631–17659–4
   1. Garliński, Józef.   2. World War, 1939–45 – Underground movements – Poland – Warsaw.   3. World War, 1939–45 – Personal narratives, Polish.   4. Warsaw (Poland) – History.   5. Soldiers – Poland – Biography.   6. Poland. Polskie Siły Zbrojne. Komenda Główna – Biography.   I. Title.
   D802.P62W3369   1991
   940.53'4384 – dc20
   DNLM/DLC   90–14548
                                                                                        CIP

Typeset in 11½ on 13½ Garamond by Acorn Bookwork, Salisbury
Printed in Great Britain by TJ Press, Padstow

Contents

List of Plates

Foreword

Józef Garliński is an eminent historian of the Second World War. In his many books, including *Poland, SOE and the Allies* (1969), *Fighting Auschwitz* (1975), *Intercept, Secrets of the Enigma* (1979) and *Poland and the Second World War* (1985), he has set out clearly and dispassionately the tragic fate of Poland during this war. The Polish people fought from the first to the last day of the war in Europe. Their losses were enormous in lives and in the destruction of the cultural resources of the past. Their courage was indomitable and their contribution to the Allied victory out of all proportion to the numerical size of the Polish people. And yet, the fruits of victory were denied to them. Poland passed from one occupation to another and any chance of free political evolution was snuffed out.

In this book, Józef Garliński tells the story of his own role during the war as a member of the Polish underground. The Polish resistance movement, subordinated to the legitimate Polish government, first in Angers and subsequently, from June 1940 in London, was, along with that in Yugoslavia, the largest in Europe. It aimed to build a new Poland, free of the defects which had been manifest in the interwar period and which were the result, above all, of the negative effects of five generations of foreign rule. It was primarily a movement of young people like Dr Garliński, himself, who joined as soon as he escaped from the German captivity into which he had fallen as a consequence of the campaign of September 1939. Within the resistance he rose to an important position, with responsibility for investigating the fate of those arrested by the Gestapo, and, if possible, securing their release. The men and women who created the Home Army

(*Armia Krajowa*), as the resistance movement came ultimately to be known, were brave, dedicated and without illusions. Their qualities emerge clearly in this moving book. They paid a heavy price for their commitment to the ideals of national independence and personal liberty. Dr Garliński describes, without bitterness, the two years he spent in Nazi Concentration Camps, first in Auschwitz itself and then in Neuengamme. But, as he is the first to point out, in this secret war, as in all wars, a heavy price, perhaps an even heavier one in this case, was also demanded of those who remained behind. Dr Garliński left behind his young Anglo-Irish wife, Eileen. This book is, as its title suggests, a record of their love for each other and of the persistence of that love in the face of overwhelming obstacles and difficulties.

It is also a book about the persistence of hope. Dr Garliński appeals to us to come to terms with the terrible atrocities of the past in the interest of creating a better future, in Europe and in the wider world. This persistence of hope has been justified. Communist rule has come to an end in East-Central Europe and Poland stands on the brink of a new era of freedom and democracy. An opportunity has been created in that the ideals for which the soldiers of the Home Army fought, can, at last, be realized. Dr Garliński, himself, was able in October 1990 to make his first trip since 1943 to his native country, where he was widely welcomed as an unyielding fighter for Polish independence and liberty. Sadly, Eileen, who died in spring 1990, could not accompany him. But her presence now, as during the war, will undoubtedly provide him with the inspiration to seek to achieve the high goals he has always set himself.

Antony Polonsky
London, 1991

Preface

During my interrogation at Warsaw Gestapo headquarters I was asked if I had a family.

'I have a wife' I answered and at that moment I saw with terrifying clarity Eileen in our miserable flat, lonely, defence-less . . .

For more than three years I had been engrossed in resistance work and only now, in the cellars of the Gestapo, did I understand how, through all that time, I had taken my wife for granted.

Many others had done the same.

From the moment of mobilization and our departure for the front we lived with the conviction that being a soldier conferred on us some special privilege. Since we were risking our lives in the defence of our country, we were less constrained by other worries or commitments. It was not that we did not love our families, but the mood of the moment was contagious and our partings were swift, our kisses hasty and our last words brief.

Perhaps some of us paused for thought when, defeated and humiliated, we managed to escape the German encirclement and steal back to our homes. There were loving hearts and welcoming arms which embraced and soothed taut nerves with a calm caress and a much-needed meal.

Hardly had we recovered from the emotions of the front, when we were caught up in the whirl of the developing resistance movement. The war forced upon us by our conquerors recognized no frontiers or international agreements; and it did not distinguish between the soldier and the woman. Our mothers, daughters, sisters and wives found themselves with us in the front line, which ran through the whole country. The dangers which awaited us also stalked them. Arrest threatened them at all times. At any moment they could find themselves in the hands of the Gestapo, in prison or concentration camps.

As I now sit in London, my thoughts turn back to Warsaw. We used to rush off early every morning to our places of work in the resistance, hungry but full of energy, tired but with a sense of the importance of our work, in danger but on the wings of hope. Behind us in our empty flats were the women. On their frail shoulders lay the burden of holding our home life together, finding food, looking for coal. The resistance reached out and set them secret tasks, of which even we were unaware. Yet they had to stay silent and suffer alone, in fear for our safety, and their hands could not betray any emotion when we came home at night. Without their love and without their silent, unseen sacrifices we would have got nowhere. To them I dedicate these memoirs, mostly written immediately after the war, while still strongly under the influence of my experiences.

I wrote what I saw and felt then; this is how it really was.

My memoirs, although written chronologically, are divided into chapters with separate titles. Each of these chapters is in itself a whole and that is why certain fragments, such as my arrest, the transport from prison in Warsaw to Auschwitz, are repeated.

J. G.
London, 1991

Introduction

The Second World War was started by Hitler when, on 1 September 1939, he attacked Poland. Before this attack he secured the co-operation of Soviet Russia and after the September campaign, up to June 1941, Poland was occupied by two powers. Only after the German attack on the Soviets, was Poland completely in Hitler's hands.

While in the West, in France, Belgium, Holland, Denmark and Norway, life under the German occupation was, to some extent, normal, things were different in Poland. There the Germans were looking for new land for expansion, and for cheap, almost slave labour. Therefore they furiously attacked the leading and educated classes. All universities, theatres, museums, radio stations, newspapers and even secondary schools were closed.

It was no wonder that, when underground activity in the West was concerned above all with sabotage, diversion and propaganda, in Poland it had to defend almost all the elements of normal national life.

Not only political activity, not only the army and propaganda connected with the war, but also education, the courts, the publication of books, the protection of cultural relics, theatre and the press had to exist as underground activities.

It is easy to imagine how partisan units operated, how the saboteurs attacked the German lines of communication, but it is much more difficult to understand how secret schools or secret theatres were organized. There were groups of students, no more than ten in each, who attended lectures in private flats and houses. Groups of actors produced plays in private homes and cellars.

1

Secret papers were printed literally 'underground' on presses hidden under blocks of flats and factories. Books were published in the same way. The most difficult problem was the delivery of the paper and distribution.

All these activities were difficult and dangerous because the Germans penetrated Polish society with the help of individuals, many of them Polish, prepared to betray their own people. It was nothing unusual. Occupying forces always use collaborators – without them occupation would be almost impossible.

In 1939 I was mobilized as a second lieutenant in reserve. On the same day that I left Warsaw with my regiment, I married Eileen, an Irish girl born in Liverpool, after we met through the most extraordinary coincidence. A distant female relative of mine had met her in England and invited her to Poland. We met and were engaged. I spoke no English. Eileen no Polish. We communicated in a mixture of German and French supplemented by the odd word of English or Polish.

Our marriage was the first of this kind between a British girl and a Pole during the Second World War. Eileen had been invited first to Katowice, in Polish Silesia, the most westerly part of the country. But the country house where we met was very different, typical of that part of Poland to the north-east of Warsaw which had been under Russian rule for more than a hundred years. There was no running water, no electricity, no bathroom, an outside lavatory, but there were a telephone and radio, horses and saddlery, a dozen dogs, a big garden and servants.

When I was fighting on the front Eileen worked in a military hospital in Warsaw. I was wounded and captured by the Germans, but escaped from a hospital which was under German supervision and returned to Warsaw. Eileen, thank God, had survived the siege and we were reunited – our first stroke of luck.

Many young people were leaving the country, trying to reach France where a new Polish army was being formed. We decided, however, to stay in Warsaw and to join the anti-German military underground movement.

After the first secret contacts and minor posts, I was nominated head of the security department of the headquarters of the 'Home Army', the secret military organization controlled by the Polish Government in London. My function was to protect the headquarters from the Gestapo, the German secret police.

My most important task was to make contact with the people who had fallen into the hands of the Gestapo. They were kept in the political prison, called *Pawiak*, or in the cellars of the Gestapo headquarters. The Germans were keeping Polish warders and Polish doctors for the time being and these were helpful in secret contacts. Another task was to penetrate the German police ranks, as well as to collect information on what was going on in the city. A special unit was used to liquidate the most dangerous spies after they were sentenced by the underground military court.

In April 1943 I was arrested by Gestapo agents, betrayed by my former schoolmate, but very fortunately that man did not know of my underground activity. The Germans were looking for somebody of the same surname.

I spent three weeks at Pawiak prison which was located in the centre of the Jewish district and exactly at that time the Jews started an uprising against the Germans.

The climate of terror was such that without any proof of guilt I was sent to Auschwitz.

There I was subjected to the most difficult ordeal, being sent to the penal company which was situated in the sub-camp Birkenau, where four big gas chambers and crematoria were in operation and where about three million people were killed.

We were allowed to send and receive one letter per month. The Germans were facing defeat, munition works were built in many camps and prisoners were allowed to receive food parcels to help to keep them fitter. I got many parcels from Eileen and my mother. This was also a link with them and with the free, outside world.

The first of August 1944 was a dramatic day. With the Red Army on the east side of the Vistula river, the Home Army started an Uprising against the Germans. I was sick with despair at not being there, fighting the Germans, but at the same time deeply fearful, because Eileen was there, at the heart of the fighting city.

Once again providence was on our side. Eileen survived the Uprising in which some 250,000 were killed, and I survived Auschwitz, having being sent to another camp, Neuengamme, near Hamburg. Finally, at the beginning of May 1945, I was freed by the American Army.

When the Red Army had totally occupied Poland, Eileen met up with some freed British prisoners of war and with them, as the only woman, travelled to Odessa in a Russian cattle truck. From there, on a British ship, *The Duchess of Richmond*, she travelled to Glasgow, where she landed in April 1945.

As she was the only non-Polish witness of the new Soviet occupation of Poland, she almost immediately began to travel around Britain as a member of the Duchess of Atholl's League of European Freedom, explaining to the exasperated British why Poles did not want to return to the Soviet 'paradise'.

At the same time, working for the Americans as interpreter, I contracted typhus and very nearly died of it. But I survived and finally got permission from the British authorities in Paris to go to England.

It was on 15 November 1945, that we were reunited in London: an unforgettable day!

During the Second World War about fifty million people were killed and many more suffered. Fate scattered them and created situations in which some perished and others became anonymous heroes of the world's folly.

If Eileen had not been invited to Poland, if we had not met, she probably would have served in the WRNS during the war or gone through it as a housewife, completely unknown.

But fate threw her into the very centre of the cyclone and then it transpired that in her frail body beat a big heart. Her loyalty to the country of her adoption, her courage, her trust and her love appeared to be stronger than the surrounding brutality, terror, suffering and death.

All this happened fifty years ago, but now, when so many changes are taking place in Europe, when so many countries that had been left in Stalin's hands regain their freedom, it seems that the sufferings and sacrifices of that time were not in vain.

We should not forget what happened at that time and it is our duty to hand down a precise picture of these events to the coming generations, but we should not give in to emotions when we return with our memories to the past. First of all we should forgive and rid our hearts of feelings of bitterness, which are destructive or the human tendency for revenge could well provoke these frightful things to happen again.

As a former Auschwitz inmate I am of the opinion that we should abandon the pursuit of war criminals and the hunt for the people responsible for the sufferings of others. It is almost impossible to prove their identity so many years after the war and a constant return to past atrocities makes understanding and good relations between nations very difficult.

One hopes that the unification of Europe is not so far away. When this happens, the nations of our continent will not only be safe from another world war, but they will have the chance for peaceful economic and cultural development.

Frontiers will not be important, revisionist problems will fade and rankling historic hatreds will die.

Chapter One

What of Tomorrow . . .?

We run through the streets, feverishly looking for a taxi. At last, a ramshackle old thing, with the driver sitting dejectedly at the wheel: no petrol. Today is 4 September 1939, the fourth day of the war. Warsaw has already experienced the first shocks of the approaching storm, decree upon decree has been imposed upon the city; the private life of the inhabitants is completely disorganized. Everything that breathes, walks, moves – everything of any value – now serves one cause alone: the war.

Although only the single star of a second lieutenant shines on my shoulder, my officer's uniform inclines the filling station to give our Ford a little petrol. We race to the Narutowicz Place. It is already 1.40 p.m. and our wedding is to take place at two o'clock. Eileen, small and fragile, has grown thin during the nervous excitement of the last few days, and sits beside me cuddling up to my arm. In an hour's time she will be my wife and ten hours later I shall leave the city to catch up with my regiment which is marching out this evening.

I still find it difficult to believe that I am marrying not a Polish girl, but one from distant England, which I have never visited and of which I know very little. I have only just begun to learn her language, she does not yet speak Polish, so we communicate in halting German. Her coming to Poland at the invitation of my distant cousin, our quite unexpected meeting, the mutual feeling which sprung up between us so quickly, all seems to me now almost unreal. Sometimes I have the feeling that I am standing outside my own body looking at myself holding a girl with black hair gently by the arm.

The formalities in the vestry take some time; war has hastened more than one decision. Young couples are crowding into the small waiting room, the clerk's pen flies over the paper until perspiration stands in beads on his forehead.

With a few of our closest friends we wait for the priest, who has disappeared somewhere. My father, also in uniform, is there, having arrived unexpectedly from Poznan the day before. He is only fifty and a major in the reserve, so he has been called up to a staff post.

'Your regiment is leaving Warsaw today?' he asks me.

'Yes, we are going to get our second line into formation'.

'For the time being that will be staff work. You are getting married today and at such a time one must live for the day. Perhaps you will be able to find a room and have your wife with you, while you are doing instructional duties.'

Among us there is a friend of my father's, the deputy chief of anti-aircraft defence for the whole country.

'What are our chances, colonel?'

The large face lights up in a cheerful smile. 'Fine, couldn't be better.'

At last the missing priest turns up. We go into the Gothic red brick church with its characteristically unfinished twin towers. They look, with their tops cut off, as if the infectious touch of war has already been in contact with them.

'Please be careful here' says the priest. Lying by the side door is a large unexploded bomb. I can't keep my thoughts from wandering. In front of the altar I try to put my wife's ring on my finger.

The mysterious future lies before us. The world is rocking on its foundations and seducing our young hearts with the promise of adventure. A period of trial is approaching which will sweep away, destroy, maybe the best, the most worthy to live. I can feel Eileen's fingers trembling as she touches my hand. Yesterday they trembled still more when, with bowed head, she listened to the voice from her distant homeland crackling over the air. Would England declare war, would she keep her word?

The ceremony comes to an end and at that very moment we hear the wail of distant alarm sirens. We go out in front of the church to see what is happening.

The square is empty. The last passers-by are running quickly into doorways, the unharnessed horses are standing quietly facing the carts and cabs, the air raid warders with armbands on their left arms and faces turned upwards are the only people on the pavements. More and more sirens take up the broken wail.

The sky is bright and clear and we can easily pick out a flock of silver birds. They are German Heinkels, circling over the city, coming lower and lower, surrounded by white plumes of exploding shells from ack-ack guns.

In front of us, in the centre of the city, clouds of smoke billow upwards, the ground quivers, the walls shake.

That evening I took leave of my father with few words, not thinking for a moment that I would not see him again. And a few hours later, as I was walking out of the door, I was momentarily detained by my wife's last words: 'I shan't make any attempt to get away, I shall stay in Warsaw. I will wait for you . . .'

The dawn was pale red; dew covered the still sleeping trees. I hurried through empty streets towards the unknown morrow.

Chapter Two

Tears

My injured back made it too difficult for me to bend down, but
fellow soldiers helped. They took off my trench coat and shirt,
which they tore into strips and used to tie up my bleeding
shattered foot as best they could. We were in a shallow ditch and
movement was restricted. Bursts of German machine gun fire
flew just over our heads. We had tried to break out in the
direction of the woods, but thick and tangled blackberry bushes
made it impossible. All we could do was wait.

I thought back over the events that had led me to the bottom
of the ditch in which I was now lying. My father's conjectures had
been wrong, and the colonel's optimistic views had turned out to
be far from accurate. The second wave of our guards' cavalry
regiment had had only three days (based in some villages to the
east of Warsaw) to get themselves into a state of battle-readiness.
The German attack in the north caused us to undertake a forced
march to the south-east before we had managed to arm and
organize ourselves adequately. In an improvised cavalry brigade,
without artillery, with a handful of anti-tank weapons, with very
few machine guns and with far less firepower than a comparable
German unit, we moved at night. During the day we hid in
copses or accepted unequal combat. On 17 September we heard
with taut hearts the radio announcement that the Red Army had
crossed our eastern frontier. There were some who believed that
it was coming to help us, but centuries of experience led most of
us to expect the worst.

On the day before the last attack our regimental commander
gathered all his officers together and told them, 'We are surrounded; tomorrow we will try to break through to the south;

anyone who can, should head for the Hungarian border. I shan't issue any further orders. Whoever wants to can go on, otherwise stay in Poland if you prefer.'

Our attack on the German positions had ended bloodily. Some of my closest friends died while I, wounded but lucky, limped along the exposed hillside peppered by whistling German bullets, eventually reaching the safety of the ditch.

Several minutes passed, the firing died away and footsteps and voices were heard nearby. Unfortunately they were not talking in Polish.

'Weg, Weg! Hände hoch!' (Stand aside! Hands up!)

Bayonets appeared above the edge of the ditch, followed by sinister dark green helmets and ruddy faces. 'Hände hoch! Waffen?' (Hands up! Weapons?)

We raised our hands and my colleagues began to climb out of the ditch. Two of them helped me get up and clamber out. I put my arms around their shoulders and, hanging heavily, began to move down the hill on one leg towards the village. Men from the German infantry closely surrounded us. One of them took my map case, another grabbed the watch from my wrist. We reached a crossroads and there I was allowed to sit down on the shaft of an upturned cart.

A dozen or so metres behind me a peasant hut was burning. Two small barefooted boys were standing beneath a dwarf cherry tree staring wide-eyed at the raging fire. Nearby a young woman was kneeling on the ground against an upturned box sobbing pitifully. On the road German vehicles roared along. I reached into the top pocket of my uniform and pulled out a small wallet. When I opened it several photographs fell onto the ground. I picked them up with difficulty: Theatre Square in Warsaw, snow-covered holiday mountains, tennis in the country.

A German soldier walked over and struck me sharply on the shoulder. 'What have you got?'

He took the wallet, looked at it, took out the money, glanced at the photographs for a moment and then screwed them up and threw them on the fire. He then returned the wallet with an ironic smile.

Dusk fell. The fire behind me died slowly. The woman

stopped sobbing but did not move, as though she had lost all sense of time. The little boys had gone. In a fork of the road our soldiers, without their belts and spurs on, were finishing digging about a dozen shallow holes. The Germans brought their dead, laid them quickly in the graves, covered them over with dirt, stuck in boards with their names on and hung their helmets on top. An order rang out and two sections fired a volley in salute.

The German soldier again come over to me. 'You killed those brave young Germans. Now we must tell their mothers and wives. You bastards!'

I stared silently at his angry face. What could I say to him? Would he be able to understand that we too had our loved ones?

Chapter Three

Going Underground

The first real field hospital, set up in a children's sanatorium, contained hundreds of the wounded. Poles and Germans lay together in communal wards, tended by Polish nurses. The battle front moved on and for several days no one in authority bothered with us.

Eventually the occupiers took off their own wounded, loaded us into peasant wagons and drove us to Zamość, where several thousand wounded Poles, now prisoners of war, were assembled. Lying on the ground unarmed and incapable of much movement, we felt helpless. We already knew that Red Army divisions had invaded our country, with the complete agreement of the Germans, and in Zamość we experienced several days of Soviet administration when, as a result of frontier agreements, the town changed hands from one enemy to the other. Once again we were bundled into a convoy and transferred to a hospital in another town.

Six weeks later, when I could just manage to walk, I was discharged as unfit for active service, was given an official piece of paper and eventually, after a couple of days, reached the outskirts of Warsaw on a goods train. I knew that the city had been besieged and had resisted for many days; the whole country was full of rumours about terrible destruction and hundreds and thousands of dead.

It was 2 November and already in the ruins fires had been lit to the memory of those who died there. In the hospital I had had the time to think of my wife; I saw her slight figure as she embraced me on parting and I felt the touch of her hands. Now, my heart beating wildly, I approached the street where two

13

months before we had had to part. Was the tall apartment block still standing, did its inhabitants come through the seige, were many still alive?

This time we were both lucky. She was there, worried but well.

Without delay we set about organizing ourselves. Life as a married couple was only just beginning. We had nowhere to live, no work and no money.

Several weeks later, when we had found a small room, I came across some friends who were deeply involved in military resistance work.

'What are you up to?' they asked.

'Well, I've only just arrived and my leg is still giving me trouble. I'm trying to make ends meet.'

'But that isn't enough. Let's talk about it.'

Within a few days I became a soldier in an underground organization, which, like so many others, eventually joined the mainstream of military resistance that developed into what was later known as the Home Army. This organization was responsible to the new Polish Government, which had reformed on French soil and, after the collapse of the Western Front, had moved to London. The Polish General Staff was also based in London and new armed forces were being raised.

I did not imagine that, after my initial introduction and tasks, I would end up, at the end of 1941, in the counter-intelligence branch of the high command of the underground army, entrusted with running a top secret network maintaining communications with political prisoners in Warsaw who had been captured and imprisoned by the Gestapo. This was the beginning of a guerrilla war with the Nazi secret police, whose only rival in the field of precision and brutality was the Soviet NKVD.*

---

*Narodny Kommissariat Vnutrennich Dyel, the People's Commissariat for Internal Affairs.

Chapter Four

In the Jungle

We caught the last tram just before curfew. As usual it was full and we joined the overflow on the step, hanging on as it rattled down Czerniakow Street. Our destination was one of the outer suburbs.

Strictly speaking, in espionage or underground resistance, even the closest colleagues should not know each other's real names and addresses. But it's a small world and I was not particularly surprised one day to find that my immediate superior, Stefan,* had been forced to leave his former home and was now staying in a house opposite mine. We agreed that this proximity had its advantages. During the day the meetings we were able to arrange were always too short, so we decided to travel together on the last tram out to the suburbs where we lived. On the journey we pretended not to know each other, but when night fell we could walk about in the insignificant street – deserted just before curfew – for quite some time and discuss the day in detail. At the outskirts of the city, curfew was a rather relative concept.

That evening the sky was overcast but the frost remained sharp. It was towards the end of March 1942. Stefan let down the ear-flaps of his cap, thrust his hands deep into the pockets of his coat and carefully heard out my hurried, murmured report.

'I had the usual meeting with Sem† an hour ago: he didn't

---

*Stefan (code name) was the deputy head of counter-intelligence at the Home Army headquarters.
†Sem (code name) was at that time head of a unit responsible for the secret liaison with those arrested, and my immediate subordinate.

bring any news. Those urgent notes to the prison still haven't been sent.'

'Things have been strange with him for some time now. Have you set up your reserve liaison network?'

'Yes, but that's not all about Sem. He was very nervous today. I could see he had something important to say but at the same time I felt he was trying to hide something. I insisted he tell me everything. He had a most interesting encounter today.'

'Well?'

'Now listen, it's very important. Sem has in his unit a Pawiak prison warder whose code name is Jan.‡ He is Sem's best worker. As you know the Germans did not get rid of Polish warders and this makes contact with those arrested much easier. Well Jan reported to Sem the day before yesterday that some guy, high up in the underground and very hush-hush, wants to see Sem as quickly as possible. Anyone of us would have wanted to know a whole lot more and ask all sorts of questions. But you know Sem. He agreed to meet the fellow without even stopping to think. And that's not all: he arranged to have the meeting at his own place.'

'Well, and then?'

'This afternoon Jan piloted the man to Sem's place. He is about fifty years old, just over medium height, slim, with fairly long gingerish hair.'

Stefan clutched my arm. 'Any moustache?'

'Yes. Sem said he had the idea it was artificial, but the fellow seemed quite at ease with his long thick whiskers; said he was chief of intelligence in some independent organization and proposed that Sem collaborate with him on the prison sector.'

Stefan again seized my arm and stopped me walking. 'Can't you guess who it is?'

'No. Don't know enough about him.'

'Well, I know. I'm nearly sure it's Hammer!'

'That's impossible!'

'It's not; I am certain it is Hammer. Now, this is critical. We've

‡Jan (code name) was a prison warder at the Pawiak prison in Warsaw which was at that time controlled by the Gestapo.

got to deal with him finally, at all costs. The security of the high command depends on our efficiency. You keep close after Sem and watch him for all you're worth. He's got to tell us every detail connected with the meeting. What's very interesting is how Jan got to know Hammer? Get busy, too; set up your reserve liaison network and find out all you can about Jan – down to the slightest detail.'

That night was a rather sleepless one for me. Could the man really be Hammer? We had been trying to catch up with him for more than a year and though it always seemed to us that we were close on his heels, we had not succeeded. For that matter, we were not even sure where he was last, whether he was now in Warsaw, or what name he went under. But he was an old fox and was capable of evading us with apparent ease.

Joseph Hammer was no novice at his profession. He had been in Germany's pay during the First World War and had operated as an *agent provocateur* in Poland and the Ukraine. After the war he went to ground so effectively that his real identity was not discovered for some time; he even managed to establish relations with the Poles which were to facilitate his future activities. When the Second World War broke out Hammer at once seized the opportunity to fish in the muddy waters which had swamped the Polish Republic. He had the advantage of vast and varied experience, well-established contacts and, perhaps most important, he was familiar with the way the Germans tended to operate. Moreover he was ruthless.

The scope for Hammer's activity in Poland was relatively easy. Secret resistance organizations sprang up like mushrooms after rain from the first day of the Occupation. Most people seemed to belong to something and almost at once underground newspapers began to circulate. The cadres of various resistance units were rapidly organized and only later united and consolidated within the all-Polish Home Army. This offered a fertile field for sowing the seeds of intrigue and provocation. Within this still uncoordinated military and administrative activity, involving propaganda, information gathering and other work, an able spy could accomplish much. Hammer was now in his element. He set up a small but carefully selected staff. Some of these were agents like himself, but many of the others were well-meaning innocents who implicitly believed that their chief was authorized to carry out missions for the underground movement – the pretence he used to cover all his activities.

Hammer and his colleagues first went to work near the border. He organized pseudo-resistance, including secret societies for the smuggling of people, mostly officers, across the newly-formed German–Soviet frontier on the Ribbentrop–Molotov Line. The results came soon: large-scale arrests in the underground organizations, especially of youths, inexperienced in resistance. It was soon established that *agents provocateurs* were at work but Hammer's alibi was always unassailable. Later, when the many organizations merged into a few, it became difficult for Hammer to operate and he was forced to abandon this approach. Mass betrayals ceased on the frontiers and the atmosphere in this sector of underground activities became markedly clearer.

Suddenly, in the middle of 1941, a persistent rumour began to circulate in underground Warsaw until it reached the ears of the supreme headquarters of the Home Army. It affirmed that an unnamed colonel had come from England armed with authority from the sixth bureau of the Polish General Staff in London. He had been, it was alleged, entrusted with a very special task, a mission of supreme importance.

Our knowledge about Hammer's activity was very limited at that time; we did not link the new rumour with him, but – just in case – we approached our superiors and were told that nobody had been sent to Poland from London. Steps were taken to identify the 'colonel', whom we increasingly suspected was Hammer.

Such tasks as unmasking someone like Hammer were strictly speaking outside my competence. After many months in an autonomous resistance group I was transferred to the headquarters of the Home Army, to the intelligence department, with the clear directive to reorganize the unit responsible for contact with people arrested by the Gestapo. I had just started my work and was occupied with other problems, but the new developments were too important to be neglected. Stefan was almost certain that the man who had spoken to Sem, my subordinate and the head of the prison liaison network, was Hammer, and what Stefan said could not be disregarded. He had remarkable intuition.

The night dragged on and I could not fall asleep. My imagination was running wild: perhaps I would be the one to trap Hammer, despite the failure of our whole organization to pin him down so far.

I dozed off only a little, towards morning, and then got up and dressed quickly. My wife warmed some soup which I gulped down and then hurried to the tram stop. In spite of the lack of sleep I felt full of energy and enthusiasm. My work began with the usual daily routine: several meetings in town during the early morning followed by work in a room in a private flat which I used as my secret office, reading reports and letters from various departments of the headquarters of the Home Army with inquiries about arrested people, writing carefully encoded replies, secret letters written on cigarette paper, to be smuggled into prison, and then finally sending out the mail through a liaison messenger girl already waiting in the gateway of a house some doors away. All the correspondence I received daily, and there was a lot of it, reached me by a complicated chain of contacts and was collected by me or my deputy from a messenger girl outside my 'office'. Then, until late evening, meetings, conferences, conversations, briefings, oral reports, discussions. We worked without respite and without eating; for these there was no time nor money.

A meeting between Sem and myself had been arranged for 4 p.m. that day in one of the rooms that he kept in various flats for such occasions. I got on to what was on my mind after a few polite preliminaries. 'Will you, please, describe again your meeting with this unknown man, down to the last detail?'

'I told you all I could, yesterday.'

'Well, how did Jan get acquainted with him?'

'Right, I forgot to tell you that. Jan was so nervous yesterday, he shook with excitement.'

'But where did he get to know the man?'

'He didn't explain that clearly. Said only that he was very highly placed and a very important person.'

'Did they come together yesterday?'

'Yes . . . that is . . . no. Jan came a few minutes earlier to make sure everything was ready and then, a little after, the fellow with whiskers knocked at the door.'

'Were you covered? Did you have any guards around?'

Sem looked at me with surprise in his kind, blue eyes. 'What for? He's our man.'

'How do you know that? How can you be certain? Well, let's go on. How long have you known Jan? Is he absolutely a hundred per cent dependable?'

Sem jerked up with indignation. 'If you please . . . I'm as sure of Jan as I am of myself.'

'Good, but how long have you known him?'

'Must be getting on for a year. He's my best contact.'

'Did you swear him in?'

Sem blushed. 'Well . . . that is . . . I mean . . . I couldn't demand that people like Jan take the oath. I trust him absolutely. Why, it would be insulting him even to propose it!'

'Have you any other contacts who haven't been sworn in?'

'There's the women's section – but all of them are superlative workers.'

Sem continued, getting increasingly disquieted. 'I can't go on with this . . . It makes me . . . Won't you please stop this interrogation?'

'Just a moment. Was there anyone else present during the conversation?'

'Yes, my assistant, Diana. It was in her home that we had the talk.'

'One more question, the last one. What propositions did the man put to you?'

'He wanted to collaborate with my network of secret contacts with the Pawiak prison.'

'That's all?'

'Yes . . . well, rather, no. He asked if we could help him – just mentioned it by the way, you know – to contact supreme headquarters. Said one of his liaison lines had been broken.'

'All right, I see. And now listen carefully, please. Nobody suspects you or any of your colleagues, but something is wrong. The talk you had yesterday may be nothing at all, but it may also have the most serious consequences for the whole of supreme headquarters. I have been ordered to sort out this affair immediately. So please go straight home and contact nobody at all. We'll meet at the same time tomorrow at my place on Belweder Street. I'll see that you get a written order from the chief of intelligence. And before you get going, tell Diana that she's to vacate her home right away – you know, the place where you met Jan and this fellow. And here's money for that.'

Sem paled and began to fold and unfold the wad of banknotes in his hands. 'What's up? Why?'

'I'll tell you tomorrow. Don't forget to come punctually. So long.'

Late the same day I had a meeting with Stefan. He promised to send me a written order from the chief and once again told me to be very careful, 'Well, I think Hammer's gone too far this time. Sem and Diana must leave Warsaw tomorrow and you will take over their liaison network. But be particularly careful – the whole business stinks.'

On the following day Sem received an order from the chief of intelligence to hand over all his contacts to me and to leave Warsaw immediately. Diana was to do the same. The conversation we had was not a pleasant one.

'Can't this be fixed up in some other way? I can't sit around now doing nothing.'

'That can't be helped. How could you agree to meet an absolute stranger? You've exposed yourself. And what made you give away your contact point, and expose your assistant too? You've been terribly thoughtless. This is important work. We are all lucky that matters are no worse!'

'But it was Jan, Jan who introduced him to me and Jan has no doubts.'

'Now listen. It's the fourth year of the war. Haven't you gone through enough yet, haven't you learnt anything? And remember, the chief's order is clear. It's no joke.'

'Yes, yes, I know . . . O, Lord!'

He introduced me to Marcelle, who was to turn over all his contacts to me and the date and hour of the next meeting was fixed. Marcelle was scared. I went out feeling it would be very difficult to take over the whole system now put under my control.

For some weeks after that I was swamped with work. It was necessary to build up a new system for liaison and intelligence with the prison – one which could cope with everyday tasks and at the same time supply reliable information about Sem's co-workers. The field was a very complex though limited one. The Pawiak prison continually received an endless stream of new victims, and it became more and more difficult to establish contact with them. Yet this was essential for security reasons. The men's part of the prison was strictly guarded and here the difficulties encountered were particularly great. Every step had to be carefully considered, every situation sounded out. It was important too, that the new contacts should have no links with the old ones – those organized by Sem.

At the same time I had to investigate his network through Marcelle in order to find out just what was happening, and to what extent our people, including Marcelle, understood that something was wrong.

I had two meetings with the head of the women's section. She appeared to be an idealist, but was unrealistic, and had no idea of our present situation. It was almost certain that her network was infiltrated, that her contacts with the prison were in great danger and that we had to act quickly to save them. My problem was to get from her the necessary information, without telling her too much.

'Sem has unexpectedly had to leave Warsaw. Our chief has ordered me to take over his network.'

'Why has he gone away? I heard he received a special order to leave the city.'

'As you evidently already know something, or have guessed, I will tell you this: it's a top secret affair. Regardless of the outcome of our conversation, you must keep all this absolutely secret. That's the order issued by our superior officers.'

'You can be quite sure I will carry out the order. But what's happened? Why all these precautions?'

'We are afraid that our contacts with the prison have been infiltrated.'

'No, no, it is impossible! Tell me more about it.'

'I can't do it now. Listen. Taking over Sem's system, I must know whom I'm to work with. How many people have you at your disposal?'

'Five wardresses, one of whom contacts me.'

'Now please listen carefully. There's no question of my undermining the confidence that we have in you, but the situation we have to face is most exceptional. I should like to know the name of the group leader.'

'Do you want to know her real name?'

'Yes, And, in addition, her rank, age, appearance and so on.'

She looked at me coldly. 'I don't know how you can even ask. This person trusts me implicitly. How can I abuse her confidence in such a way and identify her?'

'It is a matter of security. All these people are in danger and we must find a way to warn them without causing panic. The matter is very delicate, very secret.'

'But you said that you are only 'afraid' that our network has been infiltrated. By whom? I am very sceptical about it.'

'I'm here as your superior officer and I'm acting under orders from those over me. I can only repeat my question.'

'And I can only absolutely refuse to answer.'

'This is an order.'

'I cannot help it. I am ready to take the consequences but I won't obey such an order.'

The situation was quite unbearable. The matter was urgent, dangerous and infinitely delicate. I had no right to disclose anything about Hammer at this moment, but without doing so this stubborn woman would not answer my question. Also, she was, to a certain extent, right: according to her conscience she was protecting her people. For a couple of minutes I did not know what to say . . .

'Have you any doubts regarding my service qualifications?'

'God forbid. All I want is that we should understand each other. I cannot tell you what you want. Such are my principles and I believe in them. There's nothing I can do about it.'*

---

*The woman was arrested a year later in another connection, and betrayed nobody although she was badly beaten up and then sent to Auschwitz.

Further persuasion was obviously pointless. I went out empty-handed, although I had held all the trump cards. I did not know what to do. But one thing was almost certain, there was something wrong with the women's section, although I had no concrete proof. Well, I thought, no more messages through that channel: my new system would have to do. But some specially prepared messages had to be concocted and sent through the women's section from time to time if they were not to guess that we suspected something. Moreover, we'd have to watch continuously and go on working without interruption so that externally there would not be any impression that something had gone wrong in prison intelligence. That was vital for our success: one suspicion and the enemy could be scared away and would be impossible to trace.

Underground work had its advantages. If two people wanted to discuss something they often had to ride to the other end of town or arrange laboriously-prepared meetings, complicated by the fact that sometimes co-workers would not know each other. This took a lot of time, but it gave breathing space and allowed nerves to calm down so that one could collect one's thoughts for the next difficult conversation.

I climbed to the sixth floor, where I was to meet Janek, who was assembling one of the cells in the new prison intelligence network.

Usually calm, he was anxious that day. 'Have you heard?'

'No, nothing. What's happened?'

'A lot of the warders were arrested in the Pawiak today.'

'What?'

'Yes. Several of them have already been interrogated by the Gestapo. More arrests are expected. They say Germans and Ukrainians are to take their place.'

'Oh damn! It only needed that!'

I sat limply on the couch. Well, well. We're going to look fine now. Sem's system given away, mine only just being set up and here they are picking out whoever they want to. There would be numerous orders tomorrow for urgent liaison with the prison and what could I do about them? Janek was silent: he could guess what I was thinking.

'Have you the names of the arrested warders? We musn't lose time.'

'I've got some but not all. I'm to get the rest tomorrow. Luckily, my contact survived.'

'Good, that's something. Now, please investigate all the possibilities offered by the women's department. I think it should be possible to put through some connections from there to the men's quarters. You know, safe deposits, laundry, parcel office and so on – these may be workable contact points. That's the most urgent task for the next few days. And I'd like to get further details about the warders tomorrow.'

The evening talk with Stefan was not a particularly cheerful one. The unexpected attack on the Polish warders was disturbing. They'd left the women alone but there was no saying what would happen on the next day.

'Have you any more news about Jan?'

'For the moment, only that he was not arrested today.'

'And what about Sem's network?'

'I spoke with the head of the women's section today. She refused to give me the names of her collaborators. Said it was a matter of mutual confidence. Even though I explained why I *had* to know.'

'Well, well. Nice piece of work by Sem. What did you tell her?'

'I told her to keep quiet about it all. She's slowing up the work terribly, but what can I do with that woman now? I will tell you some more. Diana, Sem's deputy, is still in Warsaw. She told somebody I know that all the alarms and talk about infiltration is only bluff, that we would like to get rid of Sem and invented all this. Can you imagine? But we simply haven't time for disciplinary action. When I build up a new network and clear the field, I'll have to get rid of the whole of that lot.'

'Yes, you are right. No use rubbing anyone up the wrong way just now. We must wait a few days and as soon as the Pawiak business dies down and we get to know what it's all about and how the future looks, we'll start again all out. I have a plan which should work.'

Several arduous April days passed. Our network of Polish warders in the Pawiak prison was completely broken up. Sub-Commissioner Spitzer was killed in the Gestapo building, and the senior warder was tortured to death during interrogation. The other warders were sent to Auschwitz and the few who remained in the prison could not understand why they had survived. Germans and Ukrainians now occupied the key positions in the prison. The situation was very dark. To make it worse there was a new wave of arrests. Day by day inquiries flowed in: messages for delivery to the prison and demands for answers from our superior officers. We managed somehow with the women's section, but it was nearly impossible to get access to the men. The work went badly through no fault of ours. Liaison had to be re-established immediately at almost any cost. This was the laconic order headquarters gave us. I patched up things day by day as far as possible and continued to meet Stefan every evening in order to establish the moves which would shed light on a number of strange patterns emerging in my section.

Stefan pointed some of these out. 'Have you noticed how arrests among women have been growing? I have in mind the group accused of code correspondence with prisoners and workers in the *Reich*. We get messages for them day after day, and day after day new arrests are made. And significantly, the arrests follow in accordance with the warnings smuggled out of the prison. Somebody is giving things away or somebody's betraying secrets.'

'Yes. That struck me too. Some of the messages still pass through Sem's apparatus. You understand the difficulty here. Some of the women prisoners have their trusted wardresses through whom they have always sent messages, and it's very difficult to stop them continuing this. I can't issue an announcement in the women's prison that messages may not be sent through certain wardresses. These things are so confidential, complicated and we must maintain silence, absolute silence in the field. If we don't, everything will collapse.'

Stefan pondered the point and tugged at his small moustache nervously. Finally, he raised his head and looked at me with determination. 'It's enough. We must act. What is your personal opinion of Jan?'

'An idealist, quite unemotional. Very respected in the Pawiak prison. Considered to be a skilful and courageous man.'

'That checks with my information. I didn't tell you but my men have also kept him under constant observation. What I suspected a few weeks ago has not been fully confirmed. But I am convinced that the man whom Jan took to meet Sem is Hammer himself. He doesn't know all his workers personally and doesn't make direct contact with all of those he knows. But Jan seems to be his main contact and is the direct informant for Hammer as far as the Pawiak goes. They've been meeting at the Bell café lately.'

'Can't he be bumped off there?'

'Of course, but there are various obstacles. First of all, the café is closely guarded. Secondly, I haven't analysed his group fully and I don't know its ramifications. Thirdly, and most important, I'm not a hundred per cent sure it's Hammer. There's been a sentence of death on him for a long time but it's necessary to establish his identity without doubt. Failing this my teams will not shoot and I will not give them orders to do so. Remember, they are all professional soldiers, young officers or NCOs in the service of the state and under very strict discipline. Do you know that they are not allowed to carry guns? By special arrangement they get them some time before an action and have to hand them in after the job is done. Otherwise it would be easy for them to use their guns for other purposes. We have had bad experiences; some people started to use their guns for robberies. We are at war and strange things happen every day. After all, we have a sentence of death on Hammer, but where is he? A probability is not enough.'

'But so many lives are in danger. Perhaps we should take the risk of killing the wrong person?'

'No, never. Once we start that, there will be no difference between us and the Germans. And we want Hammer, nobody else.'

'So what do you plan to do?'

'I intend to bring Jan over here. You and I will meet him tomorrow.'

'How shall we go about it?'

'Very simple. We agree that Jan is OK. He worked well for Sem and, even if he got tied up with somebody else at the same time, he probably thought he was serving the cause the better. All this is just guessing. Who can give us better explanations than Jan himself?'

'But what about the risk? And what'll you do if Jan refuses co-operation and continues to work with the other fellow who, you admit, is almost certainly Hammer, a Gestapo agent. What will happen then?'

'Can't be helped, we've got to take a chance – there's nothing else we can do. If we don't we'll never clear this up. There is another matter, too. You don't know this, but I have one other good contact in Hammer's group. Just about six months ago I succeeded in getting one of my people, we call him 'Kowalski', into the group. He's a specialist in faked papers. Quite by chance I learnt that Hammer was discreetly looking for somebody to direct a phoney papers workshop. Hammer is a great worker and he never wants to be dependent solely on the Gestapo. When he needs documents, he makes them himself. It doesn't matter how I managed it, but I succeeded in introducing Kowalski into Hammer's crowd as their faker. Not that I gained much by it. Hammer is so careful that he never comes to Kowalski's work-shop. Everything is fixed up by one of his men, somebody else every day. But Kowalski kept his eyes open and he secured several photos of his 'chief's' staff, including Hammer himself. Even so, of course, there's nothing sure, not a hundred per cent sure, that it is really Hammer himself. Jan might be able to throw light on this.'

'Good, but how shall we contact him?'

'I've got it all fixed up. Kowalski knows Jan from before the war. Tomorrow at six o'clock, we're to meet in his apartment. Jan has been told whom we represent and has agreed to talk with us.'

'Aren't you afraid he might tell Hammer about it?'

'Of course I am. And that's why I want you to prepare a bodyguard. Three should be enough and, just in case, we'll come half an hour before time. That may confuse them. I doubt if they would set up surveillance any earlier.'

The next day passed normally, except that I had to call off several meetings so as to have the evening free. I sent out the 'mail' and returned to my office to clear up the backlog of correspondence. At about 5 p.m. I put away all my papers into a hiding place in the room and, with the aid of a specially-prepared wire hook, pulled out a revolver and two spare magazines from under the floorboards. I cleaned the gun, loaded it and slipped it into my pocket.

In principle I believed that members of the underground should not walk about with firearms on them. It increased the chances of self-betrayal during a routine, general search or round-up by the enemy. And it encouraged unnecessary shooting which very rarely helped and could put innocent people in danger of reprisals. An analysis of many actual occurrences has demonstrated that in nearly every case when someone who does not need to shoot in the execution of his duties decides to use his weapon, he does so as a rule, too late for effective action. The delay may be a small fraction of a second but it could nonetheless decide the encounter against him. A soldier, agent or policeman, who has a gun officially and is expected to use it, shoots willingly and at once. A conspirator, pretending to be an ordinary passer-by in the street, draws his weapon only as a last resort. It was for this reason that the underground authorities strictly forbade the carrying of weapons by anyone who was not specially ordered to do so when on duty. Poison was another matter. Potassium cyanide was carried by thousands of people, who preferred a quick painless death to torture; but it was kept in inadequate containers for the most part so that the poison in time lost much of its toxic property and many attempts at suicide failed as a result.

To resume: normally I went about unarmed. But the area in which I had to operate often made it necessary to take risks which in turn demanded greater vigilance. This was the case now. I was setting out for a meeting which could turn out to be a resounding success or a major defeat. I did not know Jan personally but I was strangely sure of him; nevertheless he wasn't yet one of ours and we didn't know who was behind him. I trusted in Stefan's intuition and at the same time saw the logic of his reasoning: the fellow with the big moustaches, who met Sem, was probably a Gestapo agent. He might or might not be Hammer, but he was very dangerous to us. I found myself

wondering how Jan had got into such company and what contacts
Hammer had with the women's section. In a few minutes I would
know.

I left the house on the narrow lane near Belweder Street,
turned left and made my way up the fairly steep embankment to
reach Puławska Street. Kowalski lived here, on one of the side
streets. It was 5.25 p.m. which meant I was on time. The weather
was mild, it was warm for early May, and the sun was setting. I
put on some tortoiseshell-rimmed spectacles, which greatly
changed my appearance, and waited for a moment in the gateway opposite the side street in which Kowalski lived. I chose a
moment when the stream of bodies walking past became denser,
mixed with those crossing the street and turned left. I soon
found Kowalski's apartment and rang the bell in the manner
previously arranged. Stefan was already there – he had come a
few minutes before. Kowalski, a short, nearly hunchbacked man,
led us into the dining-room and left us alone. Stefan was puffing
away at a cigarette rather nervously. I asked if the bodyguard was
in place.

'Yes. Saw them wandering around. I don't think Whiskers has
posted anybody because my men indicated the road seemed
clear. Well, we'll see.'

I looked round the room carefully to get my bearings. It was
suitable for the occasion. Wide, modern windows threw a strong
light on the door so that those in the room, with their backs to
the windows, had their faces in shadow whilst anyone entering
the room would immediately be in a strong light. I put three
chairs around the table in the middle of the room and arranged
them so that Stefan and I would have our backs to the light. It was
just getting on for six o'clock and Stefan was offering me a
cigarette when a discreet ring sounded. We stood up by our
chairs. Kowalski passed through the room into the little hall. We
listened intently. Only one person came in, probably expected,
as no exchange of words was heard. The door creaked and
Kowalski appeared with a much taller, well-built man immediately behind him. Our host smiled and indicated the newcomer
with a sweeping gesture, as he said, 'Let me introduce you to
each other and wish you a pleasant talk.'

For a moment we stood in silence observing each other. Jan's face was open and candid; he had blue eyes and his auburn hair, brushed straight back, showed a high forehead. His small moustache, also auburn, differed only slightly in tint from his dark, sun-tanned complexion. He held himself well.

Stefan smiled and opened the conversation. 'Let's sit down. Do you smoke?'

'Thanks, I don't smoke.'

We sat down carefully still observing each other expectantly.

Stefan smiled again and spoke. 'What a fine day it has been. Real spring!'

'Yes, oh yes.' Jan answered quickly. 'You're right.'

'Tomorrow is Sunday and before the war one would have gone out of town.'

'That's right. Well, of course . . .'

'And you are beautifully tanned although the sunny days have only just started.'

'I've got an allotment on the Mokotow Fields and I go there every day after duty. Going to have my own tomatoes.'

Suddenly Stefan stubbed out his cigarette and looked at Jan sharply. 'Do you know whom we represent?'

'I do. Kowalski has made that quite clear.'

'Is Kowalski's recommendation enough for you?'

'Absolutely.'

'So, you haven't any doubt as to who we are and what gives us authority to hold this interview?'

'That's right.'

'Good. You were a warder before the war, weren't you?'

'That's right.'

'So you were a state employee, executing the will of the legal Polish authorities. Has any change taken place in this respect since the German Occupation, as far as you are concerned?'

'Well, there is some change – but I continue to be a good Pole.'

'So you recognize the authority of the rightful Polish Government in London, don't you?'

'I do.'

'Do you recognize the underground military authorities operating here on orders from that Government?'

'I do.'

'Whom do you serve? For whom are you working?'

'Just for those that are officially empowered by the Government.'

'No! You're working for a spy, a Gestapo agent!'

'How dare you? My chief is a colonel, specially sent over here by London.'

'We believe your chief is a spy, a *provocateur*. The lowest of the low!'

Stefan suddenly pulled out a photograph from his pocket and put it on the table before Jan. 'Who's that?'

Jan looked and started sharply. He took up the picture and held it closer to his eyes. I held my breath; the decisive moment had come. If he denies that he knows him . . .

'Well, who is it?'

Jan still hesitated, he was clearly struggling inwardly with himself. Finally he raised his head and said very distinctly: 'Yes, that's my chief.'

'What's his name?'

'Now, that I'm not allowed to say . . .'

'Then what did you come here for? You knew whom you were to speak with. That's enough – stop wasting our time. Come clean!'

Jan's face turned a little redder. He breathed more quickly. 'We call him Colonel . . . Baczewski and his cover-name is "Uncle".'

A flash of triumph passed over Stefan's face. Jan had responded satisfactorily and we had to act immediately and decisively.

I decided it was my turn to speak and I started in a different tone from Stefan's, quiet and more conciliatory. 'That's fine. Just as we thought, you're a decent and reasonable man. You have been of great help to us so we'll help you. You see, in undercover work various things happen – you can't know everything and everybody. The secrecy which envelops every aspect of the cause and the persons working for it produces many surprises and misunderstandings. It often happens that someone works in all good faith and then it turns out that his work is harmful.

It can't be avoided. That's how it is in this case. This chief of yours is as much a colonel as I am an Englishman or you a Chinaman. We have been tracking him for a long time; he operated as a spy on the frontier at first and then passed as a Colonel sent from London to check up on underground activities. He's got, the Lord only knows how many innocent, well-intentioned people – such as you – to help him. Oh, he's been smart all right. He's been a German agent for years and years, real name Joseph Hammer, born at Bursztyn in Silesia.'

I stopped because Jan stood up and started walking nervously around the room. He exclaimed in a shaking voice, 'I can't believe it! Uncle a Gestapo agent? He swore me in before a priest.'

'Quite possible. That priest knew as little about him as you did. But we'll prove to you what Hammer has been up to.'

It was a long list and we had everything at our fingertips. Jan had finally to admit that we were right. When we dealt with Hammer's methods of secrecy, he suddenly said, 'That'll do! You're right, absolutely right! In fact, I had my doubts at times. Says he's a colonel from London, a great conspirator, and then arranges a meeting with nearly ten people at once. And once I heard him start a telephone conversation saying: "This is Colonel Baczewski". It seemed strange to me – at Sem's they were much more careful.'

'That's right, though, even so, Sem was quite a joke as a conspirator. Well, returning to your "Uncle", you see what kind of mistakes he made. When you're playing a double game, it's very difficult to avoid making minor false moves. He has constantly to weave a way between lies and truth. He plays the role of a conspirator when with you – one who's hiding from the Gestapo – yet at the same time he has a Gestapo badge somewhere on him so of course he feels safe. And that causes him to make small but characteristic errors. Well, we'll change all that now.'

Jan cheered up as the conversation went on. We dropped our official air and he became more natural and freer with his comments.

Stefan glanced at his watch and asked, 'One more question.

How long has Hammer been operating on the prison sector?'

'Luckily only a few weeks', Jan grew despondent again, 'but how much damage he's done, and with our help...'

'Answer the question. We suspect that he controlled the messages coming and going from the Pawiak to Sem's group.'

'Unfortunately that's so. "Uncle" convinced us that he had the right to do so, that London had ordered him to go into everything. We did it in good faith. Every message was read by Hammer and later, with only a very small delay, delivered to the right place. Sem never suspected anything. I must say that although I believed "Uncle", I hated that job and often I didn't give him the messages to control. But the women gave him all theirs.'

'The women?'

'Yes. All Sem's women's section were also working for Hammer.'

Stefan glanced at me. We understood everything now. Many unanswered questions, many riddles, were now made clear.

'All right, we must finish now. From today on all that will be changed. Now to come to the last point. You have a choice: either you must throw up everything and retire completely from any kind of underground work, or you must take the oath and attempt to redeem your mistakes.'

'May I have twenty-four hours to think it over?'

'Yes, you have the right to that, to serve under us will be risky and hard. We trust you, but what we have been talking about here is deadly secret. Although you have a choice we advise you to take the second alternative, even though it will be the harder. The whole country is fighting, we need brave men of integrity, such as you.'

Jan shook hands firmly; he had tears in his eyes. Stefan in a low voice gave him the address and time of tomorrow's meeting.

The next day we got ready for the conversation in a small room behind a bar on Lwowska Street. Just in case, I had a bodyguard outside, although Jan's attitude had not aroused doubts. We had kept an eye on him chiefly to be sure that none of Hammer's observers turned up, for they might have suspected something. From our side Stefan, myself and the head of our surveillance network, under Stefan, came to the meeting.

Punctually I got a report that Jan was approaching and that he was 'clean'. It was true that the day before we had given him an alternative, but we were sure that he would choose co-operation. We were not mistaken: Jan took the oath, exchanged the traditional embraces and came to attention. 'I report for orders.'

At first we got down to a detailed examination of everyone in Hammer's group known to Jan. I took down a number of names of the prison personnel and their descriptions. Stefan was interested in 'Uncle's' staff. Then we laid down tactics for the near future. All doubts had been removed. The man *was* Hammer. Now there remained only his liquidation. This was where Jan's dangerous and difficult role started. He was still in 'Uncle's' confidence and could contact him directly. This meant Jan could steer Hammer to us, if we were careful. It would not be easy since we were dealing with a first-class opponent. At any moment Hammer might discover that he was being tricked and then Jan would be lost. But Hammer's elimination was the only wholly satisfactory solution, and Jan undertook to carry it out and even got enthusiastic about it.

At the same time we had to make other moves: firstly, to make further control of the correspondence from the Pawiak impossible and, secondly, to lull any suspicions whatever about our proposed course of action.

We proceeded along two lines: Stefan worked out Hammer's movements and got ready for his liquidation; I went on building up the prison network and finding out all I could about those of Sem's employees known to me who were also working for 'Uncle'. I discovered particulars which were characteristic of Hammer's mastery of his work. All of Sem's prison workers whom Hammer had won over were, without exception, people of the highest ideals. The 'colonel' had chosen only such people, for he knew that that way he would get the best results and, above all, maintain his fiction the longest. He had kept up appearances in every detail. They had all been sworn in with the official oath, received salaries on the same scale as in the Home Army; a special cell had been formed to help the prisoners by sending them parcels and paying in money to their prison accounts; finally, permanent assistance was given to the families of arrested and deported warders. None of those who got the money knew that it was Hammer himself who had been the means of arresting the warders. This was a master-stroke, for he was able to lessen the chances of any correspondence with the prisoners being carried out without his knowledge. Of the Polish warders there remained only those who never carried messages and those who worked for 'Uncle'. There were few others.

We had to act quickly: there could be no cessation of correspondence. Hammer would have noticed this and become suspicious. Through Jan, I engaged a friend of his, also a warder in the Pawiak, and I sent to the men's side of the prison specially-prepared messages, which had all the appearance of a normal correspondence but which did not reveal anything essential. The women's side was more difficult, for before Hammer's liquidation we dared not risk another confrontation as we had with Jan, to discover Hammer's contacts there. So we were forced to use Sem's dubious apparatus. The head of the women's section was removed and the prepared messages were sent through Marcelle, without her being aware of the fact that they were not genuine. On the other hand all the real correspondence I sent through my reserve network, which was already of a respectable size.

May was drawing to a close, spring brightened the streets and the battered houses. We worked from dawn till dusk and the loveliest season of the year passed almost unnoticed. The pile of tasks mounted up so quickly that often, being unable to get through my work during the day, I stayed in my office all night. In my department the slightest delay could not be tolerated, for the safety of hundreds of soldiers fighting in the underground depended on us. And here, in Warsaw, in the heart of Poland, all the underground authorities of the country were centralized: the headquarters of the Home Army and the Government Delegacy. This was the argument which I always used with my subordinates if I noticed any slackness, carelessness or fear. But this was rare. In a small sector were grouped people of different convictions, ages and social class. But during the years of underground struggle against the Occupation the differences were minimized. We all considered it to be our duty to risk whatever had to be risked.

Jan worked in a state of high tension, but he was stubborn and kept up. Every day he went to work at the Pawiak as usual and in the evenings met either Stefan or myself secretly. He kept up his normal contact with Hammer and played his part so well that the agent suspected nothing. The messages went to and fro as usual and Hammer read them as before. His other contacts worked as they had always done, still in ignorance of what was in the air and who the arbitrary, severe 'colonel' was. Stefan had already shown him several times to those who would carry out the liquidation. They were led by Leszek, a young artillery officer. Leszek himself took part in all the more important operations and Hammer was to be his 'patient'. The preparations were difficult and complicated, for the liquidators had first to be shown the person they were going to kill. This was hard, for Hammer and his men were always suspicious and the Gestapo were everywhere. Stefan had several times got everything ready, down to the last detail, and always some small incident had been the cause of 'Uncle' being left untouched. Jan was coming to the end of his nervous endurance and any day might make a slip which would destroy all our work. We met with him every day to keep his morale up.

The decisive moment finally arrived.

The last day of June broke, warm, bright and sunny. From early morning we had been making preparations and thinking of the events of the afternoon. Jan made an appointment for this day with Hammer in his office on Tamka Street. At 3 p.m. Jan was to wait on the first floor for his boss, who, although very careful, had to see him to talk over prison affairs. We didn't expect 'Baczewski' to be punctual: if anything he would come earlier. He might come up the road from Dobra Street; but the upper end of Tamka Street, from Kopernik Street, was also open to him. It was not out of the question that he might use the steps beside the conservatoire, and a side street, Topiel Street, had also to be taken into consideration. All these possibilities forced Stefan to set the trap in the very house where the meeting was to take place, although for the sake of Jan's alibi it would have been better to shoot Hammer a little way away.

The reconnaissance men took up their places at 2 p.m., the two liquidation teams were to come at 2.30 p.m. Stefan watched the upper end of Tamka Street, himself in direct contact with the two teams of five. The stakes were too high for us to risk failure.

At 2.40 Jan got off the tram at the stop on Dobra Street and walked quickly up the hill. He was not in warder's uniform but wore civies. He showed no sign of having noticed the observers, who followed him with their eyes and who then turned to watch the other passers-by.

About five minutes later from the direction of the Poniatowski Viaduct two men appeared. The one on the right, the shorter of the two, had luxuriant ginger whiskers; he kept looking around. It was Hammer. The two turned left and began to climb the hill. The observers carefully scrutinized the people around Hammer, but the pair obviously felt very sure of themselves and suspected nothing, for they had no bodyguard.

When they were a little way off, the observers left their places and went after them, cutting off the way back. There was a lot of traffic and the whole operation was carried out unnoticed.

The net was tightening with every moment. Already they had passed Topiel Street and were approaching the steps beside the conservatoire. Upstairs in number 52 Jan was waiting nervously. In the gateway of this house the first team of liquidators was lying in wait; on the other side of the road Stefan was flattened against the wall; near the steps circled the second team of five.

Hammer, suspicious of nothing, confidently approached the familiar gateway, which he had passed through so many times. Suddenly from the direction of the steps came the ominous words: '*Hande hoch!*' But it was our men speaking. A German soldier had unwittingly walked into the middle of our operation and was now standing facing the wall with his hands stiffly up. He was trembling.

It was a short scene and quietly carried out, but Hammer heard it. He hastened his footsteps and tried to pass the house which he had been making for, but as he passed the gateway, two shots rang out. He clutched himself, ran a few steps and fell heavily on to the pavement. His companion attempted to flee but he too was hit. Tottering, he hid himself on the stairway of number 52. Hammer lay on the stones of the pavement, wounded but conscious. He tried to get up. Leszek knelt down and shot him in the ear. He quickly took Hammer's papers, rose and made a sign. Within a few seconds all those involved in the operation faded away and the street was almost deserted.

On the steps against the wall the bewildered German soldier stood, not knowing what to do with his aching arms, still held high above his head. Hammer died an hour later in one of the neighbouring clinics. Over a million zlotys was found on him in dollars, diamonds and gold. It was the day before pay-day.

Chapter Five

By Permission of the Gestapo

After Hammer's liquidation Jan returned to the Pawiak as if nothing had happened. He had every right to refuse further service in the prison and demand a change of environment, but the brave man, although exhausted and continually in the front line, decided that he might still be useful and stayed at his post.

His alibi for the Gestapo was still intact. At least so it appeared. When Hammer was shot, his adjudant, 'Captain Maciejewski', although wounded, had managed to escape. Jan had stayed calm, played out his role excellently and did not betray himself, even though he had been waiting for them. 'Maciejewski' had good cause to be suspicious, but first of all, he was seriously wounded and, secondly, it was most unlikely that having been brought up in 'Uncle's' tough school, he was ready to rush off to the Gestapo. The whole game after all depended on retaining as much independence as possible.

Of course the boss's death did not automatically spell the end of the whole gang and Jan could well become a target for an attack by the other side, but we assumed that his alibi in that direction was adequate, at least for the period of 'Maciejewski's' serious illness. Stefan hoped that when the gang recovered its composure a little and began operations, Jan could once again be useful.

That same evening as usual I met Stefan. The Hammer affair had brought us even closer together and we were now firm friends. We grasped each other's hand.

'Well, how's Jan? Has he recovered from the initial shock? Is he bearing up?'

'Yes, he's a tough man.'

'OK. Now something else.'

'Yes?'

'As you know, before we fixed "Uncle", I had a good look at his team, as I knew that things would not end with him. The most dangerous shark has been killed, but a whole lot of little sharks are still alive. One of them is "Colonel Dobrzański", who was Hammer's second-in-command, but who never appeared out front. I have a feeling that his ambitious boss wouldn't let him. Now this "Dobrzański", although badly frightened and gone to ground, is beginning to stir and start things moving with a certain "Colonel Zawadzki" and his adjutant Edward Zajaczkowski. The last name is real. "Maciejewski" is no longer in Warsaw. I'm keeping an eye on all of them, so please don't worry yourself on that score, but I do have some new things which require swift action from you.'

'Well?'

'In Sem's section there were, if you remember, several women prison warders, whom we've left on one side for the moment. Now that Hammer has gone, we have to look after them.'

'Of course, I've already taken the first steps. The leader of the women's section, whom I've relieved, used to get in touch with the warders not directly, but through one of them who is also their official superior, for she is in charge of "Serbia"* and is a deputy superintendent in the prison service. As you know, the Germans left all the women alone, including her. They continue to trust her.'

'Have you access to her?'

'Yes, through a friend of hers in the same rank, working on another prison. She has already taken the oath and is working superbly.'

'Good, we'll go and talk to her together. What's your opinion of her?'

'The highest, but we won't find it easy, for she apparently still believes that Hammer was an outstanding and honest man.'

'She's not the only one – we've still got a great many difficult

---

*The nickname of the women's part of Pawiak which had once been a hospital for soldiers wounded in Serbia.

things to do. We were lucky to get hold of 'Uncle's' papers for they show irrefutably that it really was him and that he really had been working for the Gestapo. Amongst those he won over there are bound to be a few who, out of pure ambition, will claim that we eliminated an honest man. There are also those who would willingly rejoice if we had made a mistake. I've already heard a rumour that we got rid of someone else and that Hammer is still alive and working peacefully.'

'I'm not quite sure I understand.'

'You're still too young and you know people too little, but never mind. Will you please fix a meeting with the officer in charge of "Serbia".'

Several days later we met at Mokotów in a new contact point indicated to me by our intermediary. Stefan was tired and therefore angry and impatient. 'I hope somehow we'll be able to convince her. I've had just about enough of all these highly-strung women.'

We heard the arranged knocking. Two knocks, silence and once again two more careful knocks. There were just the two of us and so I headed for the door. Our visitor was to have been brought only as far as the main entrance of the house and then she was to go on alone. I had been given a detailed description of her, but, just in case, we had a password. As soon as a slight figure appeared in the dark entrance hall I slammed the outer door and threw a short question. I received the expected answer and we entered the room in which Stefan was waiting. Both of us immediately looked at the new arrival. She stood in the full sunlight of a fine day. It was clear that these circumstances upset her and made her shy, but simultaneously she indicated a sort of inner strength. She looked us straight in the eye with a bold, calm gaze; her prominent nose did not spoil the harmony of her regular features and her blond hair and light colouring made a pleasant and appealing impression.

For a good minute we said nothing.

Suddenly and quite unexpectedly Stefan smiled and said jokingly, 'And so you are the dangerous opponent we were meant to convince today?'

The woman smiled back, and her smile was captivating and somehow warm and sincere. 'Convince or shoot.'

Stefan made a threatening face. 'Quite right and straightaway, but we expect that persuasion will be enough.'

The conversation turned out to be very much easier than we had anticipated. Our intermediary had done her work well and really only details remained for us to sort out. Our visitor no longer had any illusions about Hammer, but we returned once again to his activities, in order to dispel even the smallest doubts. Stefan's fears turned out to be unjustified. We were dealing with a charming and gentle woman, who was also practical and not in the least highly strung. We were thus quite quickly able to get through the difficulties inherent in such complicated and unusual cases. We swore her in and got down to details of work in the Pawiak. Who could provide us with better information and give us better advice?

After a dozen or so minutes Stefan took his leave of us, since he had already found out all he wanted to know, and I stayed behind for some time, for our co-operation had to be very carefully planned. Taught by experience, I had decided that my prison net would be divided into the smallest possible groups, which would be unaware of each other, even though they were operating side by side. Therefore I did not tell her of my other contacts in 'Serbia', although, naturally, she guessed I had some and would have liked to take them over. Finally we ended this first meeting deciding that my new friend would adopt the code-name 'Karol', but that to her closest colleagues she would be known as 'Danusia'. Contact between us was to be maintained by means of pre-arranged regular meetings. Just in case, I gave her my reserve emergency meeting point.

Travelling to the other end of town by tram I pondered the results of our conversation. It had brought quite an easy success, but I was not one hundred per cent pleased with it. Danusia, who had a few trusted warders, immediately became my best contact in the women's section, but at the same time she was in charge of it and was thus directly responsible to the Gestapo. She was an exceptionally valuable contact, but not for work of a specifically intelligence nature. Sooner or later she had to make a mistake and then the Germans would treat her in their own way. I admired her bearing and self-control, but would she endure any interrogation? I could not even imagine it. It was lucky that I had not given her all my female contacts. They needed to be expanded, but by whom? 'Serbia' was already completely infiltrated.

It was late summer of 1942. The Germans were besieging Leningrad and were trying to reach the Caucasian oilfields, but things were going slowly for them and so they were rampaging on the internal front and above all in Poland, through which ran their vital and very extended lines of communication. Warsaw was the centre of all the most important threads of underground propaganda, diversion and sabotage, and so time after time blows fell on us, filling up the Aleja Szucha* and the Pawiak. I was literally going out of my mind.

I met Stefan less frequently, for he was completely engrossed in chasing after Hammer's men. We usually caught the last tram giving us the opportunity to exchange a few words.

Suddenly one morning he appeared in person at my emergency meeting point, whose whereabouts, naturally he knew. Our meeting lasted only a few minutes. Stefan was excited as was his wont when he was going to take some important decision. He loved his work and to some extent treated it as an absorbing and exciting game.

'Tomorrow, if all goes well, I shall at last establish "Colonel Zawadzki's" address. Jan has again turned up trumps. He's in touch with Zawadzki and they trust him.'

'Once you get the address does that mean immediate liquidation?'

'That's possible. Do you know that Jan has been given special permission to join the execution team? He's a really good sort.'

'Good and very proud. Let him just come through this in one piece.'

Stefan once again had set everything up perfectly. As soon as Zawadzki and Zajaczkowski reached the first floor of number 9 Marszałkowska Street, the waiting five-man team was informed. This time the job was to be done indoors. Weapons were

---

*The name of the road where Gestapo headquarters in Warsaw was situated. It has, ever since, become a name for the Gestapo itself.

distributed, the observation net was tightened and the order was given to carry out the operation. The team secured the stairs and then three of them, lead by Jan, moved upstairs. They broke into the flat and shots were heard. Zawadzki was killed immediately and Zajaczkowski was seriously wounded. He lived for another ten hours and saw his wife in the hospital to which he was taken. It was a most dramatic meeting, since the wounded man confessed that he knew for whom he had been working and that he had expected just such an end. We had our people in the hospital and I later received a report giving all these details.

After this operation Jan did not return to his post. It had been decided beforehand that he would immediately drop out of circulation and hide up using previously prepared documents. His family (he had a wife and two small children) was also meant to go into hiding, but his wife objected and swore that she would not leave her flat. We would have preferred it otherwise, but what could we do? In fact the danger was not too great, since Jan's alibi for the Gestapo was still intact. Naturally enough leaving his post was a serious and suspicious step, but we launched a discreet rumour in the Pawiak that he had gone away somewhere fearing further arrests and the sacking of the remaining male Polish warders. The rumour caught on. The Gestapo sought Jan and would willingly have laid hands on him, but their inquiries were not extensive and the whole case was handled in a very desultory fashion. His wife and children were left alone, although there was certainly some sort of surveillance on them. So be it. We were by then too smart to be worried by such things.

Meanwhile Jan holed up in a good hideout in the outer suburbs and hardly ever went out into the street. He shaved his head, grew a moustache and you could only recognize him by his blue eyes. When sometimes he had to go out, he put on overalls and pretended to be a workman.

He was of course 'dead', but he knew the Pawiak area so well that I expected a great deal from his advice and instructions. It was time to give him some task, otherwise he could easily be wasted. He had lived too intensively over the last few months to be able to endure complete inaction patiently.

That day I was travelling through his suburb and so I dropped by for a few minutes.

He was depressed and out of sorts. 'When's it all going to end? I won't be able to stand much more of this.'

'So what, you're not the only one.'

'I'd surely be better off in the Pawiak.'

'In a warder's uniform, but not in a cell. The Germans would have fun with you.'

'The war is still on and I'm just wasting my time here doing nothing.'

'It's not so bad. It just happens that I've got an interesting job for you. I've brought a map of the Pawiak.'

Jan livened up at once. 'Ah, then some big operation is in the air?'

'Unfortunately, not quite the sort you're thinking of. I must go through this whole map with you because I have got to find new ways and means of getting in touch with the men's section. All my contacts have been blown. I do have a couple of channels, but they're very restricted. And anyway there are lots of camp transports and new arrivals. I must have someone to give me lists of those sent off and brought in. Can you give it a thought?'

I left Jan in a much better frame of mind and went off to meet Danusia.

I used to meet her regularly and had grown very fond of her. I just could not understand how such a young and attractive woman had joined the prison service before the war and had been promoted to be in charge of the Pawiak women's section. During the war the situation changed dramatically and the prison contained the elite of our society, but in peacetime it had housed mainly common criminals and only occasionally political prisoners, usually communists. Looking after such people could not have been pleasant or easy for such a small and physically weak woman of deep sensitivity. Only great self-control, and an exceptionally strong will allowed her to carry out this arduous work, which during the Occupation became a nightmare. In her I had a colleague of the highest calibre. There was no task which she would not undertake, no risk which could restrain her. I marvelled at her ability to deal with the Germans and to manoeuvre in such a difficult and dangerous area where so many different and usually competing interests converged. Every day she went off to work as if to the lions' den, and yet she would return calm, good-tempered and full of hope for the next day.

At our meetings we discussed not only current matters, but also in theoretical terms what else we could do. I compared her comments and ideas with Jan's opinions and thus had tried to build up an objective vision of what was necessary and also feasible.

Jan's comments when I returned to see him were not optimistic. The depository was the nub of the Pawiak – everyone brought to the prison had to go through it, and the lists of camp transports were made up there. But the whole thing was run by Germans and Ukrainians. It would need a miracle, Jan thought, for us to get a contact in there.

As we all know there are no miracles in everyday life, but if you want something with all your heart, after a certain time you begin to believe that, nevertheless, some supernatural forces are operating and will suddenly provide essential assistance.

So it was with me. I sought, puzzled, met useful people, worried over the problem with Stefan, tormented Jan and Danusia with questions, strained my willpower in one direction only, and suddenly, the miracle came!

One day, when I had had nothing but failure and was so exhausted that not the slightest spark of optimism burned within me, I found a small card at my emergency mail point. One of my women workers, a deputy superintendent in another prison, requested an urgent meeting with me. I did not really want to meet her. She was an ambitious girl tormented by the thought that as she was not in the Pawiak, she was outside the mainstream of our work. I did not expect any revelations, but the day had been dreadful and her card was urgent. It was worth a try.

Helena was already waiting for me at the meeting point.

She was very excited, trembling in fact from emotion. 'Ah, thank goodness you've come. There's a chance to get somebody into the Pawiak.'

'The Pawiak? To do what?'

'To work, of course, as a warder.'

'Is that all? How?'

'Through the Gestapo.'

I lost control and leapt up in rage. 'I'm desperately tired today and you drag me over here for some kind of joke.'

She blushed and looked down. Her enthusiasm evaporated immediately. 'Since you don't believe me . . .'

My anger subsided. 'I didn't mean to hurt you, but all this is so silly.'

'Please let me finish. I expressed myself badly, but I do so want to pass on this information to you.'

Suddenly a glimmer of interest broke through into my tired brain. 'I'm listening.'

'I have a friend who before the war was controller of prisons and the Germans have let him keep his job.'

'Impossible! How did he manage it?'

'I don't know. Perhaps they trust him or maybe he is simply useful to them. After all, as well as the Pawiak, Warsaw does have criminal prisons.'

'How do you know him?'

'We . . . know each other . . . People sometimes do . . .'

'And is he to be trusted?'

'If you trust me, that will do. He is under my influence.'

'What is he suggesting?'

'The German criminal police have already approached him several times requesting help in staffing the other prisons. He told me yesterday that this time it's the Gestapo.'

I leapt up, my tiredness had suddenly disappeared. 'Well?'

'They asked whether he could find a woman to serve in the Pawiak?'

'Impossible.'

'And yet it's true. What do you think?'

'I'm dreadfully sorry. Yes, this is first-rate news. Can I count on you?'

The girl blushed, but this time it was a triumphal blush. 'That's just why I'm here.'

'I must see this friend of yours. There's not a minute to be lost.'

'I fixed it all up, just in case. You could meet him tomorrow at my place.'

Naturally I told Stefan of this godsend. He was tied up with other matters and so reacted rather more philosophically than I had expected, but he was pleased. He advised me not to go to the meeting alone and to be careful. Unfortunately, he himself had no time at all. I realized that this was something of a compliment to me.

The following day Helena introduced her friend to me and my closest colleague. He was a middle-aged man corpulent and self-confident. He was relaxed and gestured self-importantly, but at the same time he gave us short questioning glances, which showed that our conversation both excited and worried him. He gave the impression of a man who had decided it was time to change course and was doing just that, but was uncertain whether he had taken the right path.

'You gentlemen already know who I am and what my proposition is. Helena' – he threw her a meaningful smile – 'has been kind enough to put me in touch with you. I hope that your organization will be interested in what I have to offer.'

I didn't care much for him, but he could be exceptionally useful. I realized that it was essential to make the right impression so that he would allow us to use him to the full.

'It might be. We know the Pawiak area well and everything about it. We've already had many suggestions, which later only gave us more problems. Would you be so good as to tell us exactly what this is all about?'

He was a little taken aback. He had probably imagined that we would leap at his suggestion with loud protestations of gratitude, and yet he was met with indifference and suspicion.

'Helena was meant to have warned you and explained everything. I was led to believe that the organization, that you gentlemen were interested . . .'

'That's quite possible, but what exactly is your proposition?'

'The Gestapo has asked me for a woman to work in "Serbia".'

'What for? Can't they find a suitable German?'

'Apparently not. You just can't imagine the problems they're having. Germans are afraid of jobs like that.'

'And would you be able to get our candidate in?'

'That's just what I want to suggest. Naturally the person concerned would have to be accepted by the Gestapo.'

I thought for a long moment. Heavens above, what an opportunity lay before us. We could get our woman into 'Serbia', someone reliable, in touch with no one else and all with the Gestapo's permission. Was it all nonsense or the easiest thing in the world? I looked carefully at the man. He was wriggling on his chair and giving us uncertain glances, but he didn't look like a scoundrel. He appeared very keen to do something for the common cause.

'All right, I agree. But, you know if . . .'

He leapt from his chair and came over to me. 'I know, I know, you don't need to finish. Would I be such a fool as to do anything so stupid now, in the second half of 1942? I am a Pole and I want to work with you. Perhaps it's a bit late, but I haven't come empty handed.'

We parted on good terms. I went out and immediately jumped aboard a tram. Conflicting emotions warred within me. I realized that an exceptional opportunity presented itself which I must use, and yet at the same time I was plagued by doubts and worries. Firstly, we had to find the right woman: no easy thing. Where were we to find a girl ready to agree to this kind of work? Not only did joining the Pawiak prison staff and immediately starting to lead a double life entail the most frightful risks and require iron nerves, but it also meant working for the Gestapo. This would incur everyone's contempt and, by posing thus as a traitor, such a woman would risk both her life and eternal shame.

Had we the right to make such a proposition, could we accept such a sacrifice?

I reached Jan's hideout with a heavy heart. If anyone could help me, he could.

The first few minutes of our conversation calmed many of my fears. His eyes shone, when he heard about the project. 'We'll really hit the Krauts! Don't worry, your woman will be just fine.'

In fact, very much sooner than I had anticipated, Jan brought along his cousin, Marysia, to a meeting. Again my fears returned, and I went to this meeting in an undecided frame of mind, but as soon as her calm, brave eyes looked at me and I heard the low voice and felt her firm handshake, I was suddenly strangely certain that she was the one to handle this and that she would endure anything.

I had planned to give her some time to think the thing over, but she settled it in a few words: 'I'll hand in my notice at the shop tomorrow and within a week I shall be ready.'

The three of us had a long talk. Marysia was given all the necessary instructions, took the code name 'Wojtek' and became Jan's first contact in his new role. He was to watch her every step, keep up her spirits, protect and advise her.

I went home under the influence of this conversation, which had deeply shaken and moved me. What riches, what boundless strength lie in the human heart and within the apparently frail human frame. What forces are concealed in the minds of our people – a people so difficult to fathom and yet so ready to make sacrifices. We were herded into patriotic meetings and made to declare our love for our country; we were encouraged to make public protestations of emotion, while, close at hand, true patriotism, untainted by thoughts of personal glory or success, lay in the hearts of simple folk, who were used to a hard life and who received neither fame nor honour.

Our hearts beat strongly when Marysia put on her uniform for the first time and went off to work at the Pawiak. She could break down at once, my contact could turn out to be a catastrophe. Fortunately, our fears were unfounded. Marysia survived the first few days well, no one suspected her and none of the Polish staff knew of her double role. Within a fortnight or so she began to do things for us and always faultlessly. She was calm, self-possessed and careful. The Germans had nothing to complain of, her Polish superiors came to recognize her worth and the prisoners knew that they could rely on her without fear of an unnecessary reflex or a careless slip. She became my firm contact whom I used in the most difficult cases.

After the last blow the remains of Hammer's gang no longer had the courage to undertake any new activities. 'Maciejewski' did not return to Warsaw. 'Dobrzański' also vanished. We finally had peace from that quarter.

My prison network was supplemented by a couple of doctors who went into the prison from outside and rendered useful service. We were completely in control of 'Serbia' and communication with the women was no longer a problem, but the men's section continued to require further contacts and work. In my search for additional sources of help I grasped at any idea and was on the point of using a sensational method.

There was an electrical engineer in the Pawiak at that time. The Gestapo had recently put him to work in the radio cell, where they were repairing and modernizing their equipment. I got in touch with him through one of my contacts and he proposed setting up radio communications. He would construct a small transmitter with a range of a few kilometres, while we on the outside were to fix up some sort of receiver. The project sounded fantastic, but I tried to get it going and had a few discussions with general headquarters' radio production section. I was told that there would be considerable problems, but that they could be solved. The matter progressed very slowly and just when it appeared that something might come of it, the whole thing was nipped in the bud in a most unusual way.

A diversionary unit of scouts captured a Black Maria taking prisoners from Gestapo headquarters to Pawiak and amongst those set free was my engineer! I must surely have been the only Pole in Warsaw at the time who bore some sort of grudge against those brave boys!*

Manœuvering through my numerous contacts, having frequent meetings with Stefan, Jan, Danusia and Marysia and many others, my thoughts constantly returned to the depository, where all prisoners had to leave their valuables. I dreamt of them as one dreams of a beautiful woman; a small prison hut appeared in my dreams and in optimistic moments I could see someone there working for me and sending out priceless reports and information.

I was naturally also meeting Helena, since her friend had carried out his first task reliably and it was quite possible that he might again appear with a similar suggestion.

If I myself had not experienced it, I would never have believed it possible, but facts speak for themselves. Yes indeed, a suggestion did come, but somewhat different from the first. The Gestapo was looking for a female clerk with a reasonable

---

*This was a famous clandestine action in Warsaw, which took place on 26 March 1943. Twenty-five political prisoners were set free.

command of German. To work where? In the Pawiak, in the depository!

This time Jan could not do much for me and so I had to look elsewhere. The experience with Marysia was reassuring and I looked with greater optimism.

Several days later my deputy and I set off to meet a potential candidate who was apparently ready to join us, but as yet unaware of what exactly this would entail. An essential rule for success was maintaining secrecy.

We met a young, flaxen-haired girl with a gentle oval face and calm, trusting eyes. Her name was Jadwiga and no one had yet involved her in any of our clandestine work. I felt that it was better to be as careful as possible and so I resolved not to tell her the whole truth at once. Our conversation began rather lamely; I was taking a long time coming to the point, for I wanted to see whether she wanted to work with us at all and whether she was prepared for such dangerous and unpleasant work.

I struggled in this way for several minutes when suddenly a gleam of laughter appeared in Jadwiga's eyes. 'Please stop making things so difficult for yourself, I know very well what all this is about.'

'Well in that case what do you think?'

'What do I think? You know, if we knew each other better, I would be quite offended. You see I have already handed in my notice. You just have to take me!'

We were all three of us about the same age, we were young and so we allowed ourselves a moment of relaxation. Hard times lay ahead for Jadwiga, so what was the point of talking about them now? Warsaw at that time isolated itself from the pressures of war with a deluge of humour and laughter and we had no lack of subjects.

At last the depository was under our control. Jadwiga assumed the code name 'Ryszard' and went off to her new job. I gave her clear instructions to spend the first month getting into the work and to forget about our affairs, but this order was disobeyed the very next day. She brought me a complete list of all the new arrivals and was so delighted with her success that my reprimand was useless. She was working in difficult circumstances, since she shared a small room with two others. Her direct superior, a Polish deputy superintendent, who had somehow survived, was so frightened that he might even be dangerous. He had to be avoided like the plague. If he spotted anything, that would be the end of our little game.

We tried to cut down the risks. We had some special buttons made to match Jadwiga's coat, which could be unscrewed to make a hiding place which was almost impossible to discover. We produced a handbag with a hollow clasp and our locksmiths made us some keys with screw-on heads. All this, however, did not alter the fact that these aids facilitated smuggling our reports, but not obtaining them in the first place. Jadwiga had to make notes and copy out names at her desk right next to the prying eyes of her superior and the hostile eyes of the Gestapo. At the end of January 1943, when over three days more than 1200 prisoners were taken off to Majdanek concentration camp, within two days I had a complete list of their names from her.

How did she manage this colossal task? I never did find out. We met many times and a firm friendship grew up between us.

My network was now working efficiently and adequately. I picked up a couple more important contacts, got another girl into 'Serbia', completed my outside team and was ready for even the most difficult assignments. I was certainly entitled to feel some pride if the thought had come into my head at the time. But in those days it was quite the reverse. Success deprived one of peace of mind and instilled caution. The smile of fortune was not lightly earned.

I felt that I was living life to the full, and yet fears and forebodings filled me. It seemed to me the whole time that someone was watching and following me and that he was right behind – invisible and intangible.

My instinct, sharpened by years of war, was right. These were the last days of my underground life.

Chapter Six

Piotr and Ola

One day a goods wagon of coffee for the *Wehrmacht** disappeared at the Eastern Station in Warsaw. In occupied Poland this sort of thing was considered a great joke, but the humourless Germans saw it rather differently and were furious. They called out the police, turned the town inside out and got on the trail of the perpetrators.

At the very moment when a flat on Hoża Street was being searched and its residents arrested, a man obliviously approached the entrance to the block. He was of middle age and medium height, of good bearing and with a calm face surrounded by a bushy and almost red beard. In his pocket he carried documents stating that he was Piotr Katuszewski and that he worked for a trading company. However, this was only a cover concealing an air force officer with a surname quite well known in Poland.

As he entered the main door, the caretaker looked out from his room and made a meaningful face, but Piotr failed to understand and turned into the stairwell. He had reached the second floor and was just about to ring the doorbell, when he heard some noises which made him hestitate. He was about to turn back when the door suddenly opened and two uniformed Germans jumped out onto the landing.

'*Komm, komm!*'

They both had machine pistols at the ready. There was nothing for it but to accept their invitation.

In the hall stood a couple of men with their hands up and their

*The German armed forces.

55

faces to the wall. Piotr recognized one of them as his Air Force subordinate and friend.

He was ordered into a room on the right, where he was immediately searched and his wallet taken from his pocket. He was then shoved towards a table at which a tall, greying civilian was sitting.

'Are these your papers?'

'Yes, they are.'

'What's your name?'

'It's on the papers you're holding.'

'What's your name, I'm asking you!'

'Piotr Katuszewski.'

'Where are you living?'

He gave the relevant address.

'Mother's name?'

He also answered.

'Where did you go to school?'

For a moment Piotr hesitated, but gave the correct answer.

The civilian looked piercingly at him. 'Well, we haven't time for chatting now. We'll talk later. Who's that beard meant to fool?'

'I've got eczema and I've had a beard for years.'

His interrogator waved vaguely and mumbled something to his uniformed colleagues. They handed Piotr back his wallet, then pushed him into the hall and stood him next to the others with his face towards the wall.

Once arrested, prisoners were usually taken to Gestapo head-quarters and sometimes straight to the Pawiak, but Piotr was lucky. The case was handed over to the criminal police and they were all taken to Mokotów Prison. The large prison on Rako-wiecka Street was naturally under German control, but the warders were all Poles and since the prisoners were not accused of political activity, the Gestapo did not bother about them. Piotr was put in a communal cell and the interrogation began. This is never pleasant, but Mokotów methods were bearable.

Several days later I was informed through the underground post that a representative of one of the departments of Home Army high command, whom I knew personally, would be wait-ing for me in a certain café at an appointed time. I went to the agreed place and met my friend, who quickly told me what it was all about. He firstly gave me all the above details and then asked if there was any way of getting Piotr out of Mokotów.

'He's very important to us. He's a first-rate worker and also an honest man. He has a great number of friends who would do anything for him.'

'Yes, it is possible, but it's bound to be difficult, tricky and expensive. I must first of all get permission from my superiors.'

'Naturally. I'm sure there won't be any difficulty.'

'So am I, but before we do anything, I have several questions. You realize that a prisoner's release can be obtained only by his family or friends, but they must be friends of Piotr Katuszewski and not of a pre-war air force squadron leader. The alibi must be one hundred per cent, or else we'll blow the whole thing and it won't do Piotr any good. He's inside because he got mixed up in that business of the wagon load of coffee, but he could easily be done for resistance work and living under an assumed name. Have you got some suitable people?'

'First of all there's his wife, who changed her name when he did and who has been living with him. No doubt there'll be others.'

'Good. When I get the go-ahead, I'll ask you for a contact. I'll then have to meet someone who will put in the official request. I understand that you'll provide me with someone suitable. This sort of thing isn't easy.'

A week passed and I was introduced to Piotr's wife in another little café. From that moment the intermediary's role was over and he took his leave and went out.

For several minutes we drank our coffee in silence. I glanced a couple of times at the woman sitting next to me. She must have been around forty, but the oval of her face was still gentle and in her eyes there was a lively and resolute look. I could see that my youthfulness embarrassed her, she was hesitating and did not quite know how to start the conversation. I had similar doubts, since I was uncertain whether my companion would be able to accomplish the task before her, and so we both said nothing.

Eventually I instinctively chose the right approach. 'I'm pretty sure that you're wondering at this moment how old I am.'

'Of course not.' Her face turned red. 'Why should I?'

'After all we are talking about your husband's life. I'm very well aware of that. But please don't worry. My role will be insignificant compared to what you will have to do.'

'Why is that?'

'Because I shall be working undercover, while you will have to come out into the open to go to a German lawyer I will direct you to. You will have to deal with representatives of the *Kripo*,* and if the smallest thing goes wrong, you will attract the attention of the Gestapo.'

Quite unexpectedly, the woman smiled for the first time. 'My name is Ola and please call me that. I'll do everything you tell me and I am ready for anything. I love my husband and must help him. Also, this will be my first job for the resistance. My husband felt that not everyone could be in the resistance and that if he was in it, I was to stay clear. But I want to do something, I'm also living in an occupied country.'

It was now my turn to smile for the first time. 'Excellent. In that case, here we go. We have to tackle this thing from two angles. You will act officially on behalf of your husband who has been unjustly implicated in the coffee wagon business, while I shall provide you with all the necessary information and finance and will also set up a group of witnesses, who will testify that they have known Piotr Katuszewski for years and that he has always been an honest Warsaw businessman. Furthermore, we'll have to fix him an alibi and find people to swear that he was a long way from Warsaw on the day that that wretched coffee disappeared. For this I need a close friend of your husband who knows his present name and whom we can trust.'

'Right, that can be arranged.'

'When can I meet this friend?'

'Probably within a few days. I must look round. But what shall I do in the meantime? This inactivity is killing me.'

'We'll come to that in a moment. I was going to mention that we've received two notes from your husband. His interrogation is going quite well. He didn't have anything to do with that

---

*The criminal police.

wagon and he really was going to meet a friend, so he's sticking to that story. The other accused are not implicating him and so there is a chance of success. The real danger is that his resistance role might be discovered and so we must move carefully but fast. Here is the address of a lawyer called Schmidt who specializes in getting people out of prison for money. He's a German who lived in Poland before the war and so he has an excellent knowledge of the area and the language. I've checked him and know that in criminal cases he's really very useful. Naturally we must assume that in some way or other he works with the Gestapo, therefore you will have to be extremely careful and play your role well.

'You are Aleksandra Katuszewska, the wife of a Warsaw businessman, and nothing more. You will have to remember day and night your new birthplace, your parents' and grandparents' Christian names, the names of all your schools, your former addresses, the names of your friends and neighbours, in a word, everything. Fortunately your identity cards were well made and are registered at the local council. The records are also all in order. Schmidt might turn out to be useful, but he will certainly also be very inquisitive. Do you feel up to all this?'

'Yes. I'm ready.'

'In that case I would like you to go round to him at once today and raise your husband's case. As I mentioned, the whole thing runs on bribes and so Schmidt will immediately want a deposit for expenses. I have here three thousand zlotys for this. If and when you want it, there will be as much money as you need. I've been given full authority in this case.'

I handed her an envelope with the money. She blushed like a schoolgirl. It was clear that she was finding it hard to accept this initial payment. I also gave her the address of a tobacconist's stand which I used as a contact 'mailbox' for special assignments. We fixed an approximate date for our next meeting and it was time to leave.

'If Schmidt should ask about more money, please tell him that you have a couple of pictures which could be sold. Good luck.'

Two days later my 'mailbox' signalled that Ola would like to see me again. She came with a man, whom she introduced as Mr

Batycki. He was a friend of Piotr's from even before the war and was ready to help in any way. Since I didn't yet know him, I was loath to say anything in his presence and I learned only in passing that the first visit to the lawyer had gone well. He had accepted the case, which was already an achievement, and the deposit had only been two thousand. Ola wanted to give me back the rest and she suggested a receipt, but I convinced her not to do this for the time being. We took our leave and I remained alone with Batycki.

He was at least forty years old, slight, lean and restless. After only a few minutes it seemed safe to assume that his attitude to life was not too serious and that he had no idea of underground work. It later transpired that he liked eating and drinking well and his weakness for the fair sex was quite alarming. He looked at every girl in the street, while time was for him a relative concept. He was capable of being not minutes, but hours late. This was a serious failing on account of my great workload and the basic rules of security, but this shortcoming, like many others, was balanced by his determination to rescue Piotr for whom he felt not only friendship, but also a special sort of respect.

Batycki was to find people who in case of need, would be ready to testify that they had known Piotr for years and that he was a businessman. After several fruitless meetings, he eventually took me to a couple of shops where I met some corpulent and gruff individuals who had promised to help. We talked in small back rooms. It was essential to accept the offer of a little pickled cucumber washed down with a few glasses of some stuff or other, but this ritual worked wonders, for the shopkeepers brightened up and in a flash realized what was required.

'What do we need all this talking for? I've known Katuszewski for twenty years. It's all fixed up.'

Things were looking quite good here, but Batycki's behaviour was worrying me a little, since he wanted to impress our contacts and would interrupt from time to time to say that we had some directive.

'You mustn't say things like that. They have got to take us for members of the family or friends.'

'But surely they must suspect otherwise.'

'We can't stop them suspecting things, but our behaviour must not arouse any suspicions. We'll only spoil Piotr's chances.'

'All right, all right. But do you know who we're going to see today?'

'No, and I can't even guess.'

'You see, old Batycki does have his uses. We're going to see a certain gentleman who will swear that on the critical day in question Piotr was out of Warsaw doing business for him.'

'Is this gentleman reliable?'

'I wouldn't advise doing business with him, but as far as the Germans are concerned, he's solid as concrete.'

We entered a doorway and climbed up to the third floor of a secluded outbuilding. An elderly woman opened the door for us and silently let us into a room where a grey-haired man was sitting behind a desk. His face was creased and contorted in a grimace and his right shoulder was high and stiff. He didn't get up to greet us, but only nodded and held out his left hand. I examined the stranger carefully; he was not sitting in an armchair, but in a wheelchair and the whole right side of his body was paralysed and lifeless. Only his left hand had any life in it.

After a normal greeting we all sat down round his desk and Batycki began the conversation. He didn't even reach the end of the first sentence before our host struck the table with his good fist and grated, 'You always talk too much, Batycki. I've already told you that your Mr Katuszewski was on a business trip to Lublin for me. You can rest easy, I do business with the Germans and the proofs will be cast iron.'

Our mission was to all intents and purposes over, I felt, however, that we owed it to our host to spend a couple of minutes talking about business.

'You mentioned business. What exactly is your line?'

'Line of business? Anything: if you want I can fix you a case of Chimneys.'*

'No thank you, that's not my field.'

---

*'Pistols' in underground slang.

'Suit yourself. I can also sell you a desk, a roll of roofing felt, a gramophone. I've also got some good German watches.'

The matter was settled and it was time to go. Before leaving, I bought a small wristwatch. The very same day its glass fell out in the tram and the hands came off and were lost. This was hardly an encouraging omen and yet I had a strange certainty that we could count on this man in Piotr's case.

I was dreadfully busy, but I managed to meet Ola quite frequently and she brought me news of her conversations with the lawyer. I marvelled at her cheerfulness and self-control. Schmidt did not suspect anything and had even developed a certain affection for his client. He was hopeful of a successful conclusion to the deal. Messages were regularly coming out from Piotr and from them it transpired that his interrogation was proceeding rapidly, and that he had been implicated in nothing.

I was handling a number of quite separate cases and so there were days when I completely forgot about Piotr and Ola. It was on one of those mornings that I found in my 'mailbox' a card requesting an immediate meeting. Batycki arrived. He was very excited, since the matter of Piotr's release had made so much progress that he was expected out any day now. At least that was what the lawyer promised, but at the same time he was demanding a quite considerable sum of money.

I met Ola the following day. She confirmed the previous day's conversation, but when she got to the actual details she stopped and said nothing. I finally got the truth from her: Schmidt was demanding 30,000 zlotys.

'I'll never be able to repay such a sum, even if Piotr really is released. And what if the lawyer tricks me?'

'There's no question of you having to repay the money. High command has given instructions that in cases like this, where there are some chances of success, quite a good deal of money can be spent to help prisoners. That is General 'Grot' 's* view and this aspect of our work is based on it. In any case we all take the same view.'

---

*The Commander of the Home Army.

Ola was very embarrassed when I handed her a wad of five-hundreds. 'Am I really to pay this money?'

'That's right, so long as you feel that Schmidt isn't lying.'

'I don't think so. Yesterday he showed me a letter from the *Kripo* which said that Piotr had been eliminated from their enquiries.

Two more days passed and Friday, Mokotów prison release day, came. Batycki was to meet Piotr and take him to his home. I was to go there in the afternoon.

Just in case I ordered a little observation and at the appointed hour I set off cheerfully for our meeting. I expected success and was in an excellent mood. After all it wasn't every day that one had the opportunity to meet a man whom one has freed from gaol.

Batycki opened the door and in a glance I knew that we had succeeded. At the other end of the room by the window stood a close-cropped balding man. I quickly went up to him and sincerely held out my hand. He took it, but said not a word and began to examine me. This greeting chilled me. After several moments of awkward silence Piotr said, 'Do you always do things like this?'

'I don't understand.'

'That's bad. You see two of us were arrested, me and my friend Andrzej, also an airman. You worked on my case, but what about him? You hadn't the time for him, then?'

For a couple of seconds I was speechless. Finally I regained my voice. 'To be precise, five of you were arrested and not two.'

'Yes, yes,' quickly interrupted Piotr, 'but those other three had nothing to do with us and anyway they're civilians.'

I had regained my balance by now. 'I have no intention of starting a discussion on who those other three were and whether they deserved help. In their statements they didn't implicate you and that's already a lot. I handled your case, for that was what I was ordered to do by my superiors and that was also the wish of your friends. There was some hope of success, since you were in Mokotów all the time. Are you aware that your friend has been transferred to the Pawiak?'

'And so what? Pawiak or not, everyone deserves to be helped.'

I felt myself growing angry. 'You're talking like a child. The Pawiak prison is under Gestapo control and there is no question of getting anyone out of there by legal means. And in any case do you really imagine we spend all our time thinking only of you and your friend?'

'No, and since you don't want to help, I'll get Andrzej out myself.'

'I never said we didn't want to. If high command agrees to your request and I receive the relevant orders, then I shall help you as much as I can. The case looks almost hopeless, but that doesn't mean anything. I'm here to do what I can.'

'Quite right. In any case I might not need you at all.'

'Wrong. Without me you won't get far. Oh, and one more thing. I am in charge of the Pawiak and I am responsible for it. If high command gives the order, we do it, if it doesn't, we don't. I warn you now there will be no one-man shows, for you'll get into trouble.'

For the first time, Piotr hesitated and said nothing for a moment.

'You're right there, I'll have to do it officially. But I'll get my friend out.'

I looked at my watch and started to say goodbye. Batycki tried to keep me and offer me a glass, but I refused and left. I was furious and my good humour had vanished like the mist.

The same evening I reported everything to Stefan. He listened, shook his head and said, 'You handled it right. If only some people would realize in what conditions we have to work.'

The following day I received a card from Ola and met her at the agreed spot.

She arrived trembling and almost in tears. 'Oh, what has Piotr been doing! I must apologize sincerely to you for him. If only he knew how much goodwill and effort you have put into his case. It all comes from group loyalty and also the spirit of his branch of the services. He quite simply is ashamed that he is free, while his friend is still inside.'

'I can understand that a little, in any case I'm not doing this job for gratitude. My promise of help, naturally, still stands.'

'Thank you very much. Piotr has already let me into his plans.'

On parting I held her hand for a moment. 'We've worked together now for some weeks and we surely trust one another. If your husband should start acting on his own, please watch him. Make sure he doesn't make wild plans. He must beware of bravado. He has almost no experience of these things.'

The necessary permission was given and Piotr set about his task. He had not forgotten our conversation and approached me for a great deal of information and for a map of the Pawiak. I gave him what he wanted and he disappeared for a while. Eventually my 'mailbox' came to life again. The airman arrived at the meeting place in a bad temper, he was gloomy and at a loss.

'It all looks bad. How can you get out of the Pawiak?'

'If it were easy, there wouldn't be anyone in it. Better people than we have already racked their brains over it.'

'Does that mean there is no way?'

'There is one, but it's pretty tricky and not always successful.'

'Well.'

'As you know, the Germans are terrified of contagious diseases and so when anyone catches, let's say, typhus, they at once isolate him.'

Piotr immediately brightened up. 'What then?'

'Even before the war there was a special hospital in Warsaw for all seriously ill prison inmates. It still exists, it's called the Saint Sophia Hospital.'

'Aha, then Andrzej is to catch typhus. That's easy.'

'It won't be the first time we've tried this. We send a small container with fleas infected with typhus and the prisoner catches the illness from them. Naturally, he could die or there could be other complications. I know of a case when the Germans brought a particularly important prisoner suffering from typhus to this hospital, but they chained him to the bed. The same could happen to your friend, although I don't expect it to, since so far his case doesn't look too serious. He's still in under his assumed name; they haven't rumbled him.'

'All right, let's assume that Andrzej falls ill and ends up in this hospital. Can we get him out of there?'

'Much more easily than out of the Pawiak, for the hospital is not in the prison grounds, although it's still in the ghetto. If we could enlist a member of the staff there, we might manage to arrange an escape.'

Piotr was very excited and he grasped me by the shoulder. 'So, what are we waiting for? Action stations. What are your plans?'

'Since you have undertaken to rescue your friend, let's leave it that way. I'll use my contacts to get in touch with him and ask him if he's willing to take the risk, while you better try to fix up something in the Saint Sophia Hospital. Documents, clothes, getting him out of the ghetto are all less important matters.'

We didn't see each other for several days, but news reached me that Piotr was working very hard. Meanwhile Andrzej had indicated that he accepted any risk to get out of the hands of the Gestapo. Ola was also helping us and so I met her several times. She was full of verve and the joy of life. Her husband's return and the chance of helping in our work made her look many years younger and her enthusiasm was infectious. Nevertheless, she remembered my request and surrounded Piotr with essential care, protecting him from mistakes and unjustified optimism.

Eventually the airman informed me that the contact in the hospital had been arranged. It was a young girl in the main office. He had got hold of her through some of her close friends and she had promised to help. She was to prepare clothes for Andrzej and help him out on to a first floor balcony. How? That was her problem.

Once I had received this information, I made a whole range of minor arrangements with Piotr; he supplied me with a photograph of his friend for an identity document, and it was time to begin.

I was provided with a container of typhus and, using one of my best contacts, I got it into the hospital in the men's section of the Pawiak. We awaited news impatiently. Eventually we heard that Andrzej was ill. It was typhus. Again we had several days of uncertainty and then a further report. The Germans had transferred him to the Saint Sophia Hospital; he was very ill, but they were not particularly guarding him.

The first part of the plan had been accomplished, now the rest had to be arranged and we could only pray that the ill man would overcome the crisis and begin to recover. The girl in the hospital turned out to be invaluable. Not only did she provide us with every bit of information, but she also looked after the patient, bringing him food and medicine.

The crisis passed after a fortnight and the day for decisive action was approaching. It was essential to time it right so that Andrzej was still ill enough not to have to go back to the Pawiak, and yet strong enough to make an escape. Piotr was ready and was waiting for the signal.

At last the girl brought us the news: tomorrow.

Piotr, disguised as a driver, set off in a van for the ghetto. In his pocket he had documents stating him to be a food supplier for the hospital and indeed the van was loaded with potatoes, carrots and other vegetables. In another pocket he had a concealed identity document for his friend, together with an entry pass into the ghetto and various police papers. Punctually at the appointed hour he arrived, left his load in the correct spot and drove into the street, stopping under the balcony. A moment later Andrzej appeared, climbed with difficulty over the railing and fell in a heap into the truck. Piotr helped him up, sat beside him, gave him his papers and set off. The police posts let them through the gates of the ghetto without hindrance.

They headed for the hideout.

For the second time within a few months Piotr had had incredible luck. He had achieved what others, certainly more experienced and better prepared, had tried unsuccessfully.

Life, however, is harsh and so now really was the time to take stock and wonder whether fate should be provoked in this way. But who can restrain an optimist? In any case there really was a reason for rejoicing. Several days later all four of us met. Batycki was already drunk, Piotr was radiant and Ola was smiling like the spring. Andrzej did not come, since he was still too ill. I suggested that all three of them should leave Warsaw, if only for a few days: they deserved a rest.

Piotr patted me on the shoulder. 'Don't worry yourself about us, young man.'

We shook hands again and went off our separate ways. A mountain of work had accumulated before me.

One morning I received a report that, on the previous evening, there had been a scene in one of the police stations in the town centre. Apparently the Polish police had brought in a man wearing a leather jacket and carrying a briefcase who had made so much noise that eventually the Gestapo had taken him off.

I was dreadfully busy and this report just didn't make any impression on me. It was only the next day, when I received an urgent request for information, that something began to dawn on me and I demanded further details. These I received together with a card from Ola that she must see me immediately.

For a second I did not recognize her, so much had she changed. She was grey, trembling and helpless. 'Piotr has disappeared, I'm sure he's been arrested.'

With difficulty I managed to get out of her the necessary details which, together with the report I had just received, gave me a picture of what had happened.

Piotr's friends had decided that his double success merited a party. When men get together like this, naturally they drink. This time was no exception. The bottles circulated and Piotr had his fair share. The party took place at Andrzej's hideout and when the curfew approached, Piotr realized it was time to leave. His wife was awaiting him at home. His friends tried to stop him and make him spend the night there, but he was drunk and insisted, while the others were also no longer in control of their actions.

The airman caught a belated horse-drawn cab and ordered it to go at full speed. The curfew was upon them and the city was becoming deserted. It seemed to Piotr that the cabby was going too slowly, and so he tore the whip from his hand and began to urge on the horse himself, spurring it on with shouts. A Polish police patrol happened to be passing. Trying to protect him from meeting a German patrol, they manhandled him to the police station and tried to put him into a cell for the night. Unfortunately, Piotr was no longer in control of himself and began to make a terrible scene. The policemen were patient and might have managed him on their own, but his shouts echoed down the empty streets. It was his bad luck that a German military police patrol was passing by. They entered the police station and saw three policemen struggling with a man. Again, he might have got off, but, seeing the German uniforms, Piotr screamed '*Raus!*'

('Get out!'). This was too much, the Germans knocked him down, searched him and one of them opened his briefcase. He looked through the papers and immediately rang the Gestapo.

I looked silently at the woman sobbing next to me. My mind worked feverishly looking for some ray of hope in this gloomy picture. In vain.

'I'll do what I can, Ola, I'll try to find him and probably will, but it won't be the Mokotów this time.'

'Is there, is there still any hope?'

'While there's life, there is always hope.'

I sent this matter round my Pawiak network, giving both Piotr's names: his assumed and his real one. I also gave the order to look elsewhere, including the court medical centre which took the bodies of people killed in the street.

Some days passed: nothing. I began very carefully to sound out the Gestapo headquarters. Yes, a man in a leather jacket had been seen there. He had apparently been confronted with someone, cruelly beaten and was being held in an underground cell. Was it Piotr? Apparently it was.

For a fortnight or so I was busy with other matters, but I continually enquired about new arrivals in the Pawiak. Eventually my girl from the stores answered. A man in a leather jacket had been brought in, he was quite blue and could barely stand up. She gave me a name, which was Piotr's real name. So he had been uncovered.

I had the signal ready and so I immediately sent a message. A reply returned quite soon. It was barely legible. Piotr wrote not to bother with him, since things were hopeless. In his briefcase he had been carrying documents which had completely given him away. He had tried to maintain his fictitious identity, but he had been placed face to face with another prisoner who had known him before the war. He further sent his wife greetings and commended her to God's protection.

The necessary warnings had been sent out long before and so there was very little else that could be done in Piotr's case. Batycki of course appeared demanding some task, but what could I give him? All he could do was look after Ola.

To a certain extent I also had to look after her. It was clear that what had worked the first time was quite out of the question now, but human nature refuses to the last to face defeat. Ola often asked me to meet her and from these short conversations she drew strength to continue and endure. I brought her the most recent information about her husband (and how rarely could I tell her the truth) and tried to comfort her as best I could in the way I had had to so many times before.

Unfortunately, she was not the only wife with whom I had to have such painful and sad conversations. With difficulty I tried to ignore the persistent thought that I also had a wife who waited each evening at home for me and that there might come a day when I too would not return.

It was the spring of 1943 and Warsaw was throbbing with feverish activity and reeling from the blows which plucked the best from among us. I worked ceaselessly, but even then the day had only twelve hours and there was never enough time.

It was, I think, 15 April when I once again received a card and met Ola. Easter was approaching and so she brought me some trifle and asked me to remember her and Piotr. She was going to the country for Easter to stay with some friends who had a little land and plenty of food.

She looked at me carefully and tried to smile. 'You don't look well. What is the matter?'

'Nothing, it's just that I have a great deal of work and, as you know, it's not easy work.'

Ola gently touched my arm. 'Look after yourself. We have already lost so many . . .'

I quickly turned away, so that she could not see my expression. She again attempted a smile, but was no longer looking at me but somewhere into the darkness around as if searching for a disappearing light, as if a vision of the future were approaching . . . We quickly took our leave and the spring mist immediately separated us.

Five days later I was picked up on the street. Ill-treated and miserable I sat alone underground at Gestapo headquarters.

We were brought to Auschwitz on 13 May at midnight and hustled into an empty hut. The following day we were in quarantine in Birkenau. Next to us, in the same hut were prisoners who had come from Warsaw two weeks earlier.

For several days we did not have to go to work and so we could visit our neighbours. Entering the hut I saw a small group of men sitting on the floor between the bunks. Amongst them was Piotr sitting hunched up and cross-legged. I immediately recognized him as he did me. A sudden flash of surprise ran across his face and for a moment he froze.

I casually went over to him. 'Surely we met in the Pawiak?'

'Yes, that's where it was.'

Piotr got up and we went outside. I quickly gave him my name, which he naturally had not known before and told him that I had been arrested accidentally and for something quite different. He was the only one in the whole of Auschwitz who knew my real identity. Piotr nodded that he understood. A whistle sounded and we had to go. This time he shook my outstretched hand very warmly.

We didn't see each other too frequently in Birkenau. Piotr met some friends and got a good job, while I, with a dozen or so others, was sent to the penal company and was cut off from the rest of the camp. It was only several months later, when I was selected for a transport and driven back to the main Auschwitz camp, that I again met Piotr, who was also leaving. We waited a week for a medical examination and did not have to work; there was time to talk.

We had exchanged information for the first time while still in Birkenau, but now we could get down to more general subjects. Already after our first conversation I realized that I was dealing with a completely different man. The old self-confident Piotr, who had been polite, but rather cold and who always tried to express his superiority discreetly, but clearly, had disappeared. I was now talking to a man who only physically resembled the former air force officer. This change struck me immediately. It was not difficult to guess its cause.

Piotr had been brought up in a certain traditional way and his later life only reinforced the views he had inculcated from an early age. Perhaps he had not tried to curb them, perhaps there had been no need for him to do so, perhaps his mind, trained in one direction, was unable to appreciate the evolution of the world around him. Thus he had lived for many years when suddenly the cruel war had struck us, and him no less. The front, combat, dying soldiers, danger – all this would not have changed his deep-rooted views, but fate decreed that Piotr was to follow a path which no imagination could have foreseen.

The sudden collapse of the world in which he had lived and believed, the circumstances of his arrest, the cruel interrogation by the Gestapo, the solitary confinement, the sight of the sufferings and the heroism of people whom previously he had regarded as his inferiors, the truly noble reactions against a background of extreme bestiality – these were all blows which destroyed the hard exterior of his long-established routine, faulty views and habits. When the scales of this hard exterior came off an honourable, upright and pure heart appeared.

In the course of our long conversation we naturally discussed the future of Poland, looking back and making comparisons. If in a moment of annoyance I sometimes blurted out some over-critical or perhaps too hasty opinion, Piotr would carefully lay a hand on my shoulder and quietly ask, 'Please don't talk like that . . .'

In his distressed state he had a vision of his country as a rainbow illuminated by the glory of victory, bathed in the glow of grandeur and power, free from error and meanness, with justice towards all: a truly caring country . . . Through the harsh camp days he strove for such a Poland, and he was ready to suffer and die for such a country.

The transport separated us for several days, since we were in different wagons, but we met again in Neuengamme. Once again we were in quarantine and there was a chance to exchange views. Discipline in the new camp was less rigorous and it was possible to visit without difficulty after the evening roll-call.

We were to all intents and purposes friends, but Piotr continued to maintain a certain reserve towards me. The reasons for it were different from those in Warsaw. What separated us was the fact that I knew the details of his second arrest and all the circumstances surrounding him. He could never forget this and I was well aware that he suffered whenever those days came to mind.

This was understandable. He was tortured and grieved with shame that he, a soldier of the Polish Republic, an officer of the proud Air Force, had allowed himself to be caught by the Germans in such a dreadful fashion, particularly when before he had almost miraculously managed to escape from their barbarous hands. Once captured, he had left the ranks and no longer counted as a fighting soldier, and it was his own fault that this had happened. I knew what was on his mind and tried carefully to allude to the subject, convince him and explain things, but Piotr would not listen to anything.

We never talked about our dear ones and Ola's name never came into our conversation. It was too painful a nerve for me to touch.

In February 1944 I left for Wittenberge, a small sub-camp of Neugengamme. After a year I returned for a short while to the main camp, but immediately chose another transport, believing that it would be safer to do so. I again met Piotr in passing and urged him to leave, but he had a good job and preferred to stay in familiar surroundings.

The end of the war was fast approaching and eventually the last days of April were upon us. The Allied front ran just by Neuengamme and anything was possible. Himmler had already issued instructions quite some time before that, if the camps were threatened, they were to be evacuated and that if this should prove impossible, the prisoners were to be liquidated. Not everywhere was this order obeyed, but in Neugengamme the master of life and death was a fanatical young SS officer called Thuman, a former *Lagerführer* (camp commander) at Majdanek, who would stop at nothing. When the liberating tanks were approaching the Elbe, he ordered the prisoners to be marched outside and divided into two groups. The first group of about two thousand was taken to one side and riddled with machine gun bullets. Not a prisoner survived.

Was Piotr among them? Had fate decreed that, just on the threshold of freedom, he was to endure another and final test: to stare down the barrel of a loaded weapon held by his executioners.

The rest of the prisoners were marched in the direction of the sea. They were herded onto old barges which were pushed away from the shore. The SS were going to set them alight, but just before they began their task some Allied aircraft arrived and, unaware of what was happening beneath, dropped their bombs. The barges burst into flames and began to sink, merely a few kilometres offshore. Panic seized the crowded and exhausted prisoners. Some died in the crush, others leapt overboard, while others trying to organize an escape, were trampled by the terror-stricken mob. A few managed to grab planks and pieces of wood. Hanging on, they clumsily tried to make for the shore where they were met by withering fire from the waiting SS men's machine guns.

Was Piotr there? Did he with numbed hands try to grasp the floating timbers, or struggle with the waves which washed over the wrecks, or like others was he tossed and turned by the whirlpools created by the sinking vessels for so long that eventually his strength gave out and he sank for ever into the chill depths of the hostile northern sea?

Who knows?

Chapter Seven

Betrayal

It was already February 1943 when emergency liaison brought me a very alarming piece of news. For some months now I had been in contact with the Government Delegacy security department and they notified me that the Delegate, Professor Jan Piekałkiewicz, had not come to an agreed rendezvous. He had presumably been arrested.

The Polish Government was in London at the time, directing the struggle of the entire Polish nation, while all Poland was occupied by the Germans. There was not only an underground army, but clandestine schools, university, publishing firms, courts of law, political parties, everything that the Nazis were endeavouring to eliminate and destroy. For that reason the Government was represented on Polish territory by its Delegate, who was formally number one there.

The head of security met me as soon as possible and showed signs of considerable agitation. 'The professor failed to keep his appointment, and he has never been late. He's obviously been arrested'.

'Where was he going? Whom was he supposed to meet?'

'He was going to meet a Ukrainian, a representative of Roman Szeptycki, the Metropolitan of the Greek Catholic Church in Lwów.* The Delegacy was engaged in difficult political discussions with him.'

'Where were they going to meet?'

'In Rakowiecka Street, by the tram stop. He was due to have another meeting straight after, on his own premises this time'.

*Roman Szeptycki was the spokesman of the Ukrainian nationalists.

'He could have been arrested, but he could also have had a heart attack, or an accident in the street, or he might have been caught by the criminal police. I must check. Tell me what he looks like, and the name his papers were made out in. In a few minutes time I'll hand it to my street surveillance group, then pass it on to the Pawiak liaison network.'

We parted, for time was pressing. We arranged an emergency telephone liaison so I could quickly give the results of the initial search were they to prove positive. I had yet another way of finding out what had happened to the Delegate, but I kept quiet about it. This was my own personal contact whom I kept strictly for myself, as he was hard to come by and the situation was exceptionally delicate. I had inside information into what went on in the cells, in the vaults of the Gestapo headquarters in Aleja Szucha.*

How had I achieved this? Well, in real life there are sometimes situations of which one usually reads in bad novels about counter-espionage. One of my people reported to me that he had contact with a woman whose husband was in German captivity, and who in order to earn a living had started a laundry service from home. She took in linen from lonely men and one of her clients was a *Volksdeutscher*† from Silesia called Schmidt, who was cell keeper in the vaults of the Gestapo. He had been sent to Warsaw, and was completely alone here; he was bringing his laundry to this woman, and sometimes hanging on for a chat. He was complaining about his low pay and low-grade work. He once dropped the remark that the Germans were treating the Poles badly.

I realized that here was an opportunity not to be missed. The woman was embarrassed by the German guard coming round to her in uniform and was looking for some way out of this awkward situation, some moral justification, and the *Volksdeutscher* needed money and did not feel either German or Polish. I established with my informant that I would give him several

---

*There is mention of this on page 44.
†A person who opted for German nationality, but was regarded as a second class citizen even by the Germans.

thousand zlotys, a considerable sum, which he would hand on to the woman with appropriate instructions. She was to lure the guard into greater intimacy and later offer him a little financial help. Once this was accepted the ball would start rolling.

And that is what happened. Schmidt celebrated Christmas with our woman, and spent the night with her. He accepted several bank notes, and this was repeated on a number of occasions. A few innocent questions about the Gestapo were asked, which he answered, and I already had a highly promising contact. I had no intention of sending letters through him, and I stuck to my guns, but I received verbal messages regularly. Not in person, of course, I never met our woman, my trusted colleague always acted as go-between.

As the surveillance network and Pawiak liaison brought no results, I now waited all the more impatiently for contact with the guard. After twenty-four hours had gone by, thanks to Schmidt, I already knew that the Delegate was in solitary confinement in the Gestapo vaults and that he had been arrested under his real name. Just before this a list of new prisoners, men and women who had just been brought to the Pawiak, reached my hands.

I read it through impatiently for two reasons. I was looking for the names of people who might be connected with the Delegate. And – understandably enough – my thoughts were also for Eileen. She had been translating texts for the Delegacy. The man to whom she delivered the texts could have been caught; and he knew that she was British. I knew him, and I knew where they used to meet.

Luckily his name did not figure on the list. But the Delegacy security chief found several names from circles close to Professor Piekałkiewicz. One of these raised by alarm: Tadeusz Kobylański, head of the Delegacy propaganda department. He knew Eileen's contact man. Late that evening when I returned home dog tired and we sat down to a bowl of soup, Eileen and I discussed her situation. Fortunately the man contacted by her knew neither her name nor her address. Otherwise we would have had to move out of the flat and have papers made out in a different name, and that was not so easy. Eileen had an identity card with her name changed to Helena and proof that she was born in Błonie near Warsaw, but this was only through the good services of an acquaintance who had entered her date of birth in the registry for 1912, when that part of Poland belonged to Russia. These were tricky matters and I was relieved to know that Eileen was not endangered. Nevertheless she had to suspend her contact with the Delegacy.

The question now was to establish contact as quickly as possible with people from the delegacy who were already inside the Pawiak. They had been through preliminary interrogation; a lot could be inferred from the questions they were asked. The most important point was to find out who had led to the arrest.

Four men and one woman had been seized and it was from her that the first news came. She had been arrested in the street, she had been with one of the arrested men and with a young priest of the Greek Catholic Church – the same priest who was supposed to meet the Delegate.

That same day the head of street surveillance brought me a report that complemented the information received from the Pawiak. The Delegate was arrested in the street, he had been with a man aged around thirty-five, of middling height, with raven hair and sallow complexion.

The affair was of extreme urgency, a secret letter went straight off to the Pawiak, to the women's section, to find out what the priest who had been arrested with the woman looked like. At the same time, through the emergency telephone, I summoned the head of Delegacy security to meet me.

After I had described the young man he said in a tone of great excitement, 'We know him, he's a Ukrainian, an ex-Catholic priest, who has changed denomination. He mixes with Poles, mainly among the aristocracy, he had close contact with the Delegate and his circle.'

'And what's your opinion of him?'

'Hard to say. He is very shrewd, he is also supposed to be liaison man between Metropolitan Szeptycki and the Pope, he apparently goes to Rome via Berlin, he has a good alibi with the Germans.'

This news alarmed me considerably. We already knew that the Delegate and several other people had been arrested whilst meeting the priest. The Ukrainian's role began to assume more

and more distinct contours. I came to an agreement with delegacy security and we decided that evidence pointing to the
Ukrainian as responsible for the arrests called for immediate
action. Those who might have contact with the priest had to be
warned. It was a complicated task, for although it was forbidden,
the same people belonged to the Home Army, worked in the
Delegacy, and often were active in the political parties and even
in other underground organizations.

I was sorting out dozens of problems all at the same time, but
the next few days were devoted to the delegacy. Schmidt brought
information about Professor Piekałkiewicz. He was still being
kept in solitary confinement in the vaults of the Gestapo, and was
subjected to cruel interrogation. He resisted and refused to
accept food. He had been confronted with several people, who
had been beaten in his presence. From the letters we received
from delegacy workers arrested in the Pawiak we knew that the
Gestapo was aiming to break up the representation of the Polish
Government in London and to infiltrate Home Army headquarters.

Our emergency system had functioned efficiently. After initial
arrests the danger did not spread, there were no further losses,
but for how long? Imprisoned people could break down, torture
could force them to confess, they could incriminate others.
There was nothing we could do about that; but the Ukrainian
priest was still active and within our reach. The head of counter-
intelligence, to whom I was answerable, issued an order to
concentrate on the priest and collect all information that could
provide the basis for a sentence and execution. Special military
courts operated in the underground, and it was only after their
verdict that our execution squad could shoot the condemned
man.

At the time I was so frantically busy and scarcely able to cope
with day to day business that I had to use a false night pass and
sometimes spend the night in the centre of the city, in a rented
room. It was then that the great blow hit me: Janek was arrested.*

Fortunately his arrest was not connected with our work and

---

*Janek was one of our best workers, a key liaison man in my secret contacts
with the Pawiak. His story is told in chapter eight.

there could be no danger from there; the trouble was with his wife. Her despair was understandable, her frantic attempts to rescue her husband were also justified; but she was a well-known doctor and under her maiden name of Dr Pawłowska had direct contact with the Commander of the Home Army, General Stefan Rowecki. He was in the prime of life, but he had some complaint of the alimentary tract, and Janek's wife saw him quite often. She wanted to save her husband, and in spite of my warnings she sought contacts with the Pawiak. She was going about it in amateurish fashion and treading on very dangerous ground, as the Hammer affair had shown. I was afraid for her, or rather of her, and of the results of her activity. What would happen if she were arrested? After the Delegate affair we could easily be saddled with the Home Army Commander affair. And that is what nearly happened.

I had to go and meet her. The moment I entered her room, her snow white face with wide staring eyes emerged from the gloomy interior.

'I'm just back from Aleja Szucha!'

The news was so staggering that in the first moment I did not understand what she was on about. 'From Aleja Szucha? From the Gestapo?'

'I was arrested!'

'I don't understand . . .'

'I was arrested and released. Wasn't that a miracle?'

It transpired that she was on her way to give an injection when the Gestapo encircled the flat and carried out a raid. She was taken off to the cellars of the German Headquarters of Evil, she had been detained overnight in a cell to which fresh victims were brought, and several questions had been promptly asked.

'Do you realize, I was in the Gestapo cellars, where Janek was held and tortured. Do you realize?!'

The next day she was interrogated, but not beaten. Obviously her personal data were taken down (she was already on false papers), and she was asked about people she did not know. She lived through a traumatic moment when a butchered man was brought in and in the first instant she thought it was her husband. Fortunately it was someone else, who was asked if he knew her, which he denied with a movement of his head, then fell. She was ordered to sign some paper, and warned that everything she had seen down there was secret; and then she was released.

It was a perfectly incredible story. But I now knew that I must control the activities of Janek's wife, as things could turn nasty. I gave her the key to a room that we used in cases of emergency and recommended her most resolutely to hide there, while I supplied her with some documents made out in another name within the next twenty-four hours.

This affair was not connected with the arrest of the Delegate and several of his people, but it was, so to speak, a warning. We had to sort out the affair of the Ukrainian priest and execute it as quickly as possible.

My people collected the necessary information quite quickly. After we had received contact points from Delegacy security the priest was subjected to surveillance, his itineraries were identified, and the hunch that he was a German political agent turned to certainty. I was just about to send all the facts to our special department that prepared such cases for the military court when I unexpectedly received new instructions. The head of staff at Home Army headquarters decided that the entire matter had to be handed over to Delegacy security.

This was predestined to be one of my last actions as head of security at Home Army headquarters. Only after the war did I discover what had been the fate of the Delegate and the people arrested with him.

Professor Piekałkiewicz proved to be an exceptionally tough and generous man, defending the dignity of his office to the bitter end. My own experience in the field had taught me that almost everyone breaks down under physical and psychological pressure. We used to assume that a man could hold out for twenty-four hours, a woman twice as long, though it might have seemed that it ought to be the other way round. Without going into long psychological discussions we knew that women were more straightforward, more loyal to the cause for which they were fighting, and withstood torture at the hands of the Gestapo longer.

The Professor was detained in solitary confinement for several weeks in the vaults of Aleja Szucha. Yet he did not break down, and he betrayed no one, even though he had extensive contacts, was in touch with the Commander of the Home Army, with representatives of underground political parties, and with many other important people. By refusing to accept meals he reduced his organism to such a state of emaciation that when he was transferred to the Pawiak on the last day of May 1943 he was at the end of his tether. Even then the Gestapo did not allow him to be transferred to the prison hospital. He died in solitary confinement on 9 June 1943.

Other people who had been arrested over the same affair found themselves in Auschwitz. Tadeusz Kobyłanski was one of the prisoners whom I met there in a penal company.

Chapter Eight

Janek

In the Botanical Gardens a young, tall man, who had some contacts with the prison, was introduced to me. As I was trying to gather all contacts into my hands, I was catching hold of anything going. The intermediary was my closest friend, an experienced conspirator and infallible in his estimate of people, so that any trap was out of the question.

After a few words of recommendation we remained alone. Before the first words had fallen from my lips, I had given a careful glance at the face and figure of the unknown. He was probably a few years younger than I, the same height, but better built, with an oval face, regular features and quiet, trustful eyes. He did not smile, but one could see that his attitude to others was based on trust and friendliness. He made a pleasant, convincing impression, although it was hard not to think, that he might be credulous. Before the meeting I had been told his real name, so I knew what class he belonged to.

'I have been told that you have a contact in the Pawiak prison.'

'Yes, I know a warder, with whom I have been working for some months.'

'May I know for whom?'

'For a group of people with whom I worked in a secret printing press. After a number of them had been arrested, I was told to try to get into touch with them.'

'Was your group connected with any other?'

'Yes, but that is of no importance, because they have come to an agreement and have joined up with the whole military underground.'

'That's enough for me. I have heard a lot about you from the man who introduced us. Have you been told which branch I represent?'

'Yes.'

'Would you like to work with me?'

'If possible, yes. Very much.'

'And what about that other affair? You are not in any danger?'

'No. There were no further arrests. And those who survived have been sent to concentration camps.'

'All right. We will start tomorrow.'

The next day my new co-worker took the oath and the code name 'Janek' for his personal contacts with me.

He was an excellent worker, accepted every commission quietly and carried it out perfectly, he was realistic, exact and careful with his words. From the beginning he grasped the essentials of our work, knew what was important and what not, was able to select reports and when necessary could show ingenuity and initiative. At first he worked with only one warder, but his contact was very enterprising and got more 'letters' in and out the prison than could be expected. After a few weeks I gave him a second contact and in a short time he himself widened his possibilities and formed a cell, which was an important part of my reserve net.

I grew to like him very much, but relations between us were still official, for Janek rarely smiled, never mentioned personal matters and never complained. He gave the impression of a man, who lived his own life and treated his underground work as a duty, to be performed faultlessly, but without any sentimental links with his new environment. Anyway that was the impression he made on me. I knew that he was very honest and that he would never deceive me in our work, but I could not help thinking that he was hiding something from me.

In underground work you could never be too careful, especially in work of my kind. Sometimes personal affairs could have a fatal effect on a man's duties, so I determined to sound out Janek a little.

One morning we met near the Mokotów Fields. It was glorious spring weather, so we sat down for a time near an allotment and turned our faces to the sun. Once our official conversation was ended, we could rest for a while. Janek was exceptionally talkative and gay that day, he even made a joke, so I felt that the time was propitious and put the question.

'Are you contented with life?'

'Yes, very.'

'Why?'

'Because I am doing what I ought to be doing.'

'Our work, you mean?'

'Yes, I was thinking of that.'

'And yet you give the impression of a man who is worried.'

Janek looked at me carefully, as if he was hesitating, but said nothing.

'I shouldn't pry into your private affairs, but we are in such close relationship, we see each other every day, that surely you have learnt to trust me. Besides sometimes personal matters affect our work.'

Janek again looked at me and bristled. I put my hand on his shoulder cautiously. 'We ought to be friends and we are already. Something is worrying you, something is upsetting you.'

'Me? No, no. It just looks like it.'

'I don't think so. Yesterday, for instance, you were very depressed. It was obvious. Such a mood is dangerous, not only for you, but for our work.'

'Do you really think so?'

'Of course.'

The young man was quiet for a moment and ruffled his hair nervously. At last he obviously came to a decision, for he said, 'Since you think that our work might be endangered, I will be quite open. Yes. I am worried about something.'

'Something strictly personal?'

'No, not quite. When I was still a small child, my parents adopted a little boy, an orphan. We grew up together, like brothers. There was never any difference made between us. Our characters were not very compatible, but that happens even among near relations. My foster brother was by descent a Ukrainian and we put certain differences between us down to this. Up to the war our life under one roof was amicable, but when the Germans came in, everything changed suddenly.'

Janek stopped talking and mused.

'What changed?'

'Perhaps my suspicions are unjust, but I can't help feeling, that my foster brother is up to something. He has left my parents' house, I have seen him several times in the company of Germans. He has become insolent and arrogant. It is tormenting me, I do so hate suspecting anyone.'

'Do you think, that he might co-operate with the Germans?'

'Unfortunately, yes.'

I looked at my watch and got up. 'We must go. It's well that you were straight with me. This is very important news. In our work we must be alert to suspicions. You are certainly in danger and, through you, our work. Do you live with your parents?'

'No. I am married. We live on our own.'

'Do you know this Ukrainian's address?'

'I do.'

'Good, I shall need it. Please give me also his detailed description. We must take a look at him. As for you, once more I thank you for your frankness and I will repay you with the same. You are a very good worker and a decent fellow, not merely my subordinate, but a comrade, a friend, and therefore I am giving you a clear instruction: please break off all 'contacts with this Ukrainian and cease to meet him. If he knows your address, please change it and your name, as well. You must also stop visiting your parents, at least for some time.'

'Very well, I understand.'

Weeks of hard, nervous work passed. Janek went on working excellently and his relationship with me became much more cordial. We kept the Ukrainian under observation. This was organized by the chief of my external network 'Ernest', an excellent and very devoted worker. Janek's suspicions began to look well founded. His foster brother was, in fact, in contact with the Germans and lived fairly well, although he was not actually doing any work. Naturally these were only signs.

The summer of 1942 was coming to an end. One morning I climbed up to the sixth floor to our contact flat. We rented a room from a poor woman on the pretext of trade contacts. A few rags gave us the appearance of second-hand clothes dealers. I was late, so I expected that Janek would be waiting for me, but no. It was a good half hour before he showed up. He was very excited, his hair untidy, his face grey.

'What has happened?'

'During the night the Gestapo arrested my father.'

'In his flat?'

'Yes. My mother escaped, because she has just gone to Kraków. I have already sent my wife to warn her.'

'Was your father engaged in any underground work?'

'I know that he worked in the Government Delegacy.'

'Did he know your last address?'

'No, but what does that matter?' Janek covered his eyes with his hand.

I put my arm around him firmly. 'Don't worry. While he is alive, all is not lost. And I am asking these questions, because I must. Your father may have been followed, he may have unwittingly led the Gestapo to addresses that he knew. Do you know how they got a line on him?'

'I can only guess. A few days ago my father told me that he had met my foster brother and tried to persuade him to break with the Germans. My brother was furious and began to threaten him.'

'That doesn't sound too good. I must order a closer watch to be kept on that man and, for God's sake, don't you go near him. This last blow was too close. We have to guard others from danger, not get ourselves locked up.'

Having taken farewell of Janek, I mused for a while, none too happily. I was sorry for him, but at the same time I could not forget that I was his superior officer. I did not at all like the whole situation. The matter of the Ukrainian must be cleared up as soon as possible.

For some days I waited for news from the Pawiak prison that Janek's father had been taken there, but in vain. I tried very cautiously to get something out of my *Volksdeutscher* from Gestapo headquarters. He was my latest contact, very risky, and therefore kept at a safe distance, requiring several intermediaries. After some time he sent word that there was in the cellars a tall man whose description resembled that of the man I was looking for. A few days later he sent word again, that this man had allegedly been killed during interrogation.

I said nothing of this to Janek, because, after all, there was no certainty. But he must have heard something himself or guessed, for he asked me straight out.

More or less at the same time the external intelligence group found out more about the Ukrainian. While he was out of Warsaw for a few days, they managed to search his flat and take away a number of compromising documents. I was brought a Gestapo identity card, made out in his name, and a few other papers, which unmasked him completely. I told Janek about it and once more warned him to be careful. The whole matter was in Stefan's hands.

There was more and more work. Constant meetings, dispatches, conversations, discussions, constant changes of contact points, new faces, new people. The whirl of work gathered me in and absorbed me completely. I had no time for my own worries, my own personal affairs, so it was not strange that Janek's cares slipped partly out of my mind, faded. I watched over him and his work, as far as possible, but without overdoing it. I thought that, when new trouble came, it would come from another direction. Life was usually like that.

And yet no!

It was evening when I was brought a list of the people who had come in to the Pawiak prison that day. Among the women's names I saw Janek's surname. It might be his wife, it might be his mother. It was too late to catch him that day. I met him the following morning. When I told him the full name of the arrested woman, Janek went white. Yes, that would be his mother. She did not live with him. It was a few days since he had seen her. He gave me the address. I, at once, passed it on to find out what had happened. A few hours later I received a report. The Gestapo had been there three days ago and taken several people. Our suspicions became certainty.

Poor Janek, how sorry I was for him. He tried to keep himself under control, but it was obvious that this blow had wounded him profoundly: his father and mother arrested within a few months, his childhood playmate in the pay of the Gestapo. Only his wife was left. I kept silent, waiting for him to speak, for what could I say? Janek kept silent too and stood with his head hanging down until at last he asked quietly:

'Do you know anything about the Ukrainian problem?'

The question astonished me. Where were my friend's thoughts running? 'Yes, I do and I am interested in it. I was born in Kiev. But I don't understand . . .'

'You see, I know that many Ukrainians are pro-German and therefore work for them. I can't believe that the same man, who betrayed my father, has now given away my mother. After all she looked after him, when he was a child. She loved him like her own son . . . Perhaps he also, perhaps an idealistic motive . . .?'

'Idealistic motive? What could be more holy than to love the people who took the place of his parents? Will vile – the vilest – treachery bring freedom for the Ukraine nearer? Can it right the wrongs, of which he is the author? For heaven's sake, don't be sorry for him, don't try to justify him! He is scum, the lowest of the low!'

'Yes, yes, I understand, of course. You are, you must be right, but it is very hard to reconcile oneself to it.

Necessity forced us to turn to official matters. I recommended Janek to go into the city as little as he could and promised that I would get in touch with his mother through somebody else. Janek wrote a short message on a piece of tissue paper, giving the password that would assure the recipient that the contact was genuine, and went out.

I was left alone with my gloomy thoughts. Janek's drama looked more threatening than I had supposed. The loss of his nearest ones was a heavy blow, but not the heaviest. This upright lad's outlook on the world had been turned upside down, his faith in men, in the victory of good over evil, had been shattered to dust. Could he, in this state, still carry on his difficult duties? I knew that to remove him from his work would finish him off completely, but what did one individual matter in the face of the struggle in which thousands perished day after day? The near, heartfelt, problem of one man and the problem of the universal ends at which we aimed, stood before me in all its majestic terror. I felt that my young heart must make an even greater effort than ever to find strength for the days that lay before us.

A few days later we got the first message from Janek's mother. She wrote secretly from the Pawiak prison, that she had been arrested for being in contact with Swedes and that someone must have pointed her out to the Gestapo agents, as she had changed her name and address after her husband's arrest. Further correspondence, which gave us details of her interrogation, showed clearly that the same person was the author of it all. It completed the material already in Stefan's hands. He informed me that the case had been sent to the underground military court and that when the sentence was pronounced, he would see that it was carried out quickly.

Janek still performed his duties. I kept a sharp eye on him, ordered him to change his name and address again, but did not remove him from his work. His father was dead, his mother arrested for a quite different matter and the accursed Ukrainian had been warned and was under our constant observation. I could expect that he would draw in his horns a bit. We had a few quieter weeks and my friend slowly came to himself. His mother had been taken in the meantime to Berlin, for the centre of interrogation in the 'Swedish' affair was there. This was on the whole advantageous, for the Warsaw Gestapo had the worst reputation and it was hardest to keep alive in prison there.

It was March 1943. About ten o'clock in the morning I went along to the normal meeting with Janek. I was just turning into the gateway of the house where our contact point was, when suddenly somebody grabbed my arm. I looked round. It was the owner of a shop that I had just passed. She knew me by sight. Sometimes I bought rolls and margarine there.

'Don't go any further. Germans!'

'Where?'

'Here, just round the corner. A moment ago they arrested a young man.'

I thanked the woman, turned round and jumped on the first passing tram. Some minutes later I got off the tram, went into a café and telephoned the place of our rendezvous. Nobody answered, so Janek was not there! I at once dialled another number, which was Ernest's alarm centre, and ordered two sacks of potatoes. This was our agreed signal.

When we met, I told him to get all the details of this arrest on the street and went off myself to another contact, to order a search for Janek in the Pawiak prison.

That same evening I got a report. A young man, answering Janek's description, had met another man of more or less the same age. As soon as they greeted each other, three agents had jumped out of the gateway, handcuffed Janek and taken him off in a car. The other man had been left to go free. The informers were not able to give an exact description of him.

Three days later a message came from the Pawiak. Janek wrote, that he had spent forty-eight hours at Gestapo headquarters. He had been interrogated brutally, asked about his father and the printing press. Nothing at all was asked about our work. The same Ukrainian had given him away.

So it had happened. Janek was no longer among us. He was at a distance, behind walls and bars, at the mercy of cruel people, all alone against violence and the problems that lay heavily on his young heart.

From further messages it transpired that he had arranged to meet the Ukrainian and had been arrested then. Why had he met him? Why had he broken his promise? I could not find out.

For the time being I had to take over all his contacts. I had to look after his wife, which he fervently asked me to do in every message. This was not an easy task, for Janek's wife, considerably older than he, loved him with a fierce love mingled with maternal feeling. She was at the end of her nervous tether, fluttered about like a wounded bird, asked impossible things of me, put forward ideas, which were not even worth discussion, and demanded that I should take her to do her husband's work. I did what I could to comfort her. I brought her Janek's messages to be read and destroyed immediately. I told her stories of prisoners being released unexpectedly, made out that his case was not serious, talked about the war ending soon. These were nightmarish days, filled with nervous work, thousands of meetings, repairing the broken network, chasing time, of which there was always too little. And after the day, which left me ready to drop, came the night and the turning over of piles of reports in a secret office, without sleep or rest.

How could I know that a thunderbolt would suddenly fall and that in a very short time fate would once again unite me with Janek?

Chapter Nine
Drama and Providence

I looked round surreptitiously and got quickly onto the tram, which was just beginning to move. It was crowded and only with difficulty was I able to shoulder my way inside. Out of the corner of my eye I tried to look discreetly over my shoulder; it seemed as if someone was groping in my pockets, but not really like a pickpocket.

'Get on, get on! Don't block up the doorway', grunted an unpleasant-looking young man, pushing behind me.

I was struck by the wolfish glitter in his eyes, which he averted as soon as he saw me looking. God alone knew who he was. I had an uneasy feeling. Not that there were any definite signs of danger. It was the sort of feeling I would have if I thought someone was following me, as if a pair of invisible eyes were watching my every step. I stood tensely for a while, but nothing happened. The grey walls of the buildings slid monotonously past the windows of the tramcar. I calmed down and opened the newspaper.

The tram ran the whole length of Pulawska Street and stopped at the small station. I climbed off and walked to the right. I was going to call on a friend, something personal, not connected with my work. The road was short and empty.

Suddenly I was conscious of someone behind me. Then I heard footsteps. As I turned my head I heard, '*Halt! Hände hoch!*'

Two young men rushed towards me, the dark metal of revolvers in their right hands.

I stopped and slowly raised my hands above my head. I was unarmed and had absolutely no hopes of getting away. In a daze I tried to control my muddled thoughts. They took away my walking stick and searched my pockets (one of them had been next to me in the tramcar, the one with the glittering eyes).

'We must phone for a car. No, we won't bother, we'll go by tram. You can't get away from us.'

They led me back towards Pulawska Street. My head was still in a whirl. I had so often read reports with the details of arrests that this didn't seem real. Was I really being led along with a gun pointed at my back? Was I really in this situation? Would I now be the subject of a report?

The two men pushed me onto the front platform (the front half of the trams was reserved for Germans only), and made me sit down on the end seat; they sat down on either side of me. We looked like three not very high-class *Volksdeutschers*, unable even to speak German.

I recovered my composure and collected my thoughts. I was in a bad way. Three-quarters of an hour earlier I had kept two appointments and received material, which I had on me. In my sock I had two reports and in the left pocket of my coat, crushed in my handkerchief, were hidden four *gryps* (notes from prisoners written on cigarette paper and smuggled out of the prison) which I was to hand on to the prison network in the evening. My papers had not yet been taken from me, but that would be done within the next quarter of an hour and they would not have much difficulty in discovering that some of them were forged.

One of the men had been looking at me for some time with a slight squint. 'Are you an engineer?'

'No. I was studying law.'

'And where do you live.'

I gave my full address. They exchanged meaningful glances.

'H'm. Our orders are to bring you to head office. Let them find out who you are and decide what is to be done with you. Would you like a cigarette?'

I reached for my cigarette case.

'Oh no. Smoke one of ours.'

I drew in a mouthful of cheap cigarette smoke. My thoughts were now clear and I felt much surer of myself. These two were not professionals. They had inadvertently told me something, and I suspected (hoped) that there might have been a mistake, that it might not be me they were looking for. So I said, 'You are looking for an engineer and you have taken me. Let's call it off. It's time to go home for supper.'

The one with the leer looked coldly at me. 'Don't you be so clever. We will take you to the right place.'

'Well, perhaps we could come to an agreement?'

'Have you got any cash? asked the other one quickly.'

I took out my wallet. They looked round the tramcar and one of them pulled out the banknotes. He hastily separated the 500 zloty notes and put them into his pocket. The smaller notes he gave me back with a crooked smile. Again they exchanged meaningful glances.

'That's fine. But you just try to mention this in Szucha . . .'

'In Aleja Szucha . . .?'

'What did you think? The money is for us to give a favourable report on you. But that's where you're going.'

The tramcar was travelling round Unia Lubelska Place. I completely forgot all about the *gryps* and took out my handkerchief. For a moment my heart stopped and I held my breath: four tiny rolls of cigarette paper slipped out of my pocket and, like leaves in the wind, fluttered to the floor. Two I managed to trample surreptitiously under my foot and, still holding my breath, waited to see what would happen. But my neighbours didn't as much as blink. To this day I don't know whether they really didn't notice anything or whether this was their way of 'paying' me for the stolen banknotes.

We came to Litewska Street. 'Out we get.'

The one with the leer gave his companion my stick and remained at the stop. 'You take the patient where he has to go and I will go on.'

This worried me. I was sure he had noticed the *gryps*, had pretended not to see them and now he was going to get back into the tram to collect them, so that after a couple of weeks interrogation they would be shown to me. 'You say you are innocent, that you don't know anything? And what is this may I ask?'

I knew all about such tricks. Yet in this case it was not so. Out of the corner of my eye I saw the tram going off while he stood at the stop. My first success? Or perhaps just providence.

We went down Litewska Street. A man came out of a gateway

and followed us at a convenient distance. We had crossed the frontier into the undisputed territory of the Germans.

'You go in front', said my companion. And a moment later added, 'Perhaps it is a mistake, if so you have the devil's own luck.'

We turned left and again left, and entered a building up several steps. We were in Gestapo headquarters.

In the dark anteroom the windows of the spacious inquiry office sparkled, and inside a sleepy NCO on guard sat by the telephones. The man escorting me said a few words to him and pointed to the stairs on the left, leading down into the cellars. We went up to the iron bars and my guard rang a bell. Keys rattled and a dishevelled NCO in bedroom slippers (it was after 6 p.m. and duty hours were over) opened them. My guard again whispered a few words and quickly withdrew. The bars grated open, then shut.

The NCO gave me a bored look of dislike. '*Komm.*'

We turned left along a pale narrow corridor, rather poorly lit. The left-hand wall consisted of iron gratings which formed the doors of four windowless cells. 'This must be the famous tram-car' I thought. I knew the Gestapo building fairly well from the numerous reports I had received.

Beyond the last cell was a small room with a typewriter and a large wireless set. I felt myself growing tense. Only a few seconds divided me from events which would decide whether I was to live or die. I was completely clear-headed, and gathered myself together, as alert as I could be, to be sure not to miss the smallest detail of my surroundings and of the behaviour of the Gestapo.

In the room there were two men. One, in uniform, was sitting by the typewriter, the other, a civilian, was manipulating the dials of the radio. At the sight of me they got up without any enthusiasm. The NCO escorting me whispered something to the civilian and then went out into the corridor.

'Take out everything you have in your pockets.'

I began to take out various trifles. When I produced my cigarette case, the civilian pounced upon it, took out the last two unfortunate 'Egipskis' and immediately tore the paper and emptied the tobacco on to the table. I was not surprised at this.

It was the result of my behaviour in the tram. My captor had repeated everything faithfully and here they were now rummaging uselessly in the pile of tobacco, looking for something which I was suspected of wanting to burn. Another favourable coincidence. The cigarettes were quite innocent and the fruitless search would improve my position in the eyes of the searchers.

The civilian finally left the cigarettes alone, rubbed the tobacco off his fingers, put his hands in his trouser pockets and turned to me. 'Got your papers?'

I handed him my wallet. My real identity card was there besides a forged night pass, employment card and an identity card for the *Ostbahn**, with a photograph. The civilian, yawning, took out the employment card, looked at it, put it back, dug out the pink *Nachtausweiss* (night pass), put that back too and threw the wallet on the table.

'Take away that stuff, you will give it in tomorrow morning. Give your personal details.'

The typewriter clattered. Without any haste I picked up the wallet from the table and carelessly put it into the pocket of my jacket. Here again I had been in luck. But I still had the reports in my socks. My feet burned. What was to be done? I decided to take the initiative. Seeing that the Gestapo men were bored, I began to pull off first my coat and then my jacket.

'Have you gone crazy, or what? Do you think this is the bathroom?'

'I am getting undressed, ready to be searched . . .'

The man in uniform got up from behind the typewriter and slapped me on the face. 'Wait till you're told, scum. That's our business, when and how.'

He looked enquiringly at the civilian.

'*Warte etwas* (wait a while). We'll see to you tomorrow.'

He looked at his watch and went up to the radio. A noisy, dance tune blared. The civilian revived a little and began to tap his foot. 'Also *schlafen gehen* (go to sleep). Which cell shall we put him in? *Mit Musik*? (with music?)'

They led me out into the corridor, opened the grating and

*The name given to the Polish State Railways by the Germans.

pushed me inside. I sat down quickly on a bench with my face to
the wall. This was the cell 'mit Musik' – it was only separated by a
wall from the room with the wireless and the noise could be
clearly heard.

Reaction followed. I felt my forehead covered with perspiration and my lips feverish and dry. To what did I owe these
favours of providence? I still had the night before me and the
night can be the ally of those who are defenceless and at bay.

The bench, made out of narrow boards, was small and uncom-
fortable. But we had to sit still for behind our backs, on the other
side of the bars, a guard paced up and down, observing us
constantly. Anyone who attracted his attention was led out to do
'gymnastics', from which he returned breathless and with redde-
ned cheeks.

My 'tramcar' was nearly empty. I was sitting in a bad position,
next to the wall; there was no question of looking round, so that
my field of observation was very small. Beside me, on my right
hand, a well-built man in riding boots was dozing, just behind
him a grey, bent old man, with definitely Semitic features, sat
motionless. Except for them the cell was empty, as I had noticed
coming in.

I looked at my watch: getting on for seven o'clock. Good Lord!
Five minutes walk from here, at the corner of Mokotowska and
Krucza Streets, my next-in-command was waiting for me. He had
the mail for the day, which today, as an exception, he had
collected from the 'box'. What a coincidence! I felt a sudden
wave of longing. During the last two hours, in this inundation of
events, which had brought about so many changes, I had believed absolutely that it was only a mistake, an accident, that I
would be free and able to get back to work. It had seemed to me
that it would only be necessary to make one effort, one minute
reaction, to free myself from the shackles of reality. I could not
accept that I could give in, just as in 1939 when, with a damaged
back and a shattered leg, I had tried to push through thick
blackberry bushes to rejoin some of our men in a lost position.
But then the German fire had been too murderous. And today?
Here I was deep underground, bars behind me, beyond the bars

an armed vulture and above a network of guards, guarding Aleja Szucha.

No, my next-in-command would not see me that day and would be shaking his head, wondering at my extraordinary carelessness at leaving him, just before curfew, to walk nervously up and down the street with his pocket stuffed full of letters and reports.

Behind our backs the keys rattled. Into the cell waddled a tall man with a huge paunch, in high boots and a brown shirt. From his right wrist dangled a hide whip, to his circular lips was stuck the remains of a cigar. 'Eh, who wants to go out?!'

I sprang up. I had to seek any means of getting rid of these papers and this was also a way of getting a glimpse of the other three cells of the 'tramcar'. I was not yet sure how things were going. If I was the only one here, everything might turn out all right, but if some of my fellow workers had been taken . . .?

We turned right out of the cell and marched along the corridor beside the bars. I could not see any familiar silhouettes, but otherwise the excursion was not very successful, for the man with the paunch did not leave us alone for a single moment. On my return I managed to change my seat to one a little nearer the bars.

I looked again at my watch. Curfew. My next-in-command must have given up long ago. Stefan had waited in vain at the stop of the number two tram and my wife would be looking out of the window, time and again straining her ears to catch the familiar footsteps on the pavement. Enough dreaming, there was no hope of my being free quickly. After all it was only by a miracle that I was still keeping up my pretence. I must get rid of the reports and forged papers as quickly as possible, my luck might turn at any moment. There was no use in shutting my eyes to the fact that my life was at stake.

I sat motionless, waiting until sleep overtook my neighbours and to see if the guard would put out the light. At about ten o'clock he came round all the cells again, looked at our eyes, muttered something coarse and turned off the switch. The corridor remained lit up.

I waited for another half hour. At last both of my companions began to snore. Slowly, listening all the time, I leant down, rolled up my trouser leg and slipped my hand into my sock. The reports, written on thin paper, were easy to hide but they rustled. I crushed them into my hand and carefully straightened up. I had to swallow the papers but at first there was an unforeseen difficulty. In my excitement I had not noticed that my mouth was completely dry; I could not make one drop of saliva. For several long minutes I struggled with the reports in my mouth and at last managed to get them down my parched throat.

I breathed more freely. The worst was over. Even if they took me out now to search and question me, they wouldn't find much. I still had three forged identity cards in my pocket-book but I could always maintain that I had bought them on Napoleon Square, the centre for black market forged papers. I would get a good beating but they would not get any leads from me, I hoped.

Of course I meant to do my best to get rid of the forgeries too. That was not so easy, as the identity cards, made of thick paper, were impossible to swallow. Putting my hand into my inside pocket, I tore off bits and put them into my mouth. After chewing them thoroughly, I made little rolls with the wet paper and, bending down carefully, rolled them on the floor, which was covered with a dark, greasy polish, like that used in barracks or offices where a lot of people go in and out constantly. When the roll was black and in no way resembled the original, I pushed it into the crack between the wall and the floor. In this way, in a few hours, I got rid of the employment card, the night pass and the *Ostbahn* identity card. I did not have much time to spare as it was nearly 4 a.m. – when the guards did their night rounds.

Soon noises were to be heard, a bell rang and the brown-shirted, fat guard stamped along the corridor, swearing and rattling his keys.

The grating clanged to, behind new victims. In a few minutes the bell rang again and again the bars clashed. Outside, the city still slept, the breathing of the sleeping people rising and falling rhythmically, children turning over in their beds dreaming of games and good things to eat. It was Wednesday of Holy Week 1943. In the Gestapo cellars, in the basements of the world, everything began to awaken; a new day was beginning.

The guard allowed us to leave our cells again. Once more I could see no familiar profiles. Good. I managed to change my place again. I left the seat beside which my documents lay hidden in the crack, and sat down beside the bars.

Avidly I took in every sound, and out of the corner of my eye I observed the bustle in the corridor, constantly on the increase.

An oldish man with a picture under his arm was brought in and behind him two middle-aged men, probably from the train, as they had bundles and a suitcase. A little later three women: two very young with wide-open eyes, the third older, pale as though there was not a drop of blood in her face (mother and daughters probably). Again and again the bell rang and unpleasant-looking civilians, mostly young, with cruel expressions, led in new victims. The fat guard seemed to know these civilians well and exchanged a few words with each of them, laughing loudly and slapping them on the back.

At last the little room with the radio came to life too. A cheerful tune rang out, mingled with the noise of the typewriter. Names began to be called out.

The day guard (small and thin – the opposite of the night fat-man) gave everyone a piece of bread. From one mug we all drank hot coffee. It gave me strength, for after the excitement of yesterday and a sleepless night I was feeling very tired.

The cell 'mit Musik' became quiet. In the little room next to it the radio was turned off and the occupants got down to work. One could hear curt questions, the murmur of low answers and, again and again, the sound of blows, after which came a shriek, often a woman's sob, clutching at our hearts and impeding our breathing.

It was nine o'clock when my turn came. In the room were the two Gestapo men who had been there yesterday, as well as a big fellow in uniform and a small, dark curly-haired civilian with a sullen look. He addressed me in good Polish:

'What were you arrested for?'

'I don't know.'

'You lot never know. Got your papers?'

I gave him my wallet. He took my identity card out of it and the card of the Association of War Invalids.

'What is your profession?'

'Before the war I was studying law...'

'Aha. And why have you got a false Christian name on your identity card?'

'A false name?'

'You are Tadeusz and not Józef.'

'I was christened by the name of Józef and I have lived as such for twenty-nine years.'

'Don't lie, I'll find a way to make you tell the truth. Why did you change your name, I am asking you?'

The man in uniform, standing behind me, came a step forward. I knew that at any moment they could start on me, but I was feeling more and more sure of myself. If this wasn't a trick, everything was going excellently. Clearly it was a case of mistaken identities (I could even guess for whom I was being mistaken), and they didn't know anything about me. I smiled in a friendly way at my interrogator.

'Please understand that I am speaking the truth. My papers are genuine.'

'And which one of you ever had forged papers? You all lie and twist and deny everything! *Polnishe Schweine*! (Polish pigs) Bend over.

I got fifteen blows of the hide whip until I was hot all over. I straightened myself with difficulty.

The curly-haired man looked at me carefully. 'Well, how do you feel, Mr Engineer?'

'I've already told you that I was studying law. What do you want of me?'

The interrogator sat down on the edge of the table, lit a cigarette and kept his eyes fixed on me. 'Where do you live?'

I gave the address.

'What have you got there at home?'

'What can I have? A few sticks of furniture, some clothes. I deal in old things.'

'H'm. Any family?'

'I have a wife...' (What are you doing now, my poor Eil, what are you thinking?)

'Give me your keys. We will see.'

Suddenly he stubbed out his cigarette on the table, got up and came up to me. 'Enough of this rot! Confess at once, or you will never leave here alive. We have proof that you are an engineer.'

'But I have been living in Warsaw for eight years. You can easily verify it.'

'Shut up. Shut up, you fool!!!'

He slapped my face twice. I was hit from behind, on my back, my neck, my head.

It could have been an amusing situation. I was being beaten so that I should confess that my authentic papers were forged, that I was not myself. I felt that in a minute I would begin to scream and at the same time I was almost happy. It wasn't an impossible position to defend.

Curly-hair quietened down a little and made a sign. The hide whip fell.

'Well? Have you changed your opinion?'

I couldn't answer at first, catching my breath with difficulty.

'The devil knows who you are but I haven't any more time for you today. We shall see each other again.'

He took a card out of his pocket and read out another name. The thing with the hide whip opened the door and pushed me out into the corridor. I returned to my bench in the 'tramcar'.

It seemed very hard and yet very cosy. Surely today they wouldn't bother me any more? I had difficulty in breathing; my heart was still beating rapidly. I felt so tired.

I sat like that for eight hours.

At five in the afternoon the guard read out several names. We were stood side by side and led through a maze of corridors onto the courtyard. There a black van was waiting for us.

It was with some relief that I discovered we were going to the Pawiak prison.

Chapter Ten

A Night and a Day

Sometimes I did not return home at night because of the underground work and the occasional journeys that I was involved in. But I always made a point of warning my wife beforehand. The times were difficult enough and we tried to shield those near to us from any avoidable suffering.

We lived on the outskirts of the city and I used to come home on the last tram before the 8 p.m. curfew imposed by the Germans. On the quiet road where our flat was Eileen would often meet me: she could hear my steps approaching. We never spoke about my underground work, but she knew that I was deeply engaged in it and that the old clothes trade was only a front to hide my activities. She herself, in spite of my opposition, was involved in similar activities, although to a lesser extent.

Holy Week of 1943 had just begun, and Eileen was doing what she could on our tiny budget to prepare for Easter and fill our ever-empty stomachs. She couldn't count on my help at all for my work absorbed me completely and I was still too young to understand that we had to relax sometimes and that the small affairs of household and holidays also have their place in life. So she bustled about our little flat, sweeping, dusting, airing and even baking with ingredients she had bought with the money she earned by giving English lessons in secret.

It was Holy Tuesday and the early spring night had already fallen. Eileen lit the primus stove and put a pot of soup on it; she knew I would come in tired and ready to eat. The rattle of the approaching tram, the last one of the day, could be heard in the distance. She looked out of the window once or twice, listened for a moment and went back to the primus, which tended either

104

to go out or start smoking. I hadn't arrived but there was no need to be anxious. I sometimes came home with my superior who, by a coincidence, lived almost opposite us and with whom I had always plenty to discuss. The Germans didn't prowl round our way and we were able to walk about for a bit.

The soup had boiled several times, and it was completely dark outside; it must have been well after eight o'clock. Somebody's footsteps echoed on the pavement and died away, someone shut a gate, a dog suddenly barked, and then silence.

Eileen felt the first, faint wave of anxiety. I wasn't coming home that evening, something must have happened. But immediately she had another idea; I had simply missed the last tram and had to stay with friends. We had no telephone, how could I let her know? There was nothing to do but put out the primus and start eating, but the soup tasted horrible and swallowing was difficult. The washing-up did not take much time and it was hard to read, for the ration of electricity had already been used up. There was a carbide lamp on the table, but it didn't burn well and gave out too little light. It was still possible that I might yet turn up, risking the march through the fields after the curfew. That had happened a few times, so Eileen went out to the front of the house once more and listened for a few moments, but again there was silence. Somehow the long, lonely hours of the night had to be got through.

The neighbours had already gone to bed; sleep would not come; thoughts went round in her mind and her imagination worked ceaselessly evoking images connecting the past with the present.

Not so very long ago Eileen's life had seemed quietly ordered when a surprise acquaintanceship lead to an invitation to go to Poland. The journey across Europe followed, and first impressions of an unknown city, new customs and noisy people speaking an unfamiliar language; but they were hospitable and cordial, carefree Warsaw had a charm of its own, and the Polish countryside was full of lovely old country houses and peasant women going to church with their shoes in their hands. How different it was from her previous life, and yet how similar to the customs of her Irish homeland. Later there was the unexpected meeting with a man and then a sentiment which caused her to stay on longer than she had first planned; then an exchange of promises, the decision to remain and suddenly – war.

Mobilization, a hurried wedding, farewells, the fight for Warsaw, my return from the army, the making of some sort of home life in the first months of the Occupation, the Germans, the sight of whom aroused sensations of revolt and defiance – it all made a great cauldron of shocks and impressions from which came a feeling of a new loyalty and strong ties uniting her with a country at war.

She already felt herself a part of the nation, in whose country she had decided to remain, and at the same time she went back in memory to past years and to her family, whom she had left in Ireland.

Her father, no longer young, had retired as a naval captain before the war, but had volunteered again and was somewhere on the seas; her mother was living in a small town in the south of Ireland; her brothers, now grown up, were surely on active service. Perhaps one of them was at this very moment flying over Germany, looking for the target for his death-laden bombs; perhaps they were fighting in the desert or perhaps, like their father, they were fighting the war at sea; the life that she had left behind seemed to her for a moment so real and near as to be almost tangible. Suddenly the air raid warning howled and Eileen quickly returned to reality and felt within her the chill of anxiety.

Sleep would not come, and outside the first grey mists of the approaching dawn began to unfurl.

Our flat was 'clean', for I kept to the strict principle that it was forbidden to endanger others and oneself unnecessarily. I never left behind any papers or objects which could give rise to suspicion, but when I came home at night I had to bring with me the last secret mail which I received just before curfew. The following morning I always made a point of taking it away with me, but it had to spend the night somewhere and for this purpose I had brought home a hollow-centered wooden candlestick with a cleverly concealed spring opening. That night it was empty, but a few days earlier the mechanism had worked slightly loose and the hiding place had become hard to shut. Eileen naturally knew the secret of the candlestick and when at dawn she began to consider what should be done, it came to her that she should safeguard it. She fixed the mechanism and lit a candle. The falling wax covered the sides of the candlestick and the hiding place. What more? There were some books which should perhaps be burnt, but a pile of fresh ashes might look suspicious. She gave up this idea and looked round the room and the kitchen, but restlessness made precision impossible. She tried to find something with which to occupy herself.

It was now daybreak. The sunlight brightened the room despite the black-out on the kitchen window. Eil opened it and everything looked a little gayer. Anxiety had not faded, but the time was coming that might bring a happy solution. If no misfortune had happened to me I would turn up shortly. I might miss the last tram but I would never allow her to wait longer than the earliest morning hours.

Housework killed time but could not kill the thoughts which went ceaselessly round and round the same question – would I come or not? Several times she went out of the house and looked towards the town, trying to pierce the morning mist. But nobody came.

Well. She would have to accept the idea that something had happened and decide what to do.

The first reaction to danger is sometimes an instinctive urge to run away and look for a safe corner. Eileen, after short reflection, rejected this idea. Her sudden disappearance might seem suspicious and make things worse for me, if I had actually been arrested. It would also make any possible contact with me more difficult. She must stay.

The morning dragged on endlessly, and the constant alternation of anxiety and hope was nerve-racking. There was no question of doing any more work.

Eleven o'clock had struck when a car came along the quiet road. Eileen felt certain that it would stop in front of our house. The gate creaked and heavy footsteps sounded on the stairs. After a moment there was a loud knock on the door.

'*Aufmachen*! *Deutsche Polizei*!' 'Open up! German police!'

In the doorway stood two men. One elderly almost grey, the other young with black curly hair. Both wore civilian clothes. They came inside, muttered a German greeting and looked hastily round the room.

'Where is your husband?'

'I don't know.'

'What do you mean "I don't know"?'

'He didn't come home last night.'

'Aha. And who else lives here?'

'Only the two of us, that's all.'

'We must search the flat. Please stand by the stove.'

The conversation was carried on in German. Eileen suspected that at least one of the Germans understood Polish and for that reason she used German so as not to betray the fact that she spoke Polish with a foreign accent and made mistakes. She was bewildered and her hopes were beginning to fade, although the situation did not seem desperate. The agents were behaving fairly politely, their questions were not thrown at her brutally. I was under arrest, that seemed clear; but perhaps things were not too bad. At least for the time being.

The Germans threw the bed clothes off and pulled out the contents from the wardrobe. Then they started going through the book shelves.

Opening books at random they found some in English. 'What's this?'

'I don't understand?'

'Where did these English books come from?'

'My husband was learning English before the war. Look, there is his exercise book.'

The elder German hesitated as if he did not know what to do with the books, but the younger one shrugged and pulled him away from the shelves. They went into the kitchen and looked for somewhere to rummage in. They peered into the stove, turned on the tap over the sink and the elder one went back into the hall. He started to go through the pockets of the coats hanging there and suddenly from one of them drew out a piece of paper. He went back into the kitchen, began to read and after a few seconds glanced quickly at Eileen. 'This is written in English. What does it mean?'

Eileen for a moment was flabbergasted. In the nervous anxiety of the long night hours she had quite forgotten a letter written by one of her pupils, as an exercise and given to her to correct. What to do? She must say something. 'Yes, that is in English.'

The German came nearer and looked at her threateningly. 'This is a letter, there are Englishmen hidden here!'

'Not at all. I am Irish and give English lessons. That isn't a letter, it's an exercise.'

The younger, curly-headed German approached his colleague. 'Show me, I know a little English.'

He ran his eyes over the paper and nodded his head. 'Yes, that is an exercise. It's full of mistakes. It is not important to us.'

Eileen looked at him gratefully. From the beginning he had given her the impression of a man who wished to avoid brutality. But the older one, obviously higher ranking, snapped at him, 'How do you know that it's not important?'

He turned to Eileen. 'You say you are Irish. Do they speak English in Ireland?'

'Yes. It is only a short time since they started to teach Irish in the schools. I never learnt it.'

The curly-head pulled the interrogator's sleeve. 'Drop it. Ireland is neutral. Mind your own business.'

The other man left the subject of English and pointed to a mackintosh cape hanging on a peg. 'That's your husband's I suppose. He is an officer?'

'No, that's my cape. You can see that it's short.'

'I am asking you whether your husband is an officer?'

The curly-headed German interrupted. 'Yes he told us so.'

Eileen again thought of him gratefully. He had got her out of a difficult situation because she didn't know what they had got out of me. At the same time a cold hand gripped her heart. The fact of my arrest was now undoubted. Arrest and the first interrogation . . .

The older German went on questioning. 'What does your husband do?'

'He deals in second-hand articles.'

'I don't see anything here?'

'What there was my husband took with him. Do you think we can afford a stock?'

The German made a gesture of impatience. 'To hell with it. You're all twisters.'

He turned to his companion. 'Well?'

'I think it's time to go. It's almost twelve.'

'All right, in a moment.'

He turned to Eileen again. 'Have you got a camera?'

Eileen took out the old Kodak, which her father had given her when she was still a little girl. The Germans looked it over carefully and the younger one muttered to his colleague, 'No, that's not the one.'

They gave it back without further comment. The older man buttoned up his coat, looked at Eileen and said, 'Your husband has been arrested and is now at the headquarters of the secret police. Not a word to anyone of our visit. And you can keep that.'

He threw the unfortunate English exercise on the table, muttered some words of farewell and made for the door. The curly-head one inclined his head, smiled slightly and went after him.

The lock creaked and Eileen remained alone. Only now did she realize how tired she was. She sat down on the divan, let her head sink forward and buried her face in her hands.

Twelve o'clock struck. The sun high in the sky had lightened the room with its bright, spring rays.

Chapter Eleven

Within the Walls of the Warsaw Ghetto

Every day up to now I had met up with my contacts some of whom had connections with the Pawiak. Since the prison lay in the middle of the Jewish district, these people crossed into it every day. They were Polish wardresses in the women's wing of the Pawiak, some Polish warders whom the Germans had left in the men's wing, and some Polish doctors.

Naturally, as well as giving their official reports, they told me what they saw in the Ghetto. My external network also brought me news concerning this problem, for as chief of security for the headquarters of the underground Home Army, I had to know what was happening in the city. I knew that in the Ghetto people were dying of hunger, that the number of over 400,000 inhabitants was decreasing, for the Germans were deporting them by the thousand. They were certainly being murdered, but at that time, up to my eyes in my underground work, I did not know the details of this crime. Only with difficulty could I perform my duties adequately. Every headquarters department demanded of me the quickest possible liaison with their people in prison. My external network, working in a city of over 1,000,000, where the German police were constantly active, could barely keep up with the demands. My whole attention was concentrated in one direction.

In the last months of 1942 I had received a report that the number of inhabitants of the Ghetto had fallen to 80,000. My contacts reported day after day that Jewish emissaries were slipping through the streets of the Aryan part of the city, feverishly buying up food, small arms, petrol and cement.

In January 1943 I had had a report that some shots had been fired in the Ghetto and that a few Germans had fallen.

I myself, for security reasons, met all my contacts well away from the walls of the Ghetto, but by coincidence, exactly one day before my arrest, I was walking there and saw Latvian guards in dirty green uniforms with black lapels, Soviet tin helmets painted black and light gaiters covering the whole calf. They were guarding every inch of the walls. It was obvious that something was in the air.

And now I was to pass through the walls of the Ghetto, but as a Gestapo prisoner, in a prison van.

We were strongly escorted, the horns blowing loudly and, as it was six o'clock in the evening and the city at its liveliest, trams stopped and cars got out of the way.

A wall, a barrier.

Over the Ghetto rose clouds of smoke. I was arrested on 20 April 1943 and one day earlier the Germans started the final assault on the Jewish district and were greeted by fire from small arms and grenades. The Jewish Fighting Organization had started to resist.

We were under a black canvas hood, but it was possible to see a little. The gloomy blocks of houses, standing close together, were shaken every moment by the nearby detonations of shells. From inside came shrieks, smothered by wild firing.

The barrier had been raised to let in our column of cars. We raced through the deserted streets, past a group of gendarmes and SS men crouching behind a wall, past some corpses.

Finally, the crazy barking of dogs, the curses and shouts of the Gestapo men, '*Raus! raus!*' ('Get out!')

The Pawiak, an island in the midst of the stormy sea of the fighting Ghetto.

The first person that I saw, when we were led into the basement of the seventh section, was Janek. He recognized me at once and his face went as white as chalk. I made him a sign to pretend that he didn't know me. After having been searched, while we were being led to the cell, I managed to whisper, that I hadn't fallen into the Gestapo's hands for our work. The organization of life in the Pawiak held few secrets for me. I knew, that

Janek must have a function, since he could move freely about the section.

We were shut in the cell for newcomers. There were four of us. The fourth was a young Jew pretending to be an Aryan. He had kept this up until a few days ago – he had had false papers. Finally he had been caught somewhere in the post office. Even in the Gestapo headquarters he had stuck to his version, but a brutal search had revealed the truth. Terribly beaten, he was thrown bleeding into the cell.

'Do you realize that at this very moment your fellow Jews are fighting to defend the Ghetto?', I asked him.

'Yes, but that won't help me now.'

We sat sleepless through the night. The firing died down somewhat but did not cease altogether. In the morning we were put into various cells. The seventh section was below street level. The cellar windows looked onto the yard, separated by a high wall from the street. Somewhere in the heavens an aeroplane was circling, invisible to us. Not far away grenades were bursting, the remains of the window panes shook.

There was a discreet knock at the cell door. It was Janek, bringing news. 'They have just brought in several Jews, some of them wounded.'

During the next few days I got used to prison discipline: at the run we rushed to the lavatory; at the run we put our bowls under the ladle of soup; rigidly we straightened our tired bodies when the door of the cell opened and a Gestapo man stood in it to receive the report.

Janek contacted me daily. Through him I sent a secret message to Stefan informing him that the Gestapo knew nothing about me, that they had taken me for someone else and that it should be passed round our men that I had left Warsaw. The least false step could unmask me. For I was in that same Pawiak which was the chief terrain of my activity.

It is hard to describe the impressions of those first days. How much effort, how many hours, how many long months I had spent in the artistic setting-up of liaison lines between the outside world and the prison, and now I am myself here. I see it all with my own eyes, I know the ways the messages come, now they are trying to get news to me by the methods which I once created and brought into being. Janek had already got over the first shock. Our contacts had enabled him to get out of the common cell and he was now as useful inside, as formerly outside the Pawiak.

After Easter the second corridor-sweeper was sent to another section and I was given his function. Again our contacts worked with Janek's help. I now shared a double cell with him. We worked together and made our secret post office more efficient. The newly arrested were generally brought to the seventh section, so we were in an excellent position. For the time being Stefan was directing our secret correspondence. In one of the messages he informed us that justice had been meted out to the Ukrainian, who had brought ruin to Janek's family. Our bullet had reached him.

New prisoners were usually brought in to the Pawiak at about six o'clock in the evening. Part of my duties as corridor-sweeper was to assist when prisoners were being searched. This took place in an alcove common to both the seventh and eighth sections of the prison. Newcomers were sent to section seven, while section eight was chiefly for Jews.

That day Lisowski, the Ukrainian, was on duty. He was a decent man who never struck anyone or raised his voice. His face, strong and pleasant, although slightly disfigured by smallpox, did not show much feeling. But by the narrowing of his eyes and the tightening of his lips it could be seen that he suffered when the Gestapo tortured their prisoners. He was a friend and we knew that when he was on duty we could open the cell doors without fear and settle our secret affairs.

I had just finished dusting, when from the staircase came the noise of marching feet. The bars grated and some men in groups of five, escorted by two warders, came along the corridor. The newcomers were told to turn to the left and stand in the alcove with their faces to the wall. To the right of the alcove there were some tables and it was here that the prisoners were searched. The escort went away and Lisowski remained alone with me and with Janek, who was also detailed to sweep the corridors.

We stood by the wall, near the first table, and looked at the newcomers. This was a very important moment. A quick decision and in less than a second we could take from one of them a secret newsletter or some other object, which would have compromised him fatally. Perhaps it might only be a trifle of personal value. At the same time we had to be careful for we could be trapped by an informer. Sometimes too, there were fools who gave themselves and others away.

Lisowski started the searching. Each of the prisoners came up to him in turn, emptied his pockets and then undressed. The warder looked over everything methodically, sometimes pulling off the lapel of a coat or undoing the lining; he looked into their mouths and ordered their hands to be shown palms upward. When other warders did the searching all valuables disappeared, but not with Lisowski. After being searched the prisoners took their clothing and went into a little room nearby for a brief medical examination and to have their hair shaved. If they were 'clean' they were shut up in the newcomers cell; if they had any skin diseases they were sent to the cell called '*Krätze*' [itch].

I lightly nudged Janek. 'Look at that one. Do you recognize him?'

Janek nodded. At that moment a stout man was standing before the warder. He was a second-rate cabaret actor, known for his smutty monologues. Once Janek and I had seen him in a restaurant where he had been drunk and was making a scene about the bill. I had not taken to him from the moment that he marched into our section with a mocking smile on his arrogant face.

Lisowski made a sign with his hand to indicate undressing, but the actor pretended not to understand. Lisowski repeated the sign and at the same time stretched out his hand for the prisoner's wallet. The actor muttered something coarse and gave the warder a sharp shove. Any other Ukrainian, not to mention a German, would have thrown himself at once onto the prisoner and beaten him. But Lisowski controlled himself, turned pale and glanced at us.

'Get undressed, you damn fool!' I spoke sharply and through my mind ran the question: an idiot or an informer?

'Keep away from me, you . . .', began the actor, but at that moment the bars grated.

Lisowski stiffened, grabbed the prisoner and tore off his jacket. Along the corridor came Thomas, a young, slim good-looking man in Gestapo uniform. His eyes were wary and cold; in his left hand he held a cigarette, the right grasped the handle of a heavy whip. He was one of the cruellest Germans in the Pawiak.

I held my breath. Now one could only keep quiet and wait to see what happened. Surely this fool had heard Thomas come in and had noticed the warder's change in behaviour?

The actor undressed quietly and was handing Lisowski his clothes when suddenly, with a rapid movement, he threw a small, glittering object in Janek's direction. Janek stiffened, but tried to catch the flying object. Unfortunately the attempt did not succeed and it fell noisily to the floor by my feet. I glanced down cautiously. It was a gold five dollar coin. Thomas of course had seen everything but he said nothing. He picked up the coin, put it in his pocket and hit Janek across the face with the whip. A bloody weal appeared down the length of his cheek at once.

The actor took off the rest of his clothes and stood naked, stout and heavy. His face was twisted as he looked at us.

Lisowski examined his underwear and was showing the prisoner the way to the medical room when suddenly Thomas came up to him. He pushed the warder aside, grasped the prisoner by his bare arm and pulled him towards himself. Without a word he took the actor by the jaw with his other hand and with a tug opened his mouth. A gold wedding ring fell onto the floor. Thomas turned towards Lisowski and looked at him for a few moments. The warder turned pale. The Gestapo man moved his eyes towards the actor. The whip hissed through the air and fell with force on the fat mass of flesh. The actor shrieked and covered his face with his hands, and then madness seemed to overtake Thomas, for he jumped forward furiously, pushed the prisoner on to the ground and began to thrash him. Within a minute the body of the beaten man was covered with red weals. The man tried to stand but the blows felled him again and he rolled around the floor screaming.

We looked on this scene in silence, knowing that the beaten man would not get away with his life. The bars grated again and another Gestapo man came in and with him the prisoner Kaminski. Just who he was nobody really knew. He had been in the Pawiak a long time, he shaved Germans, amused them with his jokes and helped to value stolen jewellery. He was useful to them and had managed to avoid transports to concentration camps. Although no saint he had helped many people in the prison.

Kaminski saw what was happening, hesitated for a moment and suddenly burst into loud laughter. Thomas ceased the thrashing for a second and looked in disbelief at him, but Kaminski caught him by the arm and, choking with laughter, began to whisper something in his ear. The Gestapo man struggled, took a step backwards, but Kaminski did not let go and finally the three of them went out together.

With difficulty we raised the blood-stained actor from the cold floor. He was breathing heavily and rolling his eyes round in a bewildered manner. We half-carried him to a nearby room where a doctor-prisoner who was jailed in our section dressed his wounds. The actor then put on his clothes by himself and went to his cell. Lisowski, who had finished searching prisoners, stood in the middle of the corridors and smoked a cigarette nervously.

Peace reigned at last in the section. When the time came for lights-out, Janek and I went along the corridor to see that everything was in order. Only the newcomers' cells remained to be checked, which we always did last.

We had just opened the first of them when Lisowski came out of the doorway and joined us. The prisoners were all lying down; only the actor sat on the floor in a corner. He saw us and got up slowly.

For a long moment we looked at each other. We were just going to close the door and turn out the light when, suddenly, the fat man moved towards Janek. 'Couldn't you catch better? Eh? My last five dollars, blast it!'

Janek quivered. The bloody weal on his face turned purple. He tried to say something, but nothing came from his constricted throat. I clenched my fists but at that moment Lisowski pushed himself in front of me.

He grabbed the actor by the front of his jacket, dragged him into the center of the cell, swung his arm and struck him hard right across his fat face.

The seventh section of the Pawiak was directly connected with section eight, for Jews only. All the time groups of them, dragged out of the cellars and ruins of their burning houses, were being brought in. They were completely exhausted and speechless with fright.

Sometimes we managed to get in touch with them. From one I did learn that he had been taken in the centre of the Ghetto, and that some Jews were still holding out there, but they were running out of food and ammunition.

These contacts, sporadic and short, were only possible when Ukrainians were on duty. The most we could do was to offer a mug of water to some of these unfortunate people. Day after day they were killed in the prison yard.

The Ghetto was burning, the fires came nearer and nearer. The houses round the Pawiak were in flames. Two fire brigades arrived and the firemen played their hoses on the roof and walls of the prison. It was evening, we were standing near the small window and watched as the fires crept higher and devoured the tall chimneys on the street.

Somewhere in the distance, further and further away – shots.

But the prison lived its own life. It had its own frightful secrets. Over each of us hung the uncertainty of the morrow, fear for our dear ones. The high walls separated us from the ruins of the Ghetto, becoming quieter, even more deadly quiet.

The first week of May was a nasty one. The Germans suddenly shot 100 Polish prisoners, nobody knew whom they would take another day. Jews were being brought to the prison constantly. They were being murdered mercilessly on the spot.

Bound to our common mutual work and common cell, I was now able to learn more about Janek. His faith in mankind was so strong, that even after his mother's arrest, he could not believe that the Ukrainian was such a scoundrel. He had written a letter to him, reminding him of the past, appealing to the brotherly feelings, which ought to bind everyone. The other pretended to be sorry and asked for a meeting. Janek went, for he believed that he could convert him.

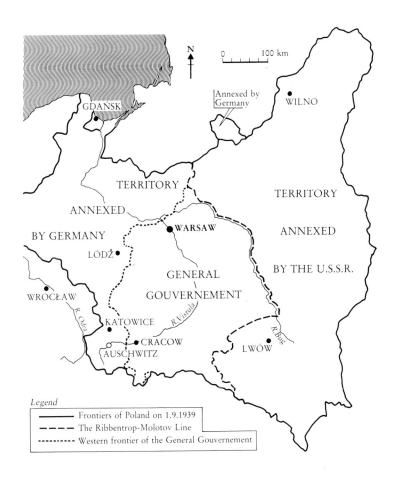

1   Map of Poland on 14 June, 1940

2　Warsaw under German occupation.

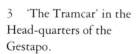

3　'The Tramcar' in the Head-quarters of the Gestapo.

4 Pawiak

5 Inside Pawiak

6 The ruins of Pawiak

7 Author in 1935

8 Author in 1985

9 Stefan 10 Sem 11 Jan

12 Janek 13 Danusia 14 Helena

15 Marysia 16 Jadwiga 17 Eileen

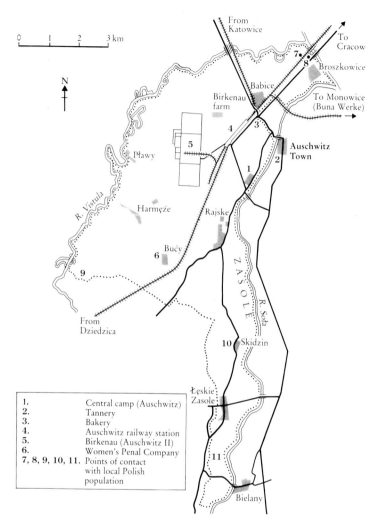

1.   Central camp (Auschwitz)
2.   Tannery
3.   Bakery
4.   Auschwitz railway station
5.   Birkenau (Auschwitz II)
6.   Women's Penal Company
7, 8, 9, 10, 11. Points of contact
                      with local Polish
                      population

18   Area under camp's jurisdiction.

19 Auschwitz: the gate to the main camp

20   Birkenau

21   Birkenau: the Gate of Death

22   A barrack at Birkenau

23   The Wall of Death

24   A gas chamber

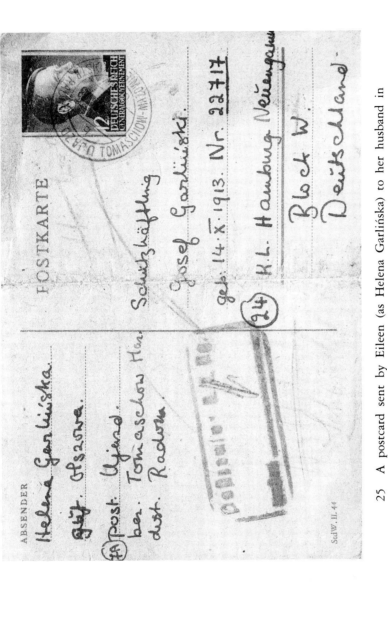

25 A postcard sent by Eileen (as Helena Garlińska) to her husband in Neüengamme.

H.Q.POLISH MILITARY MISSION
ON LIQUIDATION IN FRANCE
25,Quai d'Orsay, Paris VIIe.

Paris, 5-th of November 1945.

No.425/Transp./45.
Subject: Movement Orders.
To: Authorities concerned.

M O V E M E N T   O R D E R

The undermentioned officer of the Polish Army
is proceeding on 4 weeks leave from the present
station to L O N D O N   by authority of the General
Staff :

Lut. / J. GARLINSKI   No.1472

You are kindly requested to provide rail and
surface transportation by the cross channel service.

Anticipated date of departure: 8.NOV.1945.
Anticipated date of return   : 6.DEC.1945.

Chief of Polish Military Mission
of Liquidation in France

A. SZYMANSKI, Staff Col.

Q(M)
BRIT. ARMY STAFF
- 7 NOV 1945
- PARIS -

- 5 NOV 1945
★ PARIS ★

26   The Movement Order for the author, from Paris to London.

27 and 28   The photograph (left) is of the author in the uniform of a cadet officer, from which the Forged Papers' Service of the Home Army faked the civilian photograph (right) for a German document of a Volksdeutch. This was made ready for an attempt to escape from Wittenberge, a sub-camp of Neuengamme.

COMITÉ INTERNATIONAL DE LA CROIX-ROUGE

Palais du Conseil Général
GENÈVE (Suisse)

1 CMP 45280

DEMANDEUR — NADAWCA — ANFRAGESTELLER

Nom - *Nazwisko* - *Name* *SHORT*

Prénom - *Imie* - *Vorname* *MR.*

Rue - *Ulica* - *Strasse* *St. James, the Faley* *Wexford*

Localité - *Miejscowość* - *Ortschaft*

Province - *Województwo* - *Provinz* *Irland* *England*

Pays - *Kraj* - *Land*

Message à transmettre — Zlecenie — Mitteilung

(25 mots au maximum, nouvelles de caractère strictement personnel et familial) —
(najwyżej 25 słów, wiadomości ściśle osobiste) — (nicht über 25 Worte nur persönliche
Familiennachrichten).

*Vater, Mutter und Brüder senden die
herzlichsten Grüsse und sind ungeduldig
Nachrichten von Dir zu haben. Schreibe
an "The Folly" Wexford. Familie*

POLSKI CZERWONY KRZYŻ
Biuro Informacyjne
Warszawa

Date - *Data* - *Datum* 2 0 KW. 1940
Wpłynęło

DESTINATAIRE — ODBIORCA — EMPFÄNGER

Nom - *Nazwisko* - *Name* *Golde*

Prénom - *Imie* - *Vorname* *Frau*

Fils de / *Imie ojca* Sohn des

et de / *Imie matki* und des

Dernière adresse connue
Ostatni adres
Letztbekannte Adresse

Rue - *Ulica* - *Strasse* *Przedmieści 16/18 m 45*

Localité - *Miejscowość* - *Ortschaft*

Province - *Województwo* - *Provinz* *Warschau*

Pays - *Kraj* - *Land* *Deutsche Post Osten*

RÉPONSE AU VERSO.	ODPOWIEDŹ NA ODWROCIE.	ANTWORT UMSEITIG.
Ecrire très lisiblement.	Pisać czytelnie.	Bitte deutlich schreiben.

29   A letter sent by Eileen's mother, from Wexford (Ireland) to
Mrs Golde, in Warsaw; Eileen stayed with her before the war.

✚ 15. DEZ. 1940 ∗ 000189

ANTRAG

durch das Deutsche Rote Kreuz, Präsidium, Auslandsdienst,
Berlin SW 61, Blücherplatz 2,
an die *Agence Centrale des Prisonniers de Guerre, Genf*
— Internationales Komitee vom Roten Kreuz —
auf Nachrichtenübermittlung

PASSED
P.71

1. Absender (Name, Vorname) *Garlińska Eileen.*
   Nadawca (Imię, nazwisko)

   Genaue Anschrift *Narbutta 50 m 7.*
   dokładny adres

bittet, an
prosi

2. Empfänger (Name, Vorname) *Short.*
   Odbiorcę (Imię, nazwisko)

   Genaue Anschrift *The Folly. Wexford. Irlandja.*
   dokładny adres

folgendes zu übermitteln / o następującem zawiadomić:
(Höchstzahl 25 Worte)
(Najwyżej 25 słów)

*Quite well + happy. Have received several
letters, but difficult to answer. Very
glad that all are well. Jack wrote
also. Love to all. Joshie.*

(Datum / data) 14. XI. 1940.

(Unterschrift / podpis)

3. Empfänger antwortet umseitig
   odbiorca odpowiada na odwrotnej stronie

26 DEC. 1940

C/1555

30 Eileen's answer to the letter from her mother in Ireland.

31   Eileen and the author

Luckily I was left in peace, but over Janek there hung an unfinished interrogation and he dreaded the day when he would be called out again. 'Oh, if I could go in a transport. It doesn't matter where, it can be Auschwitz, if only to be farther from the Warsaw Gestapo.'

Unfortunately, they were of a different opinion. On 29 April a transport left, but Janek was not on the list. That alarmed him considerably. He saddened, had a premonition of evil.

During those few days I had grown to love him like my brother and couldn't bear to see his torment. Nor had fate spared me. My father perished in Russia. With all my heart I longed for my wife and my work. And yet my position was a hundred times better. The Gestapo took me for someone else, I had an easy defence. And Janek? His face still bore the marks of the cruel blows which had fallen on him the last time he was interrogated. They called him several times. He came back bruised, helpless, hardly able to speak. By a miracle he kept his 'job', normally unattainable for a prisoner with an unfinished interrogation.

On 12 May a rumour went round in the morning that the following day a large transport was going to Auschwitz. Again a spark of hope flickered. We waited with beating hearts for the warder, who was to bring the list of prisoners chosen from our section. He came in at last and handed it to the scribe. I was on the list among many others. Five hundred prisoners, men and women, were to go from the Pawiak. Janek was not among them.

Somehow we got through to the evening. When eight o'clock struck, I began to get my modest belongings together. A slice of bread, a sweater, a couple of handkerchiefs. All those going in the transport were to spend the night in another section, for the train was leaving at dawn.

Janek helped me in my senseless bustling. We felt the terror of the moments that were to come.

Suddenly the warder's shrill whistle rang out. Now!

We held each other in a last, brotherly embrace.

During the night we were counted and inspected. In the very early morning of 13 May we were loaded onto a column of lorries.

It was a lovely, sunny May day. Our vehicles moved slowly

forward, climbed up the heaps of ruins and slithered down them on to the fragments of the former streets.

The Ghetto was burning down, partly covered by smoke. There was no sound of human voices, no rattling of machine guns.

One more glance at the city, for many of us the very last.*

---

*I did not lose hope of seeing Janek again. I scanned the faces of the new transports at Auschwitz, Neuengamme and in other camps. In vain. Many months later I met prisoners from Pawiak, who had been there after my departure.

In July the Gestapo carried out mass executions in the ruins of the Ghetto. One day Janek was taken there too.

Chapter Twelve

Penal Company

They brought us to Auschwitz late at night. The train rolled onto the ramp and stopped. At once guards began shouting as they opened the doors of the goods wagons and ordered us out. All eyes immediately turned in the direction of the countless lights hanging on the high-tension electrified fence which surrounded the camp and criss-crossed it, dividing it into sectors and sub-camps and eventually disappearing into the night.

Amidst the barking of dogs, shouts and curses, we were formed into fives and driven at the double into the camp. Some of us were struck with rifle butts; some, who lagged behind, were spurred on with bayonets; and dogs tore the clothes off more than one prisoner.

We were herded into an empty barrack and ordered to stand against one of the walls. After a few minutes a senior SS officer, with a cold and arrogant face, arrived and made a short speech:

'Now you are in the care of the great German Reich. Here we shall teach you to work, you will be treated fairly and not a hair will fall from your head. Every misdemeanour will be punished and you can all cease to dream of freedom.'

Having made his speech, he rasped out a few words to the trustees and left. After many hours of travelling we were extremely tired, thirsty and hungry, but we were not given anything to eat or drink. We were made to settle down and told to go to sleep. The barrack's only furniture consisted of a few tables and two barrels as toilets, while the floor was covered in wet sand. Our chances of getting some rest did not look good, but all of us had already spent some months in prison and were accustomed to hard conditions, so after several minutes the conversation died down and people began to snore.

On the following day we had numbers tattooed onto our left forearms by a special needle soaked in ink, were issued with camp clothing (a sort of striped two-piece pyjamas) and finally we were each given almost a litre of turnip soup. We then dragged ourselves out in front of the barrack and although separated from the rest of the camp by barbed wire, we were able to examine our new home and exchange a few words with prisoners who had already been there for some time and who now were observing the new arrivals with great interest, looking for friendly faces and sniffing out the chances of a little black marketeering.

We had landed in Birkenau*, which was one of the sub-camps of Auschwitz. On the other side of the wire was the 20,000-strong women's camp and nearby three crematoria were smoking (a fourth was under construction). The low barracks stretched away in long lines, some of them brick, some wooden. It was a dry and hot May and the earth resembled an irregular threshing floor. We looked around for water, but our barrack had no taps. Through the wire we tried to strike up conversations, but mutual mistrust paralysed any real communication. All we found out was that there was almost no water in the camp, and what there was dripping from the few taps was marsh water containing so much chlorine that it caused stomach illnesses, which ended disastrously here.

In the evening we were marched to another barrack, number 26, which was a quarantine. The block chief was a French Jew, who had emigrated from Poland before the war and who could still speak Polish, and his deputy was a Pole; both were decent men. We were divided into groups of six and ordered to occupy three-storey bunks made of bare boards less than two metres wide. There were two blankets to a bunk and one could lie only on one's side; if anyone had to go outside to a latrine during the night, he had to lie down on top of his comrade when he got back.

Panting and swearing we clambered onto the inhospitable

---

*The largest sub-camp of Auschwitz, with about 100,000 prisoners at its peak, three kilometres from the main camp.

bunks. Our nerves, taut with anxiety, began to relax and an awareness of this new world began to grow in our tired minds.

The second night in Auschwitz was much worse than the first.

In theory the quarantine was meant to last several weeks, during which time we were not supposed to work. But within a couple of days trusties* from various *Kommandos* (working parties) appeared and began grabbing anyone they could. I managed to avoid this initially but one morning I was ordered into a working party which was levelling the ground next to a newly-finished crematorium. It was a large red brick building, looking rather like a small factory without windows. Bringing earth in lorries and carrying lengths of railway track, we frequently leant against its walls to take a short rest.

The days were hot and the nights cold enough for a touch of frost. We got up before dawn and went to bed late at night; there was not even enough water for an eye-wash and the daily diet consisted of a piece of bread, a very small portion of margarine and sausage meat, and less than a litre of watery soup. Our lips were cracked and all our muscles ached, barely able to react even when we wanted to move. The strain of camp life began to weigh more heavily upon us, yet we were still only on quarantine and older camp inmates claimed that we would find out what the real Auschwitz was like only when we were transferred to a normal barrack.

The time was approaching when our transport would be split up, when suddenly, during evening roll-call, a trusty accompanied by several SS men appeared. He read out a list of 78 numbers and ordered their owners to step forward. I was among these, as were Jurek and Marian whom I had met in the transport: we had by now formed an inseparable trio.

'They're going to release us', whispered someone who was quickly silent when nudged in the side.

But most of us had not the slightest desire to joke. It appeared that a different decision had been made for us.

We were issued with bread and then ordered to form up in groups of five. The block chief checked us carefully once more.

---

*Trusties were prisoners with special responsibilities and privileges.

He saw our inquiring and uncertain looks and, walking past, he grimaced as though eating something bitter and whispered, 'There's no need to wet yourselves. You're only going to the SK.' (*Straf Kompanie*, the penal company.)

Our nerves relaxed and we greedily threw ourselves on the hunks of bread in our hands.

We were led along the main camp road and were ordered to stop in front of a brick barrack with a yard, which was separated from the rest of the camp by a high wall.

The gate opened and a strongly-built man of average height, in his thirties, appeared. Seeing the SS men he took off his *Prominent*'s* black beret and looked hard at us. He was Emil Bednarek, a Silesian, block chief of the penal company and one of the camp's dignitaries.

'Come here, worms. Hey, *Stubendienst* (barrack-room orderly) where the hell is the punishment stand?'

We entered and the gate slammed to. The trusty had already dragged into the little yard a large wooden contraption, resembling a short, high bench, on which the prisoner to be beaten was made to lie down. Some sinister-looking men, also prisoners, with sticks in their hands, were hanging around.

We watched these preparations without enthusiasm. We knew that anyone landing in the penal company received twenty-five strokes as a sort of entrance fee and that he was beaten with sticks as thick as a table leg. After such treatment those of a weaker constitution got a 40 °C temperature.

'Hey, let's have the first one of you!' Bednarek was smiling in anticipation, but this time he was denied his pleasure.

The trusty who had read out our numbers, and had accompanied us all the way, went up to him, showed a piece of paper and said a few words. The block chief protested but appeared to concede defeat, casually waved his hand as if to say, 'You'll get what's coming to you', and ordered the *Stubendienst* to issue us with underwear.

One by one we entered the dim interior. The *Stubendienst* directed us to our allocated bunks. Small windows provided very

---

Prominents were prisoners who had good jobs and influence in the camp.

little light, and the few bulbs on the ceiling shone feebly. The air was thick as mercury, and out of the darkness came whispers, the shuffling of feet, sighs and groans.

A new chapter of camp life was beginning.

The following morning we were made to work inside the camp. That evening we were issued with three badges, which had to be sewn next to the number on the left side of our prison shirts. The badges were a black circle a few centimetres in diameter, which signified the penal company, another circle of the same size, but red, which was given to particularly dangerous prisoners, and finally a small patch with the letters 'I.L.' painted on it (which stood for *Isolations Lager*, the isolation camp).

The sewing was not going easily. Hardly anyone had managed to smuggle in a needle, nobody had any thread and the trusties would help only if payed. Since we had not yet received any parcels,* we had little to offer.

I was sitting dejectedly against a wall when suddenly a pale Jewish-looking prisoner with a gentle face cautiously came up to me.

He spoke in quite good Polish. 'I expect you need needle and thread?'

'Yes, but I've nothing to give in exchange.'

'That doesn't matter; it's alright. Give me your shirt, I'll sew them on.'

I looked at my unexpected friend with amazement, but quickly took off the shirt and handed it over together with the trouble-some badges. He pulled out a needle and immediately set to. It was obvious that he was not new to sewing. Within a couple of minutes it was all done.

'Thank you very much, but I really don't have anything. If you like, I'll give you my margarine tomorrow.'

'No, no, there's no need. Perhaps later when the parcels start coming, but not now.'

The man touched my arm and tried to smile. 'Remember, if

*From the beginning of 1943 the prisoners, except Jews and citizens of Soviet Union, were allowed to receive food parcels.

you should need something, I'm here. My name is Motka. Motka from Grodno.'*

Eventually everyone managed, somehow, to sew on the wretched badges. The other inmates of the penal company, and there were more than 500 of them, wore only black circles and so our Warsaw group stood our clearly. Over one hundred of us had been honoured in this way, including a number of prisoners from the previous transport who had also been assigned to the penal company. None of us could guess to what we owed this dangerous distinction, but the choice of people seemed to suggest that the officials of the Warsaw Gestapo were behind it. It seemed that we were in rather good company, which improved our spirits somewhat.

The penal company was divided into three groups. The first and the largest consisted of prisoners on their last legs who, in camp jargon, were called *Muselmänner* ('moslems').† They were usually Jews who had been brought here for minor offences and were being worn down day by day by the back-breaking work, the beatings and the hardship. The second group was made up of German criminals – various camp dignitaries – who had been caught trying to get into the women's camp, or discovered in the bread store. These were assigned the best bunks, given several blankets and were blatantly allowed to steal from the kitchen; they went out to work as supervisors, not workers. We were the last group, the red circles.

It was an interesting fact that from the moment we appeared with our red badges, the attitude of the other prisoners changed towards us. There was a hardly perceptible respect, even deference. This reaction was apparent not only among prisoners from other blocks, but also from our German criminal companions. Even block chief Bednarek was a little less brutal towards us.

We were not sure why this was. The fact that we were Polish could not have had anything to do with it, nor that we came from

---

*A town in East Poland which since the last war belongs to Soviet Russia.
†The expression had nothing to do with religion. A *Muselmann* was simply someone who was broken physically and mentally.

Warsaw. After a while the secret was revealed to us by the block scribe, a teacher.

In great secrecy he told us that we were not the first to wear red circles and badges with 'I.L.'. Several months previously another large group of Poles had been assigned to the penal company and ordered to sew on similar badges. The group had attempted a mass escape, it failed and all of them were shot, partly on the spot, partly at barrack number 11 in the central camp.*

The conclusion was obvious. The optimists amongst us tried to trivialize the whole thing, others refused to believe it; but it was difficult to ignore those who believed that we were condemned men and that our days were numbered.

In Auschwitz one was not really in a position to debate the future, so the pessimists' point of view, although seemingly justified, did not weigh on our minds too long. If we wanted to survive we had to live from day to day and not think about the distant future.

The day in the penal company started before dawn, somewhat earlier than the other blocks, for each morning there was a thorough inspection and anything of practical value was taken away. Clothes had to be in order, but it was forbidden to have either needle or thread, not to mention a knife or scissors. Although we were given a little soup for lunch it was an offence to have a spoon. The mornings were chilly, but every sweater, sock or glove was taken away. It was even forbidden to wrap old newspaper around oneself. While the sun shone, it was bearable, but in cold weather life became agony. We came back from work in wet rags and the following morning had to put on the same wet clothes.

In principle everyone in the barrack went to work outside the camp, building an earth embankment near the River Vistula. The prisoners had to stand up to their waists in muddy water in which the 'moslems' floundered and drowned. They were

*In this barrack was a camp prison, called the 'bunker', in the yard of which was the 'wall of death' where executions took place.

constantly harassed by a group of trusties who played wild games such as pushing prisoners into the water with long poles and laying bets as to who would last the longest under water. Every day a few corpses would be brought back on stretchers of sticks tied together so that the number of prisoners at evening roll-call would tally.

It turned out that, despite the croakings of the pessimists, our red circles also had some advantages. We were considered, as a group, to be dangerous and thus were not allowed out of the camp, even with the strongest of escorts and notwithstanding the patrols, dogs and watchtowers, which encircled the camp. Our group worked inside the camp and not on the dreadful embankment, under the eye of the Berlin or Hamburg pimps. They would have willingly played their cruel tricks on us, but being on the embankment all the day, they had only a little time in the evening when we all got back to the barrack.

We were assigned to digging shallow ditches which ran along the camp roads and were to act as a sort of sewer system during wet weather. The camp had been built on a swamp and the ground was marshy, becoming hard only in dry weather.

The sun had been blazing and we chipped at the surface with pickaxes, slowly moving like archaeologists sifting through prehistoric remains. The camp had been set up only a few years before, but our work was like that of the researcher trying to wrest the earth's secrets from it.

In the autumn of 1941, when Birkenau received its first intake of prisoners from the main Auschwitz complex, it had just a few decrepit huts and the whole area was covered by sickly aspens and a sodden quagmire. Work began on filling in the swamp with tons of earth, logs, broken bricks, rubbish and general refuse. The camp's sole installations were the barbed-wire fences and the watchtowers; there were no sanitary facilities, water or even a proper roof. The prisoners floundered and drowned in the mud; carts, horses, vehicles, tools and clothing were all sucked in. Digging our ditches we constantly stumbled across relics of those 'pioneering' years. Our spades brought up shoes, glasses, wheels with broken spokes, the remains of camp clothing, human and horses' bones. We were painfully constructing a new reality on the debris of our predecessors' world, putting out of our minds the thought that maybe we in our turn would come to lie in that inhospitable earth, which the next victims of German madness would turn over with their spades.

The lunch break lasted three-quarters of an hour and since we were working nearby we returned to the barrack for our soup. Not everyone received soup each day, for there were not enough bowls and there was insufficient time to pass them round twice.

The day ended for the whole camp late into the night. The returning *Kommandos* brought with them the bodies of those who had not the strength to survive, they walked the gauntlet of trusties to the strains of the orchestra,* the prisoners were carefully counted and only inside the camp did they break up into small groups which headed for their own barracks. There was an evening roll-call after which everyone received the daily bread ration. This was followed by the only moment of relaxation throughout the whole day.

The penal company returned at the same time as everyone else to its barrack, isolated from the rest of the camp. Bread was given out, but the day was not yet over for us. After evening roll-call there were still two more hours of 'work'. This consisted of physical exercises, usually knee-bends or crawling, or sometimes we were led out of the walled yard and made to carry earth. To do this we put our shirts on back to front, so the tail made a little bag in front. We then formed a long line flanked by SS men and trusties with sticks. At one side, on a pile of clay, stood a German with a spade in his hand; some distance away stood another, also on a pile of clay and also with a spade. At the sound of a whistle we ran towards one of the piles, were given a load of clay and ran to the other pile to drop it and pick up another. The SS men and trusties cheerfully beat whomever they could reach. And so the useful work carried on without a break. To fall meant being beaten. Not everyone turned out to be strong enough to get up and resume his place in the line. Our main object was to avoid being hit, and for this it helped to be young and in reasonable physical shape.

*There was a prisoners' orchestra in all the main concentration camps.

Finally night fell and the SS men, no doubt tired, went off to bed.

We returned to our barrack out of breath, clambered onto our bunks and almost immediately most of us fell into a deep sleep.

The penal company had not been allowed to write letters or to receive parcels, but by the summer of 1943 these Draconian rules began to be relaxed. We waited with longing for the day when we would be issued with the appropriate letter-forms and meanwhile we slowly starved. We were also tortured by the thought that our families knew nothing of us and must have anticipated the worst since all earlier correspondence that we had had when in prison now ceased.

Our group was composed almost entirely of professional people and although we never discussed it, all of us had been connected with secret resistance work. Amongst us there were a number of regular army officers, engineers and lawyers. There was quite a large group of civil servants, a few students, judges and state prosecutors. There was also one policeman and a Warsaw curate, and they had to keep their mouths tightly shut, for neither of these professions was held in high regard by the criminal prisoners and any indiscretion could lead to a lynching party. The group's solidarity had not yet been undermined so they were safe for the time being.

Work and hunger were beginning to sap our strength irrevocably, when one evening there arose an opportunity to improve our lot. The kitchens were situated right next to our barrack and the *Capo** approached our block chief with a suggestion that a dozen of us should work there. After the evening roll-call volunteers were called for and when a great many applied, there was a selection and the lucky ones were chosen. Marian and I were among them.

The following morning we were woken up even earlier than usual, since work amongst the pots began at 3 a.m. We found

---

*A prisoner in charge of a *Kommando*. *Capo*, an Italian word meaning 'head' or 'boss' was used by Italian workmen making roads in southern Germany. It was adopted in Dachau, the first concentration camp, and later by other camps, always spelled with a 'C' as in the original Italian.

ourselves in a turmoil of frenzied bustling, snatching cooking implements from people's hands, running for supplies, man-handling heavy cauldrons and constantly hosing down the floor.

The kitchens were ruled by the Russians, all of them prisoners of war, the few remaining from the 12,000 who had been brought to Auschwitz in 1941. Only the strongest and toughest of them had survived and finally they had been permitted to work in the kitchens (where they regained much of their former strength). They were large men, not tall, but broad-shouldered with large hands and bull-like necks, and relations with them were good. They would grasp the heaviest cauldrons and carry them, smiling at the run. Next to them I felt weak and clumsy, and the work really was too much for me. But I clung on tenaciously, for at last I was no longer hungry and I could support my comrades.

One of the first I was determined to help was Motka.

Coming back one evening from the kitchens I took a bowl of soup pulled the poor man into a dark corner and pushed a spoon into his hand. 'Eat quickly or someone might see us.'

My job in the kitchens had given me some status in the camp, but Motka would probably suffer if one of the German criminals spotted him.

To my amazement Motka took the spoon, but did not start eating at once. 'Good heavens, man, aren't you hungry?!'

'Yes, yes.'

He finally dug into the thick cold mass taken from the very bottom of the cauldron. He ate everything, scraped the bowl and returned the spoon to me with quiet words of thanks, but continued to act strangely. I could not understand why.

A few days later I again gave him a full bowl and again he was slow in starting to eat. He was so thin, his hands trembled, and yet he ate as though under duress. When he had finished he thanked me warmly, but hesitated for a moment as if he wanted to ask something.

'Well?'

'Look, I'll do anything for you, sewing, washing, but do you think you could get me a few potatoes? I don't need many, just one or two . . .'

'Yes, I can, but a bowl of soup is worth much more. You're up to something. Don't be a fool. Who do you want to take these potatoes to?'

Motka winced as if I had struck him and he tried to get away, but I grabbed him by the sleeve. 'Tell me the truth, or I won't get you anything at all. You trust me, don't you?'

'Yes, but why do you want to know everything?'

'I've got to. Who knows whom are you helping?'

'Over there, on the other side of the fence . . . my wife.'

He wanted to say more, but at that moment there was a loud whistling and then shouting, as though someone was being killed. The trustees grabbed their sticks and began chasing everyone out of the barrack into the yard. I just managed to hurl the bowl through a small window and leapt for the door. Several SS men arrived and began to check the whole barrack. They were searching for two sacks of bread which one of the German criminals was supposed to have stolen from the stores and taken into our barrack. *Rapportführer* Palitzsch* arrived, the wooden punishment contraption was brought and we were ordered to wait. Formed up in rows of ten we stood motionless, uncertain how things would develop. After a couple of minutes one sack was dragged out and then the second, and three Germans were called out of the ranks. The first one was ordered to lie on the bench while the remaining two gave him fifty strokes, after which he got up with difficulty. Then he beat the next one and finally they got down to the last one. After this Palitzsch himself gave a hand. The man being beaten was groaning, gritting his teeth; he knew that if he screamed they would start counting again.

I was not able to talk to Motka for a few days. I brought him a cap full of potatoes and a hunk of bread. He thanked me with emotion and without prompting explained how he communicated with his wife. When he had been on a normal barrack, he

---

*He was an SS NCO responsible for discipline in the camp. Palitzsch served in the main Auschwitz complex and was renowned for his cruelty, see chapter thirteen. Each of the sub-camps had their own *Rapportführers*, responsible for discipline.

had made friends with a Czech working in an electricians' *Kommando* who often went to work in the women's camp. The Czech naturally took his cut, but something always got through to Motka's wife. Since Motka had landed in the penal company, things had become worse, for his communications with the Czech were difficult and he had to pay a second intermediary, but he had no choice. His wife was in particularly poor health and had barely managed to recover from a recent heavy cold.

'Look, I expect you're sending her your bread?'

'No, no ... how could I?'

'She'll die and you won't survive.'

'But what else can I do? If only you knew ...'

The poor man covered his eyes with his hand, but immediately regained control over himself and carefully touched my shoulder. 'Listen ...'

It was already dark. The Germans were enjoying themselves on the other side of the yard and we were able to prolong our casual meeting.

Motka's story resembled that of many families destroyed by the savagery of the war.

He had lived in the suburbs of Grodno, in a small wooden house with his wife and three small children. He inherited from his father a small tailor's business and by working hard kept himself afloat and his family alive. It was a poor area, and he earned little. They had lived in poverty. But his eyes misted over and his lips quivered when he spoke of those years. It was clear that he loved the country which had become his home, and although the people around sometimes treated him as an outsider because of his Jewishness, he didn't hold that against them and he didn't blame anyone.

'If only you could have seen a town like Grodno. And what people there were living in it! I would have sewed for them for nothing if I could.'

The arrival of the war struck them like lightning. He was not in the army, since from birth he had had one leg shorter than the other; trembling he had listened to the radio bulletins describing the advance of Hitler's armies. When the Russians came, occupying East Poland in agreement with the Germans, he hid in his work, hardly poked his nose out of doors and somehow survived. The year 1941 arrived. The Germans attacked Russia and within a few days occupied Grodno. Motka was afraid but could do nothing; what chances were there of escape and where could he go with his family?

The first few weeks were tolerable, but then the hardships began. They were ordered to sew on yellow stars, they were refused rations and if they went out on the streets they were usually beaten. Motka lost all his customers – people were afraid to come to him. Dreadful months of hunger followed. There was no food for the children who cried almost continually and gradually became emaciated in front of their desperate parents. Motka used to sneak out at night after curfew, at great risk to himself, and struggle to neighbouring villages to get anything edible from the peasants in exchange for a garment.

Finally one morning their street was filled with armed soldiers; after a few minutes SS men barged into the house.

'You are to get ready in two minutes. Move!'

His wife began to fluster helplessly. Motka ran into the workshop and began to pick up some small things. The Germans looked contemptuously at the poor interior and the dirty, thin children. The two eldest ones cowered in the dark corner, but the youngest boy, not really understanding what was happening, walked up to the SS men and looked at one of the soldier's gleaming boots with surprise.

The wife went over to the children with some warm clothing, but the soldier barred her way. 'There's no need!'

'But it's cold at night. They'll be cold.'

'Only you're going, they're staying. Get out!'

She cried out and fell on her knees in front of the Germans.

The SS man pushed her away and two others dragged her into the corridor. Motka, out of his mind, followed. The door slammed, they could still hear the barking of the SS men and the sobbing of the children . . .

We had sent our first letters and, finally, answers and parcels arrived. Our group had already shrunk somewhat, but we now had a better chance of survival. It was just then I caught a chill, which developed into a slight infection of the inner ear. My temperature rose to over 39 °C, and the pain was unbearable, but there was no question of going to the hospital. We used to say in Auschwitz that you had to arrive with your head under your arm to be admitted to the hospital and, also, typhus was raging there and the inmates were dying off in their hundreds. However, since I was in no condition to continue working in the kitchens I had to drop the work there and go back to digging ditches. When things were quiet I lay down on the wet sand while my comrades kept a look out in case anyone came. Feverish at night I could not sleep on the narrow bunk, but fortunately Motka brought me some aspirin he had managed to obtain. Jurek and Marian also did all they could to help. June was warm and dry and I somehow came through. My temperature fell and the pain stopped.

Unexpectedly we received an order to move, turning our sub-camp over to the women who no longer had enough space. We were divided into teams and ordered to drag our wooden three-storey bunks, which had been knocked together by camp carpenters, to furnish the new penal company barrack. We marched along the camp road, continually surrounded by wire, to a new sector completely filled with empty wooden barracks. As before, our barrack had a yard surrounded by a high wall adjoining, on its longest side, a similar barrack. It turned out that half of this barrack was a washroom. Adjoining this, separated by a wooden wall, was a washroom which was assigned to another barrack which housed the *Sonderkommando*.*

These were exclusively Jews who worked in the gas chambers and crematoria. They were issued with special rations, including alcohol, and were treated gently so that they could carry out their dreadful work. At the end of three months the whole *Kommando* was gassed and replaced by Jews newly arrived who, in their turn, suffered a similar brutal fate. It took a particular sort of mentality to conceive of such refined bestiality. But life in the camp had a style of its own.

---

*In June 1944 the *Sonderkommando* (special working party) was moved into the area of the crematoria.

After a couple of days there was close contact between us and the Jews on the other side of the wooden wall: we talked through holes in the planks, news from the outside world was passed and many goods were exchanged. The people from the *Sonderkommando* were in touch with others who worked in the thirty huge barracks, called in the camp jargon 'Canada', where articles brought by the Jewish transports were sorted. Wealthy people, brought from all over Europe, had plenty of valuables: jewellery, gold dollars, fine clothes, food, medicines and dental instruments. There was a death penalty for taking any of these goods, but they were smuggled into and outside the camp. The members of the *Sonderkommando* were ready to bargain the linen, tins of sardines, Dutch cheeses for fresh vegetables smuggled into the camp by *Kommandos* working outside. For a small onion one could buy a gold watch, for a couple of kilos of beetroot a diamond of several carats. We ourselves were not interested in these things, but some criminal Germans started to build up a chain of intermediaries.

Before we had settled into our new quarters we were sent to be deloused. Our clothes, underwear and blankets were taken away to be disinfected, while we had some evil smelling liquid poured over us and were then left in peace for twenty-four hours and not chased out to work. We walked around naked, dressed only in wooden shoes and the thin strips of leather which usually held up our trousers. Some of us hung small mugs on these strips and nearly everyone stuffed their spoons behind them, since the camp authorities had finally allowed us to have them.

It was a warm day; we sat around in groups on the hard earth by the barrack deep in conversations, discussions and conjecture: we already knew that the Allied armies had landed in Sicily and so there was something to talk about. We were careful all the same.

In theory Nazi newspapers were permitted in the camps and sometimes a German trusty would get one; they were also brought in by civilian workers, who came into contact with some of the *Kommandos*. In our situation, wearing red and black circles, it was better not to display knowledge of the papers, but we were desperate to read whatever we could. Scraps of the

Völkischer Beobachter (*People's Observer*) or some local paper circulated from hand to hand, providing us with snippets of information from the southern and eastern fronts. The same happened at other barracks and the whole camp buzzed with gossip, predictions and so-called '*paroles*' (camp jargon for optimistic rumours) which turned everything upside down. Tired and barely living, we thought up the most unbelievable things just to keep up our flagging optimism and somehow, in this way, survive. Fanciful stories, which only children could have believed, were exchanged; yet many adults believed them.

Paroles could not, however, change the reality of camp life. Without any notice, news ran round the camp one day that there was to be a selection of those unfit for work. They would be sent to the gas chambers. No one wanted to believe it, for this practice had been abandoned some time earlier. However, the selection did take place but only of Jews and it did not reach the penal company.

Working inside the camp we were witness to the incredible sight of hundreds of prisoners being led along the main camp road to the crematoria. These were Jews mainly from Greece and Salonika. Cruelty, hunger and the terrible workload had reduced them to such a state that even the SS men lacked the courage to urge them on faster. They were terrifying shadows of people, ghosts covered in wounds and blood, dressed in rags and probably numbed and unaware of what was happening around them, slowly dragging themselves to the main gate.

The same evening Motka ran up to me in such a state that I could barely calm him down. 'What's wrong? What's the matter with you?'

'I'm alright, but my wife . . .'

'Is she ill again?'

'No, but she's weak and they've been picking them out to be gassed.'

'Yes, but only those on their last legs.'

Motka took offence, but immediately touched my shoulder in silent apology. 'I know you want to cheer me up, but what's the use? We're damned, we've got to die!'

'You shouldn't talk like that. Everything is in God's hands.'

'God, God! Where was he when my children . . .?'

I grasped him firmly by the shoulder. 'Be quiet! Control yourself! What have we got left if He doesn't exist?'

More heavy, hot days passed. Tragically Motka's intuition was right, his wife was selected. He was now quite alone. Within a short time he changed completely. He had always been pale and thin, but some fire had burned within him which had kept up his strength and nourished his surprising and continual energy. He had lost his children, but his wife still remained and the fight to save her life had been the goal which had given him that strength. Now Motka felt a great emptiness. The burden of camp life fell on him with all its weight. He shrivelled, his faced turned grey. He no longer prowled restlessly among the prisoners, looking for some extra little job; he no longer hunted for food nor made mysterious contacts to keep in touch with his wife. Previously so careful and obedient he began to be careless at work and was several times reprimanded. He suffered at the cruel hands of the supervising Germans.

I began to fear for his life.

Time after time new transports arrived and the camp bulged and expanded, even though the death rate was so high. However, not all the new arrivals reached the camp. Unexpectedly a massive transport of 30,000 Dutch Jews arrived and was sent straight from the ramp to the gas chambers. It was a mixed transport composed of old people, mature men and women, and children. For three days and nights the *Sonderkommando* worked feverishly in two shifts. The camp shuddered and waves of nervous tension began to flow through it. The authorities tried to control the situation and issued an order not to send the prisoners out to work for a few days. So we were kept in our barracks and they tried to isolate us somewhat from the crematoria, but the stink of burning bodies was so pervasive that no one was in any doubt as to what was happening.

On the third day we were ordered back to work, although the dreadful proceedings had not yet been completed.

During morning roll-call Motka's face caught my eye in the

grey crowd. It was blue and almost inhuman, only the eyes burned with feverish intensity.

That evening we came back from work earlier and had to move our bunks and clean out the barrack. Just before roll-call the *Kommando* working on the trench arrived. Once again someone was brought back on a stretcher made of plaited reeds.

When the counting finished and the evening bread had finally been distributed, I moved cautiously in the direction of the gate and looked at the motionless body. It was Motka. He lay calmly with his eyes closed, but there was still some spark of life in him, for his hands were trembling and his lips moved as if he were talking, asking for something. Help was out of the question because two Germans armed with sticks were guarding him.

I went into the barrack and sought out my friends. I felt the need to be near someone whose heart was still beating and who had not yet lost all human emotions. I tried to eat, but the bread would not go down my throat.

All the lights were out in the barrack and it was completely dark when I crept out into the yard. The stick-wielding murderers had gone to bed and I could get up quite close to look at my friend's face for the last time.

Motka had stopped moving, but his lips still trembled in their final agony.

The sky was overcast and the night was dark, moonless and angry. Somewhere in the distance a harmonica played, a train whistled and on the watchtowers the SS men shouted to each other.

The camp was asleep and only the distant noises of the crematoria drifted over. Three great pillars of fire shone from the brick chimneys and merged into a single glow which hung over the camp, a symbol of the times in which we were fated to live.

Chapter Thirteen

The Wall of Death

One morning, during the roll-call, an unknown SS man appeared in front of our ranks and read out several numbers.

Among them was mine and when I heard it, my legs literally began to give way under me. I had been long enough in the camp to know that the reading out of a number was an evil omen. It might mean execution or cruel punishment, it might mean renewed interrogation or even a return to the prison from which you had come.

I had been in the Pawiak, I had survived several weeks in Auschwitz, but as a victim of the common terror. The Gestapo knew nothing of my underground work and thanks to this I was alive. But there was always the possibility of my being uncovered. One of my people might have been arrested in Warsaw and cruel interrogation might have forced him to give my name. None of them were supposed to know it, everywhere I used code-names, but an unfortunate coincidence could have occurred. I had lived in Warsaw for several years, I had attended the university there, and the regiment of cavalry, of which I was a reserve officer, was garrisoned in the capital.

Those of us, whose numbers had been read out, did not go to work and the sullen SS man, who came to fetch us, growled that he was taking us to the main camp, to the political department.

It was a warm, summer morning, but I felt the cold sweat break out on my body. I could not stop trembling. So here it was, so this was the beginning of the end.

The main camp lay about three kilometres from Birkenau. We walked among groups of working prisoners. We were on ground under the camp's jurisdication, watched by a chain of guards and patrols with dogs. The SS man paid us no attention, we were in striped clothing, there was no question of escape.

The barrack of the political department lay outside the barbed wire fence surrounding the main camp, to the left of the gate. The SS man led us there, ordered us to stand outside the door and entered the building. We stood in silence, each one thinking his own thoughts. It was better not to talk.

Several hours passed and nobody called us. The sun rose higher and began to burn. We were, of course, hungry and thirsty, but that happened every day.

Only after twelve o'clock was one of my companions called in, after him a second and a third and I stood and waited, more and more weary.

A surprising thing happened. It was late afternoon. I could barely stand up, when an SS man with a file in his hand appeared at the door. He read out my number, looked at my shirt to check that I was wearing the same number and said there had been a mistake. I was the wrong man. Someone would take me back to Birkenau and meanwhile I would go with another SS man to barrack number 11, to the 'bunker'. Perhaps they would give me some soup, perhaps I would spend the night there and go back to the penal company the following morning.

I breathed deeply, at once I began to come back to life, I did not even feel any fear of going to the 'bunker', which was the camp prison and where, beside the black wall, executions were carried out.

'*Komm*', ordered the soldier and I followed him along one of the neat camp roads. The prisoners were at work and only here and there a figure in camp stripes passed by rapidly.

We walked along a row of one-storey brick barracks until we reached the last one. The soldier went up a few steps to the door, unlocked it and beckoned me into a windowless corridor in the barrack.

Inside I met a young prisoner in clean striped clothes who looked indifferently at me. I looked at his number. Three-digit figures showed that he had been brought to the camp in the first or second transport, in June 1940. So he had survived the terrible ill treatment of the first few weeks, he had survived the hunger, the endless beatings and the labour carried out all the day long at the double, he had seen dozens of his comrades beaten to death, perhaps he had survived the torture of the 'standing cell'. For sure he had managed to become a trusty, otherwise he would be dead. As a 'low number' prisoner he now had certain privileges, had changed jobs a number of times and had at last been appointed orderly in the camp prison, the 'bunker'. The SS no longer beat him, he no longer suffered from hunger.

Had his heart hardened, had he ceased to respond to his surroundings? Almost every day he had to prepare prisoners for executions.

'Why are you here?', he asked me in a low voice.

'I was at the political department. I have to stay here till somebody takes me back to Birkenau.'

'Fine. My deputy has been taken ill, presumably with typhus. You will help me today.'

'But I have had nothing to eat all day. At least give me a mug of water.'

He directed me to a washroom and after a couple of minutes brought a bowl of cold soup.

'Eat quickly, I hear a noise. You never know when you will have work to do.'

Several minutes passed and from the corridor we heard steps.

'Stay here and do nothing till I call you.'

I moved to the corner of the washroom, from which I could see the door and a part of the corridor.

The orderly stiffened to attention and I did the same, because an SS man appeared in the doorway. Behind him a man, a woman and a teenage girl.

As was the custom, the orderly wanted to direct the man to the washroom, where I was standing, and the woman to another one, but the SS man stopped him with a gesture:

'Take them all together.'

They moved towards me and only then did we both notice the young boy in the woman's arms. The orderly hesitated, but the young soldier said shortly, 'Do your job.'

He went quickly up to the man and shook his arm. 'You must undress here.'

'Here? All of us?'

'Yes and don't dawdle, because the SS will be here in a minute.'

His voice was hard and he tried to make it sound as indifferent as possible.

The man took off his jacket, took off his tie and began to unbutton his shirt, but then he stopped and looked helplessly at his wife and daughter.

'Get undressed man', shouted the orderly, but he realized what was the matter and turned away to the wall.

We both heard behind us the rustle of falling skirts and at the same time we listened for noises outside.

Suddenly we heard behind us a whisper and the child crying quietly. The orderly quickly turned round and not looking at the almost naked woman grabbed the boy. The little one cried out in fright and began to struggle, but at that very moment a hoarse order rang out.

'Bring out the first one, bring the man.'

The orderly quickly placed the little boy on the floor, grasped the man's hands, twisted them behind his back, tied them with wire and let him into the yard.

I shouldn't have done it, but like a lunatic I followed him.

There was a wide area between the 'bunker' and another similar brick barrack, enclosed on the short sides. Under one of them was a high, black plank wall. By it, with a small-calibre gun, slung carelessly over his shoulder, stood the camp *Rapport-führer*, SS NCO Gerhard Palitzsch. There was a silencer on the gun.

Next to him another SS NCO was looking at a piece of paper in his hand, while a little further off was another SS man, responsible for the 'bunker'. Alone, to one side stood a young SS doctor with the rank of captain. It was clear that he felt unsure of himself, for he kept taking off his glasses, wiping them and putting them back on again.

Palitzsch looked at the naked man and with a gesture indicated what he wanted him to do. When there was no reaction, he came up behind him and began to push him in the direction of the black wall with the barrel of his weapon. He stood him with his face to the board and threw an ironic glance at the doctor who was still wiping his glasses. He slowly raised the gun and let the muzzle rest against the back of the naked man's skull. It was clear that he was enjoying every moment and was intentionally dawdling.

The orderly shook my arm and pointed to the body. We removed it to the side quick as lightning, returned to the washroom and looked at the woman. She was quite naked and held the little one in her arms. She was not crying, although it was clear that she was using her last reserves of strength to retain self-control. The orderly took away the child with shaking hands, put it on the floor and silently showed the woman what she was to do with her hands. With his eyes closed he began to push her towards the door.

He returned trembling. The girl was standing up by the wall, clutching her little brother to her and trying to use him to shield her own nakedness. The orderly went up to her and put his arm round her shoulder.

'Don't be frightened, don't be frightened', he kept repeating quite absurdly. At the same time he took the child away from her and slowly pushed her towards the door.

Again, like a lunatic, I followed them.

All four SS men turned to look at her, but the doctor lowered his eyes. Palitzsch walked over to her and with his usual little gesture with his gun motioned towards the black wall and with the barrel parted her long hair. The shot was almost inaudible, but the girl's body fell face down. The SS man kicked her onto her back and looked inquiringly at the doctor.

No one moved, no one said a word, but after a second the SS man responsible for the 'bunker' appeared to wake up and turned an enquiring glance at Palitzsch.

'There's still a child, but after all . . .'

'What?! Bring the little bastard here.'

The SS man entered the bunker, grabbed the child himself and carried it outside. The young doctor looked up and on his face were reflected confusion and fear. His lips trembled, he tried to say something, took a step forward, but Palitzsch did not wait, he grasped the little boy by his legs and with all his might smashed his head against the wall.

The scene was so unexpected, so terrible that even the two SS men caught their breath, while the doctor took off his glasses and tried to wipe them again, but his hands were trembling so much that the glasses fell onto the sand. He bent down and with the awkward movements of a short-sighted person began to look for them. And at that moment Palitzsch spoke, his calm, hard voice filled with irony.

'Herr Doctor, your duty is to check whether the execution has been correctly carried out and whether those condemned to die are in fact dead.'*

---

*Palitzsch himself admitted the killing by his own hand of 25,000 prisoners. Despite the strict prohibition, he began an affair with a Jewess from Slovakia. After disciplinary proceedings he joined an SS unit fighting partisans in the Balkans. He was apparently killed in December 1944 near Budapest.

Chapter Fourteen

The Sixth Column

After three days spent in cattle trucks we were told to get our things together and get ready to alight. Marian, Jurek and I had all been transported from Auschwitz. Night had closed in on the transport, and it was impossible to form any idea of where we were. We crowded up to the windows so we could see the searchlights from the camp's guard towers. They threw streams of light, just as lighthouses send their saving beams to drowning castaways. From inside the camp we heard the shouts of command, the howling of dogs and the shuffling of hundreds of hobnailed boots. The SS men who had gone to reconnoitre came back to the trucks.

'*Rrrraus!!*'

With a clatter of wooden clogs we stumbled out and were hastily formed into groups of five and marched to the camp between two close ranks of sentries. Losing our clogs, pushing each other, hurting our feet and swearing in the darkness we approached the row of faint lights which marked the barbed wire. Here was our new 'home'. What would the following morning bring?

We had previously been in Birkenau, a part of Auschwitz, for only a short time, and the rigours of the penal company had isolated us from the main life of the camp. Here we were to have new experiences. So when the gate opened and we marched on to the concrete of the roll-call square, we glanced with interest at the rows of trusties, mobilized for the reception of the new transport.

'Look, nearly all red triangles,* somebody near me whispered.'

In truth the well-fed men with the armbands of *Capos* and block chiefs on their sleeves, were mainly political prisoners. The senior camp prisoner who came up at this moment also wore a red triangle. This was something new to us for in Birkenau we had been accustomed to criminal prisoners ruling the roost.

We were led to the showers. Everything took place without any shouting.

'Don't you notice that the trusties here are somewhat different? That there is something missing?'

Suddenly I realized what it was: they had no sticks in their hands!

In the baths our bundles were searched. In Auschwitz that would have had a sad ending; here we almost got through without losing anything.

'These are quite different people. It looks as if we haven't struck badly, boys.'

The first weeks we spent in number 4 block, which at that time was quarantine. We didn't do too badly in fact. The clerk and interpreter, specially detailed to our transport, was a Pole, a young journalist from Warsaw, and the block chief, a good-looking red-haired man, was also a political prisoner. It was whispered that he had been in the camp for seven years for fighting in Spain on the side of the Reds while he was an officer in the *Luftwaffe*.†

For several days we did not go to work. After meals we sat down outside the barrack on the narrow strip of concrete; no one shouted or swore at us as they had in Birkenau, no one dragged us to work by force. The passing Germans, nearly always red triangles, smiled and said the odd friendly greeting to us.

These conditions emboldened and yet embarrassed us. In our hearts there awoke memories faintly remembered. We were perhaps still human beings?

---

*In the German concentration camps every criminal prisoner wore a green triangle and every political a red one on his shirt and trousers.
†German air force.

Within the circle of a few friends we began to talk over these novelties. Naturally these outwardly favourable conditions resulted from the fact that the trusties were political prisoners, but what were their opinions, how had they come to be in authority and did they not abuse it in other sectors of camp life?

We discovered without difficulty that the red triangles, occupying the majority of camp 'posts', were mainly Communists. For the greater part they were Germans (the senior camp prisoner, Kirbitz, senior *Capo* Liedke, senior hospital *Capo* Mathis and many others) but there were also representatives of the other nationalities among them. In the camp office, for instance, which decided what work the prisoner was to do, what block he was to live in and whether he was to be sent somewhere else, the Belgian André was in charge. And authority did not always lie in the hands of those who seemed to be in charge. We had to look deeper into the matter.

This was something we had to do quickly because our transport had finished its period of quarantine and any day would be divided up among the barracks and working parties. Preparations for transport to reinforce the numerous branch camps were also spoken of. As a group we had developed a sense of harmony, we understood each other well, we had reached the stage of mutual confidence and we wished to defend the entity of our group.

Here we began to doubt. Among us there were a few Communists, gathered in like most of us from Warsaw. Would they break away from the general defensive Polish front? Could we count on their loyalty? At the end of September I got into a small working party which went every day to a nearby village to take down a house. It was an excellent job but it isolated me from the internal affairs of the camp. We set out before dawn, we came back just before roll-call (sometimes even after it) and besides we were divided among different barracks, where we were in touch with no one in particular. So our observations of the life of the camp were disrupted.

The good job had only just ended when I caught a chill and was stuck in the sick-bay for a couple of weeks. At this time there began a spate of transports. Every morning a long row of the chosen, dressed in new striped suits, stood on the roll-call ground, right in front of the sick-bay. SS men came and there was an inspection that lasted many hours. Carefully I crept up to the window and looked for familiar faces. Unfortunately there were many I knew. It was understandable that as our transport was the most recent it should fall victim to further transportation, but even that circumstance did not explain such a large percentage of prisoners newly arrived from Auschwitz.

I shared my observations with my friends, who had managed to visit me. They were of the same opinion and added that in the Camp Office day after day there were arguments as to who was to go in the transports to sub-camps, which on the whole had a bad reputation. It was quite clear that two influential groups in the camp were at odds with each other. Our colleagues from the building office, where specialists had to be accepted, whether it was liked or not, were in strong opposition to the well-organized and all-powerful Reds. The struggle with them was difficult, for their influence reached even outside the barbed wire, and they had held power here for some time.

Once one of my Russian fellow prisoners told me that before the war a film called *Soldiers of Mud* was shown in Russia. It was about life in Dachau.

'Germans used to give Germans good hidings there. And not only the SS men. Prisoners beat prisoners. And especially Communists.'

The film had been accurate. Indeed during the first years of the German concentration camps the Communists had been murdered *en masse*, and both SS men and their own criminal colleagues had enjoyed doing it (the latter were the worst).

The SS men, even in those blessed times, when the front was not yet crying out constantly for new soldiers, were only in the camp while on duty. They lived outside the camps and it was the particularly sadistic who prowled around inside when off duty.

But the fellow-prisoner trusties were there all the time, and the long years in prison and their criminal pasts had taught them all the tricks of the jungle. They would eat their colleagues' food; wring the last drop of sweat out of them to hide their own indolence; and in the moments of rest played cruel tricks to stop themselves from getting bored. Sometimes the scenes played out behind the barbed wire were beyond our worst imaginings.

Once, for example, the block chief was to have a birthday party, so he ordered about twenty prisoners to be killed to enable him to get their slices of bread the following morning; in another instance the *Capo* had taken a fancy to someone's sweater, so he drove him onto the electrified wires. On occasion, during the night, drunken SS men would shoot from their towers to the walls of the blocks, judging the accuracy of their shots by the shrieks. It was apparently to pass away the time.

It was inevitable that a prisoner who had no one behind him, no connections, no support, who didn't himself become a trusty, was almost certain to die. And so there began the terrifying struggle for influence, to get on top. The criminals had behind them power, a well established routine, a tendency not to feel any restraints in their behaviour, and a common identity as criminals, not being there for political or military reasons. The political prisoners, on the other hand, had a different sort of intelligence, an ability to organize and a cameraderie from their days of activity before their imprisonment. The majority of them were Communists, imprisoned for their activities before the war, so the struggle between these two groups was almost exclusively between Germans.

If the struggle for power among free men in normal civilized conditions is rarely chivalrous and clean, it was inhuman in the camps. The outbreak of war inflamed an already bitter atmosphere, as thousands of new victims came to the camps. The largest centres, like Dachau, Sachsenhausen and Buchenwald, began to be ruled by the Communists, while the criminals held sway in the smaller camps and in the new camps, although their power there did not last.

While the internal conflict took place within these camps the SS men looked on indifferently. On principle no one ever got out of a concentration camp, and inside, the most efficient killers made the best prison staff. The block chief made the best hangman, the *Capo* was the most zealous in driving others to work and the nurses were those who tortured the sick most efficiently. There were of course exceptions but very few. And those were generally in the later years, when the power of the Nazis was on the wane.

The camp authorities began to appreciate these changes in power amongst the prisoners. The Red trusties carried out their duties well and were efficient and methodical in administration. Once the war had spread across Europe, millions of Europeans, other than Germans, found themselves behind German barbed wire. Anyone who was already a Communist or who was able to ally himself with them quickly, found himself on firmer ground. The camps were in touch with the outside world via the civilian workmen, the master craftsmen and even some SS men, and the efficient Communist network built further on this.

From the end of 1941 the ranks of the Communists were swelled by hundreds of thousands of Russians and other inhabitants of the Soviet Union. Outwardly they seemed undisciplined, but they were responsive to their leaders who rarely held exposed positions in the camp but had much influence and acted adroitly undercover.

So it was in Neuengamme into which arrived five hundred of us, transported from Auschwitz.

Could one hope that in the Polish nation's struggle for life or death, in the fight waged against enormous German odds, Poles would have stuck together? Poland under German occupation was not far from this ideal. The ranks were broken only by those who looked to the East, to Soviet Russia, for inspiration.

This was particularly true in the camps. Our transport had hardly settled down when all hopes of comradeship and honesty seemed to have faded. A few Reds, led by sturdy Franek, immediately made contact with the camp Mafia, who were also Communist, and adopted similar policies. Every evening outside the camp office they held council. Plots, intrigues, favouring began. The weaker ones from the transport, scenting what was in the wind and from where it blew, joined the leaders. Only the nucleus of the transport, composed of a smaller group of soldiers and members of the underground movement, remained in solidarity. We had been together a short while but were bound together by a common past and the secret of a common service.

So the attacks of the Communists began to be directed against us. We were split up among the barracks, sent out to the worst working parties, and when the branch camps demanded fresh workers we were transported.

Lurking near the window in the sick-bay I could observe the faces of my colleagues, standing in rows every day waiting for the departure signal. They were being sent to factories, on which night after night allied bombs rained; they were being sent to earthworks, to notoriously bad camps, where drunken SS NCOs reigned, uncontrolled and unrestrained.

When I returned to the block from the sick-bay it was somehow empty and strange, although no less crowded. Luckily my two friends were still there. It was now the late autumn of 1943 and the end of the war was approaching, but we didn't believe in rumours of an early date. We felt we would have to survive for a long time yet.

'It's not looking too good, but so far we've managed to exist here and God alone knows what it's like in the branch camps. We must stay here to the end.'

'That's fine but the winter is drawing on and we are digging trenches out of doors. Do you think we can get indoor work.'

'It won't be easy especially as our 'friends' are on our heels and we are likely to be transported to sub-camps. We should try to get into a working party which would protect us from them.'

Marian nudged me slightly, 'Speak lower', he whispered.

We were standing in the narrow gangway between the two rows of three-tiered bunks. I looked around carefully. Our neighbour at the table, the Russian Kola Lazowski, was passing us. He smiled as usual, half mockingly. Jurek turned and looked at him.

'I've had my eye on Kola for a while. He's something of a mystery. He has the accent of a Russian intellectual and usually behaves well. Every evening he goes out and prowls around the camp. What sort of job can he be on?'

'I don't know but we can try and find out. I have a feeling that he speaks perfect Polish. We better be careful.'

Very cautiously we began to try to change our work. I had

been in hospital so I managed to get a permit for five days light work. After the following morning's roll-call, when the order was given for working groups to form up, I joined the column of 'moslems' who worked in the barracks twisting various types of rope from odds and ends of rubber and rags. Jurek and Marian were with me and somehow we managed to get away with it and at last worked under a roof. The work itself was disgusting, unthinkably filthy, but what a delight to hear the stove hissing nearby and to look indifferently out at the rain and hail beating on the sweating window panes. But it did not last for long. One evening Kola, sitting opposite us at supper, smiled and spoke:

'So? You've turned *Muselmänner*, eh? You're working on the ropes and that's a *Muselmann's* job. Well well.'

The following morning, when we were waiting in the ranks to go to work, a group of trusties appeared in front of us. Among them was the Belgian André, a young man, but an old Communist. He was very powerful in the department that organized work. In the glare of the searchlights which pierced the darkness before dawn he walked down the quietened ranks. He checked the numbers on the coats, comparing them with a slip of paper in his hand. Somehow he overlooked Jurek and me, but he noticed Marian.

He pulled Marian out of the row and pushed him towards a sturdy figure who grasped him by the collar and marched him away into the darkness. Marian went back to digging trenches.

In the evening Kola left us alone, but it was easy to see from his discreet smiles that he was pleased with his success. We doubled our vigilance but it didn't help much. A few days later André came to the rope-makers' barrack, and again began to pick out numbers from a list. I managed to hide but Jurek couldn't and the following day he went to work in a brick factory up to his knees in clay. His job involved carrying and laying rails under the trucks which carried sand. He came back each evening exhausted and soaked. Brief meetings with the few colleagues who had escaped the last transports enabled us to work out that the same thing was happening in the other blocks.

We couldn't see how to fight against this and decided that it wasn't worth trying. We would have had to fight our opponents with their own methods; it was one thing to break into the stores for bread, or to avoid work, but another to hunt down colleagues, to lessen their chances of survival by denunciations and dirty tricks. Seeing no hope of keeping the rope-making job I threw it up and went to work in the transport columns, near the workshops.

One day I noticed Kola there. 'Hello, what are you doing here?' I asked.

'I'm working in the locksmith's shop. Any of your business?'

Kola couldn't do much harm for I had heavy work, but his prying eyes watched me all the time and annoyed me. I was working with some Russians and a few days after meeting Kola I felt they began treating me more coldly.

In the barrack the atmosphere became increasingly strained. Lazowski was helped by another Russian, an NCO of an infantry regiment, who carried out all Kola's orders, followed us everywhere, checked on whoever we made contact with and made it almost impossible to keep in touch with our colleagues, whom we were now forced to avoid.

We wanted to find out what Lazowski really did in the camp and where the threads of his contacts led. It was already the beginning of 1944 and, in spite of everything, the end of the war was not far off. But our fate depended to a large extent on ourselves. If you could withstand starvation and the work you had a chance of surviving, for the methodical murdering of men had ceased. But we had a new anxiety for there were rumours going round of orders to liquidate the prisoners at the last moment before the Germans surrendered. If that happened then some sort of internal organization might be very important.

We decided that of the three of us Marian was on the best terms with Kola. He had a particularly quiet disposition and seldom was the object of Lazowski's jeers and gibes. There was a chance that with a little skill he might learn something.

During the following weeks, our relationship towards Marian appeared to change. We ostentatiously avoided talking to him; at table we refused to share our extra food; from time to time we made nasty remarks as if he'd changed his colours to Red of late. After supper, instead of a friendly talk together, Jurek and I went off leaving Marian with Kola and his companion. Marian treated them to his stores and allowed himself to be drawn into long ideological discussions; he would sometimes assent, occasionally protest, but on the whole played the role of the stray sheep who wanted to be put on the right road. Kola was distrustful at first but after a couple of weeks began to show some signs of thawing.

He confided briefly in Marian that he had come to the camp from a prison where he had been put after the discovery of an intelligence cell of which he had been chief. He had been an NKVD officer (Narodny Kommissariat Vnutrennich Dyel, the People's Commissariat for Internal Affairs) since before the war. He was excellently informed on Polish affairs and explained to Marian at length about the increasing co-operation between the Poles and the Soviet Union. He gave Marian many details about the Polish army under Soviet command and argued that this was the only road open to the Poles. Marian agreed and in his spare time he sought out Kola's company; they might even have been taken for close friends.

A few more weeks passed. Kola asked Marian one day what he thought about the end of the war.

'The Germans will be beaten and probably soon.'

'Of course. But that wasn't what I meant. What will happen to us?'

'How should I know?'

Kola smiled with a certain superiority. 'That's why I'm talking to you. The SS men could finish us all off but life is still sweet. Be outside the canteen tomorrow evening. We'll talk it over.'

Lazowski didn't come alone to this evening meeting. An unknown German, who watched Marian carefully, was with him. In a few words they told him that there was a secret organization in the camp, preparing to disarm the guards and defend the camp if the Germans tried to kill off the prisoners in the final stages of the war. Marian was given a small task and the conversation ended:

'Only look out for the Fascists. Who knows which side they'll take.'

Marian repeated the conversation to us. It was clear that we must be prepared for the final phase, but such preparations could only work if the prisoners stuck together; there had to be a solidarity above that of nationality or of party. However, there was little chance of this since even within the Polish group there was a split between ourselves and the Communists. We couldn't count on them so we would have to conceal any conversations we had from them and any traces of an organization, to prevent ourselves being exposed to further transportation or even heavier work.

Christmas passed and 1944 began. One morning a transport of planks came in and the wagons had to be unloaded in a hurry. The group I was with was working feverishly next to the lock-smith's workshop, from which Kola emerged now and then to talk and joke with us. He came up to me with a question about some trifle or other so I stood still for a moment to answer him. I had barely stopped when round the corner, unexpectedly, came Schramm, the worst SS officer in the camp. Kola disappeared as if blown away by the wind; I was left on the spot, doubled under the weight of the planks.

Schramm came up to me slowly, ordered me to put down the planks, slapped me several times on the face and took out his notebook. 'Your number?'

He wrote it down, pointed to the planks and slowly walked off. I stooped to pick up the wood while Kola looked on through the window, smiling.

He mouthed, 'No chance of getting out of that; he will make sure.'

A few days passed quietly until on Sunday morning I received a card from the camp office: I was to report to the camp baths in the afternoon. It wasn't hard to guess for what: a medical inspection before transportation or a beating for not working fast enough. In any case it was almost certainly Schramm's doing.

I had been given the card while the morning coffee was being doled out and it had not escaped my fellow prisoners' attention. They began to ask what it meant, to give their opinions and advice. Kola also saw it and at once left the barrack. Through a few influential colleagues I tried to find out what was going to happen and even to get my name crossed off, if it were transportation.

Before midday I heard that it was an inspection for a transport, but there was not the slightest chance of getting my name struck off, for my name and number were 'known'. Marian happened to be in hospital (through Kola's influence) so Jurek and I talked it over and with utmost secrecy sent in his number as a volunteer on the list of those to be inspected. Normally this was an easy matter for there was always a lack of candidates for a transport, but this time we had to look out in case someone was anxious to break us up. Marian's case looked hopeless.

The inspection took place two days later. We clustered in the small baths, pushed and pulled about by trusties, while outside the windows various camp dignitaries, our self-appointed guardians, gesticulated and shrieked, letting the doctors know whom to reject and whom to write on the list for transportation. The SS had not yet arrived on the scene. Since there was no chance of being rejected, Jurek and I kept together to try and get into the same group. It was possible that there might be more than one transport going off at the same time. We had already passed inspection by fellow prisoner doctors and were waiting only for the SS men to arrive and make out the final list.

At last the senior camp doctor showed up and behind him, Schramm, with his crooked smile. Lined up in a long naked crocodile we came up to the table, under the bored look of the SS doctor. André put a cross against the relevant number. The inspection and ticking off lasted a few seconds. I moved on to the next room and it was Jurek's turn. Suddenly André, who up till now had been carrying out his duties quite mechanically, came to life and stammered to Schramm, 'That one can't go. He is working in the kiln.'

It seemed for a moment that our partnership was to be broken up. But Schramm made a wry face and grunted, 'Take it easy, they can all go . . .'

Back in the block Lazowski, smiling, greeted us. He already knew that we were going together but he must have known where to, for he didn't try to conceal his joy. We were not of any great importance in the camp but along with us went many others, whom the Communist organization got rid of in this way.

Our branch camp turned out to be quite bearable.* We worked there for nearly a year and in February, three months before the end of the war, were sent back to Neuengamme, as the factory in which we were working ceased production for lack of coal.

We were in the main camp for only one week since we managed to get into another sub-camp, fearing possible liquidation at the end of the war. We were right. Our new sub-camp, although very primitive and brutally managed, survived; but the main camp at Neuengamme came to a tragic end. On 29 April about 9,000 prisoners were loaded on to three old ships, which put out into the North Sea. Suddenly some Allied planes appeared and not knowing who was on board the ships, bombed them and set them on fire. This only anticipated the actions of the SS men, who were themselves to sink the transport. Of 9,000 prisoners only about 600 managed to swim the few kilometers to the shore.

It was a sad end for people who even in a concentration camp, in the face of almost certain death, had been unable to forget their political differences and control their human passions.

---

*It was a sub-camp in Wittenberge on the Elbe river, between Hamburg and Berlin.

Chapter Fifteen

Marian and Halinka

We were crowded round the table in the narrow, low barrack which more or less protected us from the icy North Sea winds. We had been given our supper, some bread with margarine and a piece of sausage (the only food that day). We had also been given our parcels and letters, and I was lucky again.

There was a buzz around the table while we ate, eyes glittering and jaws working. One had to hurry for at any moment would come the shout: '*Licht aus*' (lights out) and as soon as we had been driven to bed in the dark, ubiquitous Russian and Serb hands would grab the priceless uneaten remains.

I had grown coarser in these months, surrounded by churlishness and unbelievable bestiality, and was not particularly aware of what was going on around me. I was gulping down bread with thick slices of ham (where in the world do they get it from in famished Warsaw?), noisily washing it down with the dark fluid in my tipped bowl and reading over and over the two small sheets of paper written by the distant hand of my wife.

Suddenly Jurek, my inseparable camp companion, nudged me gently and said quietly, 'Have you noticed, Marian isn't eating.'

I took a glance to my left. 'Yes, he's not at all like himself. Perhaps he's ill?'

Jurek put his hand on my shoulder and added still more quietly, 'He's got tears in his eyes.'

I stopped gulping slop, looked at my friend's face for a moment and all of a sudden my weary brain took in the situation. Inconspicuously I folded and put away my letter. I knew what was wrong. We all clung to those small letters, written perhaps long ago and far away, yet so near and indispensible. I had been handed a letter from my wife and for a while it seemed to me that the world was smiling at everyone. But it was not so and Marian sat with his head hung down and his thoughts centred around one, urgent question: why hasn't she written?

The beginning of Marian's story was no different from the stories of thousands of our colleagues, about whom for the most part we knew little or nothing.

Marian was a regular officer, one of the youngest in his regiment. In September 1939 he was taken prisoner in Germany and in December escaped. A few months later, having made contact with the right people, he took over a position in the military underground movement near Lublin. He was also an excellent worker. He lived alone, unburdened by a family, with few social obligations. He was a stranger in the area, and he lived only for his work. He did not get letters to distract his attention from his daily duties. In his native town in the district of Wilno he had left his mother and sister, but they had been deported to Soviet Russia and every attempt to find out where they were had failed.

In the summer of 1942 there was sudden disaster at the underground headquarters in Warsaw. A large number of people were arrested, the archives discovered and the Germans were able to strike in the provinces.

One day Marian arrived in Lublin on his motorbike and stopped before a house of a slight acquaintance. He felt something strange about the atmosphere in the street. A white face appeared for a moment at the window. He kicked the starter but at the same time heard the click-click of machine gun breech blocks. Some men, looking like gangsters, moved quickly out of a gateway on the other side of the road. In a few minutes he found himself in the cellars on Akademicka Street (the Gestapo headquarters) and a couple of days later in the tower of the castle, which was used as the prison.

It was all over. His colleagues, arrested at the same time, had broken down and confessed. There were confrontations, they were put into the same cell, they were beaten in front of Marian; he himself was beaten, starved, hung up in chains, blackmailed by promises. He gritted his teeth and said nothing. At last he was thrown into the cell from which there is only one way out, execution.

It was just then, when he lay swollen and covered with blood, on the wet concrete waiting for the rattle of keys, that the first miracle happened. In a piece of bread he found a scrap of paper on which a woman's hand had written with even letters: 'The others are all dead, but don't be afraid, I am thinking of you. Halinka.' He didn't know anyone called Halinka and couldn't comprehend who it was and how she had managed to smuggle in this mysterious message.

A week later came a second message: 'I am fighting for you, trust me.' It couldn't be a letter of an informer? Marian experienced a feeling of excitement that he had not felt for a long time. The first gleams of his lost manhood began to awake in his consciousness. Could it be that he was not quite alone?

Days passed, days of uneasiness, of nervous tension, of struggle with his weakened body and of waiting for the next letter. For so many months he had felt lonely, had passed nights of longing, of dreaming, and here in the death cell, he was getting letters written in a woman's handwriting, letters which said 'trust me, I am fighting.' I am fighting – therefore I am thinking of you . . .

Solitary confinement is often the cause of delirium, imaginings, fancies, which eat so deeply into the soul that with time they become reality. Was it love? He would not have been able to answer for sure. But he felt intense excitement when in the morning he got his hunk of bread and, after the warder had gone, feverishly crumbled it up in search of the scrap of paper.

Some weeks passed and there were no further letters. One morning the doors of his cell opened; but the faces of his warders were not threatening.

'Come along, you are going on a journey.'

Handcuffed he was taken to the station and, accompanied by only one policeman, put on to the train. They travelled in a separate compartment in an ordinary third class carriage. It was autumn and the still warm rays of sunlight fell in bright streaks on the quiet fields and countless trees, past which they rushed. The green and golden leaves of the forest, through which the railway line ran, rustled with memories of childhood and brought into his mind pictures from distant Wilno province long buried in forgetfulness. The train sped in the direction of Warsaw.

Marian didn't know whether the documents had been lost or whether a mistake had been made or whether some enormous swindle had come off. In Warsaw he was first taken to the Pawiak prison, then to another one, and finally to the criminal prison on Danilowiczowska Street. At none of these prisons did they want to take him in and the escorting policeman began to swear angrily. Marian might have managed to escape if it had not been for the handcuffs, a shaved head and his poor condition. Finally he was pushed into a communal cell, given a litre of soup and left in peace. The next morning the warder on duty called him out.

'You are wanted upstairs by the lady commissioner.'

He was led to the office where behind the table sat a good-looking woman in the uniform of an officer of the prison guard. Conditions here were fairly liberal, for the Germans didn't take much interest in criminal prisoners. After Lublin Castle Marian looked at his surroundings and was not sure how to take the encouraging smile of the eyes looking at him from under the black brows. The escorting warder saluted and left the room.

'Your full name?'

He gave the required details.

'Born?'

Again he gave the information.

'You are an officer?'

There was nothing to hide. At his interrogation everything had been discovered.

'Yes.'

'Perhaps you know "Halim"?'

Marian started. That was his code name in the underground which even the interrogator had not found out. How could she know it?

'I don't understand you. Halim . . .?'

'You can speak out, I have given the password. I have a message from Halinka.'

Marian felt himself turning red. Halinka? He didn't know her, he didn't know who she was and why she had taken an interest in him, but he had already got used to the thought that a letter might arrive, a letter which brought someone nearer, a letter which proved that somebody was thinking of him, waiting. Many a time in the loneliness of his solitary cell he had repeated this name, which began to have an exotic and mysterious sound to him, a name which had become a personification of hope, the goal of his dreams and longings.

He hesitated, struggling within himself; he thought that this might be the only chance of finding out. And he felt an overwhelming desire to exchange at least a few words about the person who, though unknown, had come so near to him and become so very important.

'I . . . I don't know any Halinka. Who are you talking about?'

'She was the fiancée of one of your colleagues, arrested in the same episode. He was shot like all the others, you are the only one alive.'

This explanation made it clearer. One of his colleagues in the underground *had* been engaged and they had often talked about his future wife, but Marian had never had an opportunity of meeting her. She lived in Warsaw and hardly ever came to Lublin.

'Could . . . could you describe a little more exactly the person about whom we are speaking? I have had messages from her, I owe her a lot, perhaps my life. And I don't know her. I don't even know what she looks like . . . and I really don't know why . . .?'

The commissioner took out of her bag a postcard-sized photograph and without saying a word handed it to him.

Large, peaceful eyes looked at him from the photograph, lighting up the severe oval of the young face. Marian felt his cheeks and forehead becoming red again. 'Can I keep this photo . . .?'

'Of course. It was sent to you. And I have a message. Miss Halinka is still trying to do something for you. She has found a way by which such things can apparently be arranged. She asks you to keep quite calm and count on her.' The commissioner smiled. 'She really thinks of you very sincerely and will be very glad when I tell her about our talk and describe you to her.'

Marian played about with the photograph nervously; at last he thrust it quickly into the pocket of his shirt.

'Thank you . . .'

In the Pawiak prison several names were read out by a guard and we stood on one side. I was among the chosen but this made me uneasy for distinction in prison is never good for any purpose: hope of regaining one's freedom was practically nil, so one expected other results, all radical and final.

At the station it turned out that my fears had been well founded. The chosen were loaded into a prison truck on a train, lined inside with tin and heavily guarded. All hopes of escape faded. We were going to Auschwitz.

I managed to sit on a little bit of bench at the end of the truck. Here I made myself as small as possible, took off everything I could (the heat was unbearable) and looked around at my neighbours. I realized I would have to be extraordinarily careful. I was in an almost unbelievable situation. The duties which I had carried out before my arrest at the headquarters of the Home Army had given me an insight into the procedures connected with arrests and what it was like for those threatened by arrest. In this prison truck were travelling some of the aces of the resistance movement who had been put out of action, so that, up to now, they had been my 'clients'. I was acquainted with all of their correspondence from the prison, and I knew their organizational contacts and links. I had never met them personally but I had only to ask someone his name and immediately I knew all the relevant details of his past.

I had to be particularly careful. I could not at any price betray the fact that I knew as much as I did or somone might unwittingly give me away. During my interrogation they had not found out my real name and my position and I didn't want anyone to know. So, there was to be no talking, nothing to make myself conspicuous and above all no unnecessary questions.

On my left were seated two young men. The taller, like myself, had managed to sit on the packed bench; the smaller, better built, was sitting on his knees. Both had some hair on their heads (a sign that they had held office in the Pawiak) and their faces were open and pleasant, their eyes calm and good-humoured, a rare thing in these circumstances. They were talking in under-tones and I strained my ears to listen.

'Do you know Jurek, that on the very last day I got a message from Halinka?'

'You're always lucky Marian. Anyway I don't know what that girl sees in you, if only you even knew each other, but she doesn't know you at all.'

Further words were drowned out by the shouts of our escort. The train stopped at a station. I waited for some minutes and carelessly turned to the smaller one.

'Don't we know each other, what is your name?'

'Marian T. I worked in the Pawiak in the prisoners' deposit department.'

We exchanged small talk during which I learnt the name of my other neighbour, and then broke off the conversation. The SS men had brought a bucket of water and noisily demonstrated their humanity in allowing us to drink in turn. The train crawled along for hours and my thoughts concentrated on our destina-tion. I felt lonely. Not so long ago I had been absorbed in my work, surrounded by friendly people, full of a feeling of force and efficiency, conscious of the value of what I was doing – and here I was on my way to Auschwitz, quite alone. It didn't do to make friends too easily, but life was too complicated to live alone, more so in the situation we were in, in which the defenceless individual is up against forces directed not only at his life, but at every thought and feeling. I had to improvise, to fill in the vacuum by which I was surrounded.

The nearer we got to Auschwitz the more this intention grew within me. And when we were unloaded on to the platform in Birkenau and driven to the camp, my intention turned into decision. After being inspected, which took many hours, we were allowed to lie down in a barrack in which the only furniture was a few tables. Under one of these we spread out my coat and Marian, Jurek and I lay down. When sleep had overtaken all and the darkness was filled with heavy breathing I woke Marian and put my lips to his ear. 'Greetings colleague "Halim".'

Late into the night the three of us whispered. By morning we were already close friends.

We had been in the penal company in Birkenau, and for a week of selection in Auschwitz followed by transportation to Neuengamme, we had managed to stick together and surmount every distressing difficulty. Jurek – the linguist, of a quiet and even temperament, a brave and sensitive heart – softened down and smoothed out all the rough edges of our relationship, neutralized my outbursts of nerves, dispersed Marian's spells of sadness, brought peace where thunder had been sown. And Marian? The shocks he had experienced had awakened in him a mystical faith in a power which he could call up by thoughts, prayer and good deeds. He was unable, he didn't know how, to take short cuts through life, to fight for his existence, to grasp at any opportunity which might give a chance of existing until our freedom came. He gave away his last crust of bread to the weaker, shared his small section of straw mattress, took on his own back burdens with which 'moslems' struggled; and Marian lived for one thought alone – a letter!

When dusk fell and our working day was over, he stood quietly in his place for the roll-call but the trembling of his lips betrayed the fight that was going on within him and the struggle with feelings which were swamped by his yearning heart. Going into the block he asked invariably, 'Any mail?' And when as a rule he got a negative reply (he was not very interested in parcels) he went inside the barrack into a dark corner and took out the creased photograph, which by some miracle he had managed to smuggle through endless searchings and inspections. He guarded it from strange eyes, but he trusted us and each time gave up his treasure boldly.

'Have you seen Halinka's photo?'

Strange were the ties which bound together people who had never seen each other before. She sent him parcels regularly, prepared with the carefulness of a mother, and wrote letters which were quite unequivocal – traced by a nearest and dearest hand, with great pains to which he responded with overflowing feelings. Was it love? Who could give an answer to that in this human antheap which deprived man of his humanity, forcing him to struggle savagely to survive until evening and a bowl of food.

The very worst that could happen happened. I was caught out in some insignificant trifle in my work and my name put on the list for transportation. In Warsaw we had a saying: if you go to Auschwitz you won't need to be afraid of round-ups. But we were wrong. What would the Germans have done without man-hunts? So in Neuengamme, which had a number of branch camps attached to it, from time to time panic broke out:

'*Achtung, Achtung*! ('Attention, Attention!') They are catching people for transportation!'

Nobody was particularly eager to volunteer for the branch camps which had terrible reputations (time and again the trucks brought back piles of men in the last stages of exhaustion, and no one knew how many had died on the spot). Besides, one was searched and lost all the treasures one had managed to accumulate, as well as other little surprises. So the teams of trusties, with the help of SS men, went the rounds of the *Kommandos* and the prisoners hid like chickens, destined for killing, seeking flight in a small hen house.

I was put on the list for transportation and sent to the baths for inspection. Jurek immediately volunteered, for long before, we had made an agreement not to be separated. We would have been quite composed if it had not been for Marian. He, who was never ill, had gone to the sick-bay for a few days with a temperature and sore throat. As soon as we could we went to the hospital windows and passed on to him the news.

'I shall go with you', he stated.

At once we got hold of a doctor we knew and made him promise that Marian would be discharged the following day. The transport was to go off in three days so there was plenty of time.

Suddenly, during working hours, an alarm went off. We received a litre of soup, our evening piece of bread and were driven to the stores. Dressed in new striped suits we stood in threes by the gate. Beside us roared the engine of a heavy transport truck. The sick-bay, where Marian lay was just by the gate, so anxiously we watched the windows for the familiar face. It was three o'clock in the afternoon and at five Marian was due to leave the hospital. What bad luck. An SS man came out of the guard room and shouted. '*Einsteigen!*' ('Get in!')

Some rugs were thrown at us. The truck moved, the gate opened. At that very moment Marian's face showed at the window. He forced a smile and waved his hand.

'Keep up, keep up, remem...'

I didn't finish my cry to him as the fist of the German standing by me knocked me down.

The clouds came lower and thick damp snow began to fall.

We made every effort to get in touch with Marian. We took advantage of every transport to Neuengamme, every possible opportunity. In vain. Later we often talked of Marian and Halinka. Our thoughts turned to her just as they did to our own dear ones and by our prayers we tried to shield her from the blows of the enemy. For she was in the heart of fighting Warsaw.

Many years have now passed, a sad English winter is with us and my thoughts again turn to you my friend Marian.

Where are you, what has happened to you. Were you beaten to death during an attempt to escape, were you dragged under the waves by whirlpools of sinking ships, did you fall from SS bullets? Or was fate kind to you, did you meet your Halinka?

How little meant the love between you in comparison with the awesome forces which brought the world to war. And yet how much.

Chapter Sixteen

Ruck-Zuck Kommando

For a few days we worked in the transport column, later we were transferred to repairing the sewers, destroyed by an American bomb, until one evening the senior *Capo* called us together, looked us over ironically and growled shortly: 'Morgen *Ruck-Zuck Kommando*' ('Push-pull working party tomorrow').

There was no question about it, the nastiest, the most hated work in the whole camp had fallen to our lot. Firstly, laying the foundations of a new factory (and it is 1944, a spring breeze blowing and bringing with it hope of a quick invasion); secondly, the merciless foreman, a withered old man with a frantic zeal for work; thirdly, the *Capo* Adam.

Anyone who has ever met a sneak-thief, a sullen gangster, short, desiccated, completely devoid of a sense of humour, with a cold glance and a decided predilection for beating, a subtle slave-driver, if possible cross-eyed – that person knows more or less *Capo* Adam. He was born and bred in a den of the Berlin criminal underworld, he had pushed his way through life with wide-spread elbows, until at last justice had caught up with him and packed him off to gaol years earlier. That kind never sink, so he had made a career there, and here he was now, the leader of a group that bored large holes in the sand and filled them with cement. *Capo* Adam had one other specific attribute, perhaps the worst of all camp vices: he was in love with his mate in the next bunk.

Next day Jurek and I stood together by the handle of the '*Wele*'. It was a windlass, like that of a well, mounted between two poles of a tall tripod, at the top of which was a pulley and a rope, wound round the windlass. Four prisoners laboriously pulled up either the drill, or the pump, which sucked up the water and sand from the hole bored and then gave way again to the drill, reaching a depth of nearly twenty metres underground. Again and again heavy iron pipes had to be brought up and lowered, with great difficulty, into the opening, to hold up the sides until the cement could be poured in. It was stint-work and terribly exhausting, all the implements weighed nearly twenty kilograms each and the frantic foreman and the *Vorarbeiter* (foreman*) (*Capo* Adam rarely stuck his nose out of his hut) did not allow the smallest breathing space.

Five of us formed the gang of our tripod: four at the '*Wele*' and Zygmunt, the leader, at the pump, pipes and drill. Misfortune had brought Jurek and I from Warsaw, Zygmunt was a young labourer from Łódź, nearby snuffled a German, Willy, and beside him, hanging on to the same handle, fumbled the Bialorussian Czornyj.

A cold hoar-frost covered the still sleeping earth, nearby stood the foreman and muttered something to the *Vorarbeiter*, a burly German with a canine face. Willy sniffed and looked with distaste at the lazy Czornyj. We grasped the cold handles.

'Ruck-zuck, ruck-zuck!' yelled the *Vorarbeiter*, the pump rose and fell with a jerky movement, the dry rope creaked.

Slowly, day by day, we dug down into the sand, slowly, day by day, we grew to know each other, to return to the past, which had formed our heterogeneity, and to look for contact among our different worlds, struggling together for a chance of survival and seeking a way of regaining freedom.

Willy had been inside for six years and was nearly at the end of his strength and nerves. He was over forty and an intellectual, a journalist from Kiel. He spoke beautiful, literary German, stressed, whenever possible, his dissimilarity from the rest of his criminal compatriots – and snuffled mercilessly, for he was on the borders of exhaustion. My nervous gaiety and the speed with which I spoke incomprehensible Polish words, drove him to distraction.

*A prisoner.

'Sss, sss!' would burst from his pursed lips when I carelessly let go of the handle and quietly watched the tripod shake and rock, jerked by the impetus of the rope.

'*Du bist, du bist . . . aber . . .*' ('You are, you are . . . but . . .'), and he would flap his hand in resignation, seeing that I was taking no notice of him and Czornyj had let go of the handle and was having a breather.

And yet in a few days we were to some extent friends and Willy became a pedagogue, polishing up my German, and a constant recipient of part of the provisions from my parcels. He threw off some of the normal camp reserve and in his tales began to go back into the past, and behold: his family originated from the Polish town Torun and his grandfather, who had emigrated to Germany as a labourer to dig the Kiel canal, had not spoken a word of German. We understood now whence came that completely non-German, unexpected and spontaneous humanity.

At the same handle, shoulder to shoulder, worked with him, or rather should have worked, Czornyj. If Willy was a bundle of nerves with a mixture of retrospection and hope for freedom, Czornyj kept an unruffled calm and there was no force on earth which could quicken his reactions or make him work more efficiently. Sometimes his slowness was exasperating.

'What a typical Bialorussian peasant', Jurek used to say.

Lastly, Zygmunt. As I have already said, he was a young labourer from Łódź, whom we hardly knew and who had greeted us coldly enough at his windlass. That was not hard to wonder at, he had been given two intellectuals, physically weak to look at, and here the work had to go like lightning, for the foreman and *Vorarbeiter* were hard drivers and completing the stint before time gave a chance of a short rest in the warm hut. When we took hold of the handles the first day and began to wind up the windlass awkwardly, Zygmunt turned green with disgust and looked away, swallowing oaths.

Our first hours were hard, for even Willy swore at us. However after a few days our partners discovered, that somehow the work was getting done and perhaps even better than before. After all we were young and in spite of everything we could cope with the heavy tools and we had grasped the essentials of the work at

once. One way or another the stint had to be worked daily, so
speed paid. After a week we were beating the other gangs
unquestionably and regularly got into the hut first, taking up the
best places, right by the red-hot stove. Zygmunt lost his first
distrust and slapped us on the back in a friendly manner. For one
must add, that he was a grand lad who, even in a concentration
camp, had not lost his enthusiasm for work and its good execution.

Both during our labours and our rest periods in the hut, we
carried on long conversations and drew close to each other, but
in spite of several weeks of working together, the ice, which
normally divides prisoners and deprives them of comradely
heartiness, was not broken. Jurek and I felt that our 'Wele'
tolerated and perhaps even liked us, but had not accepted us
wholly into their circle. We also felt that, in spite of considerable
differences, something united our three workmates and held
them together, although God alone knew what cement could
bind these three, completely different and in principle antago-
nistic, souls.

The last hours of toil are always the hardest, for hunger, cold,
fatigue and boredom become unbearable and the hands of the
clock begin to go round with impossible slowness.

It was already dusk and the spring mist had begun to envelop
the factory walls and the skeletons of the new buildings. The end
of our labours was still about two hours off, when, suddenly, a
shrill whistle rang through the air and shouts came from every
direction. Without a moment's thought we downed tools and
rushed to the usual gathering place. Instead of forming one big
column as usual, we were ordered to stand in the groups in
which we went to work. It was then that we noticed that from our
own *Kommando* a Russian, Jaszka, was missing.

'Adam . . .' I managed to whisper to Jurek and stopped at once,
for we were stricken by the dreadful shriek of a beaten man.

We recognized Willy's voice. *Capo* Adam was holding him
with his left hand and with his right, doubled into a fist, was
beating him in the face, which was already streaming with blood.

'Und du bist ein Deutscher, du bist ein Deutscher' ('And you

are a German, you are a German'), he hissed through clenched teeth.

From the barracks the camp commandant approached slowly. He was an SS NCO, and an elderly man, addicted to drink, in principle not one of the worst. Adam let go Willy, took off his cap and ran to the commandant. They exchanged a few words and the *Capo* came back in our direction. Meanwhile Willy had managed to conceal himself in the ranks.

The *Capo* stood in front of us.

'Zygmunt!'

The boy stepped out and took off his cap. Adam, without a word, drove his fist between his eyes. Zygmunt fell to the ground, but got up at once and stood in a waiting attitude.

'Where is Jaszka, du, Polnischer Karkower?'

'He doesn't work in my gang. All mine are here.'

Adam knocked Zygmunt down again, only this time he did not allow him to get up, but jumped on him in his big boots and began to stamp in passion.

Zygmunt groaned, the ranks closed up more tightly. The SS men looked coldly on at an everyday – for them – scene.

The commandant beat his top-boots with his whip.

'How many more of them?'

The *Vorarbeiter* stepped out of the ranks.

'Zygmunt's 'Wele', step forward!'

Jurek and I stepped out, without any enthusiasm.

'Come on, all of you? If I find anyone ...'

Dragging back, as slowly as possible, crept out Czornyj and stood beside us. The commandant came forward and looked at him threatingly. After a while he switched his gaze to us. Suddenly, quite unexpectedly, the halting voice of Willy, broken by a cough, rang out:

'Those two tall ones, they're new, they didn't work with us earlier.'

The commandant looked questioningly at the *Vorarbeiter*.

'That's right, they haven't been working long.'

'*Rrrausss!*' ('Get out!')

We jumped back into the ranks, as if struck by a thunderbolt. Czornyj remained on the place alone. He stood calmly, stooped and crumpling his cap in his right hand. The SS man looked him over for a moment.

'*Du bist auch Russe.* Schön. ('You are a Russian too. Fine.') Do you know Jaszka?'

'*Niczewo nie poniał.*' ('I don't understand a thing')

'*Was? Wie lange in Konzentrations Lager?*' ('What? How long in the concentration camp?')

Czornyj changed his cap over to his left hand and remained silent.

Adam left Zygmunt and came up to the commandant. 'They never understand, when you ask them. I'll open his mouth for him.'

He went up to Czornyj and with the edge of his hand struck him suddenly in the nape of neck. When the stricken man stooped forward, the SS man hit him across the face with his whip. Czornyj groaned and covered himself with his hand, but to no avail, for Adam and the *Vorarbeiter* threw themselves on him and began to thrash him furiously. In a few minutes an insensible body dropped on to the sand. The commandant turned away indifferently, looked for a moment in the direction of the barracks and suddenly yelled balefully at the trusties:

'And what are you doing? Off with you, look for him, turn the factory upside down, dig him out from under the earth! *Raus, raus!!*'

The *Capos* and *Vorarbeiters* rushed hither and thither and we were driven into the camp and made to stand in the yard. We stood like that until the early morning.

A protracted interrogation gave no results. Czornyj did not come out of it alive; Willy and Zygmunt went to hospital. All the searching was in vain. Jaszka had vanished like a stone in water.

Several months later, ill and hardly able to drag my feet, I was crossing the square of a barracks, in which an ex-prisoner of war camp was housed. A Polish soldier in American uniform passed by. I looked at him carefully: Zygmunt!

I came up beside him quietly and suddenly yelled with all my might, '*Ruck-zuck, ruck-zuck, aber schneller!!*' ('... but more quickly!')

He jumped as if electrified, but immediately got himself under control and soon we were laughing heartily.

'So the two of us survived somehow. Tell me, what was all that about Jaszka and why did they go for your lot?'

'Jaszka had to get away, because one of the German foremen had reported that he was contacting civilian workers. He was a pioneer of the Red Army and schooled in sabotage, and I knew something about that too, because I had done a course on it back in Łódź. First we worked in a group inside the factory with Willy and Czornyj. There were certain possibilities and they helped us. Nothing was ever discovered, but one day we were packed off to the ruck-zuck.'

'You were a well-matched bunch! But what earthly use was Czornyj to you?'

'That was the best of it all. You both said that he was a Bialorussian peasant to the life, and he was a Jew from Minsk!'

'Impossible!'

'In life nothing is impossible and especially in a concentration camp.'

Chapter Seventeen

A Smile

Capo Adam was not only in charge of a working party at our small camp at Wittenberge, but he was also senior trusty of the barrack, with its three-tier bunks, to which we were allocated.

Small, springy, dry and with a squint, he was a perfect representative of the Berlin underworld. He had already been inside for a great number of years and, as a habitual offender, had no hope of being released under the Nazis. So he had resigned himself to his fate and had made his life as comfortable as possible in the camp. During working hours he usually stayed in a little hut frying potato pancakes on an iron stove and when we got back to camp, he chased us round the bunks, ordering us to clean up, carry water, scrounge for coal and share out produce from our food parcels. He slept comfortably on a single bed under a pile of blankets and on a mattress well-stuffed with straw. If he got bored, there was always the opportunity to smash in someone's face or obtain, as if from the earth itself, a few glasses of alcohol.

From the purely material point of view Adam was well off, and while others were fighting for their very life and counted every day survived as a gift from God, time didn't bother him and he did not feel its weight. The only thing which really troubled him was the lack of women within reach of his rapacious hands.

The millions of prisoners filling Hitler's camps came from many nationalities and social classes. Their age span was also great. There were old men, who by some miracle managed to stay alive, while next to them were young boys in their teens who still needed a mother's care and not the swearing and brutality of the

SS. It was heart-breaking to see these children forced to do hard labour, dressed in tattered prison overalls and blue from hunger and cold. Hardly anyone made allowance for their age, no one tried to lighten their load, everyone thought only of himself and took what he could. Only occasionally and completely unexpectedly did some mature middle-aged prisoner, usually a German and naturally a trusty, come along and take one of the boys under his wing. He brought him extra food, tried to get him a better job and wrangled with the barrack chief over a better bunk. Newly arrived prisoners took this care at face value and greeted it approvingly, but those of us who had been longer in the camp, knew what was happening and what was the object of this apparently praiseworthy gesture.

The poor boy, surprised at first, naturally accepted the help of his unexpected protector. He needed every scrap of food he could get, and easier work gave him some chance of surviving. But above all he felt the lack of family love and so clung to anyone who, amidst all the indifference and bestiality, showed him some consideration.

Suddenly the moment came when the 'protector' decided that his preparations were done and showed his hand. The deceived boy tried to protest, but was then faced with the alternative of losing everything he had come by over the last few weeks. Not only that: he also gained a mortal enemy.

Could many of them resist?

We were a mixed bunch in our barrack. The majority were Poles, mainly mature men, after that there were Latvians, Frenchmen, Serbs, Czechs, a few lesser Germans and a dozen or so inhabitants of the Soviet Union, in other words so-called 'Russkies'. They were usually Ukrainians from the western part of the Ukraine, young lads.

One of them, who was about fifteen years old and slept not far from me, had attracted my attention some time before. He was slim, but well-built, he moved gracefully and had regular features making a generally pleasing impression. He stood out from his rather common fellows, but in the long run there was nothing particularly interesting about him, except for his eyes, which had a striking and intriguing expression. Boys of this age often have a mischievous, or mock-serious look, but always rather childlike and carefree. One sought in vain this look in Alyosha's eyes. He was always deep in thought, as though tensed up inside and ready to defend himself; he always looked carefully and intensely, his eyelids were slightly closed and he never unbent or smiled. It was clear that he had been through a great deal and that these ordeals had left permanent marks, which camp life, naturally enough, could not heal. No one particularly bothered him, but at the same time he did not seem to have any friends. He lived alone and in constant state of tension and preparedness, like a man expecting painful blows from all quarters.

We could receive parcels and so from time to time one of us would share his goodies with Alyosha. It had to be done discreetly since he was mistrustful and very proud. He would never accept the smallest morsel in the presence of another prisoner.

Knowing Russian quite well, I was better able than the others to gain a little of his trust and from time to time I managed to get a few sentences and a bit of information out of him. After a few weeks I had found out that he came from a neighbourhood of Kiev, that he had been taken away for labour and that later, he had been sent off to camp for trying to escape. His father was dead, and he had left his mother and younger sister in his village. Our conversations were rather halting, but our mutual trust grew with every day. My knowledge of Alyosha's life increased accordingly and formed a certain overall picture. It was as I had imagined: the boy's experiences went deeper than the war, and his present caution and reserve were not just the result of camp life.

He had been born when conditions were not too bad in the Ukraine, in other words during the period when private property and farms were tolerated. Before the Revolution his father had had a small farm. He had then lost a great deal of land, but retained enough to be able to live quite well with his family. Suddenly, when Alyosha was about six or seven, collectivization had been introduced. The peasants, naturally enough, did not want to give up their land and began to rebel. Alyosha well remembered his father meeting with neighbours in their hut, going out at night somewhere, quarrelling with his mother and swearing that he would never relinquish his land. Some strange armed men twice came to the hut, his mother sobbed and prayed by her bed and his father fell silent and was much more careful.

The village continued to live as before when, suddenly, one night the roar of car engines was heard. Alyosha leapt up, woken by a hammering at the door. Soldiers entered, ordered his father to get dressed and took him away into the night. He hardly had time to take leave of his wife and hug his children. In the morning it turned out that the same thing had happened in many huts.

His father wrote a few times from some distant unknown place, but then the correspondence ceased and he never wrote again.

Meanwhile the scourge of collectivization had struck the village like the plague. Strangers started organizing a collective farm. Alyosha didn't understand much of this, but the changes burned themselves into his memory. Their three cows were led out of the cow shed, their horses were taken away. His mother began to go to work in the communal fields and returned exhausted with despair in her eyes. There was a shortage of milk, flour and even potatoes in the small hut. Alyosha and his sister wandered around the yard, rummaging in dustbins and eating unripe fruit. In the village people began to go hungry and simply die. Later things improved a little, but the hunger continued. His mother lived in continual fear and even changed her surname. Alyosha, whose name was now Manyeta, could not properly remember his former name, although he did think it was Polish-sounding. His parents never called him Alyosha and it was only after his father's deportation that he began to use this name.

This was as far as our discussions of the past got, but at least the previous mistrust between us had gone and we were now linked if not by friendship, than at least by mutual tolerance.

A small transport arrived from the main Neuengamme camp. It brought a dozen or so new prisoners, mainly Germans. One of them stood out by his powerful frame and cheerful, open face. He was wearing a remarkably decent camp uniform and his head was not shaven, which immediately struck everyone. He was put into the German hut and allocated an excellent bunk, on the first level and with no one else on top.

Before long people began to ask who was this prisoner with unheard-of privileges and why did he have them.

I was on good terms with the camp secretary Bohdan, a Pole in his fifth year in the camp, and so one evening I struck up a conversation with him.

'Who's this new *Prominent** then?'

'He's a Baltic German from Riga called Hans.'

'How on earth did he get here with a haircut and anyway why did he let himself be stuck in that transport?'

'He says that he wanted to get out of Neuengamme, for he had had enough of things there. He's allowed to have his hair, for he's got special privileges. He's an *Ehren-Häftling* (honourable prisoner)'.

This answer told me a great deal. I had not yet met a prisoner coming under that category, but I did know the reasons for the strange concept. Such an oddity could arise only in Nazi Germany, which was covered by a network of countless camps and prisons, specialized in ways of depriving people of their freedom, which revelled in rules and regulations.

The Nazi prison system's iron principle was the permanent deprivation of freedom, despite repeated protestations that prisoners were rehabilitated and released. During the war this belief was intensified. Naturally all these regulations did not cover political prisoners, who were imprisoned for years without any trial and whose situation was one hundred times worse than that of common criminals. The latter were entitled to a defence and usually were released on completion of their sentence.

This was changed only after the outbreak of war. Concentration camps, although very much worse than normal prisons, were not considered by the Germans suitable locations for doing

*See page 124.

a prison sentence. A common criminal who was sent to a camp because his prison was full, went on a sort of bail and none of the time he spent in the camp counted towards his sentence. At the end of the war he would return to prison to complete it. It was not surprising that the criminal prisoners cursed this devilish concept.

The second painful blow to them was the law on recidivism. Formerly every wrongdoer, irrespective of the number of times he had already been arrested and convicted, if convicted for a new offence, went free after his sentence. Hitler changed this. Now, after his last sentence, a recidivist was sent to a camp where he was meant to spend the rest of his life with no chance of ever being released.

He would never be set free and yet to the Nazi mind he was something better than a political prisoner or just any criminal, who had not yet completed his sentence. He deserved special treatment and so the idea of the 'honourable prisoner' was born. This was a fine-sounding and distinguished name, although conferred on the bearer without his consent.

A criminal thus distinguished enjoyed a number of privileges in camp. He could choose his place of work, the barrack he would live in, he had his own bunk and he could always go to the kitchen for extra food. Finally, he did not have to shave his head.

I became very interested in Hans and decided to get into conversation with him. I was working as a locksmith and was allowed to go to the tool store, where the newcomer was installed. I waited for a moment when no one was moving around and then went into the store hut, greeted Hans and pulled out a cigarette.

'Want a smoke?'

Hans took the cigarette, looked for his matches, drew on it and thanked me with a smile. 'You a Pole?'

'That's right, my name's Józef.'

'I'm Hans. How long have you been inside?'

'Almost two years, and you?'

Hans waved impatiently and made an amusing face. 'This is my new profession. I was inside many times in Latvia.'

Someone came in and so we had to stop, but contact had been

made. Hans turned out to be very talkative and cheerful. He spoke a strange sort of German, intermingled with long Russian curses, and he talked frankly about his life.

He couldn't exactly remember where he had been born, but he lived in Riga for many years and worked in the docks. This was a very suitable job for him on account of his unusual physical strength. He must have weighed about fifteen or sixteen stone, but without an ounce of fat, while his shoulders and thighs were so powerful that he could, without any difficulty, throw a 200 kg sack on his back and run on board a ship with it over a moving and steep gangplank. He earned good money, enjoyed life and was already thinking of marriage when suddenly a friend with whom he had used to work started chatting over a pint of beer.

'Hans, are you making enough?'

'What do you think? Find someone stronger than me in the docks.'

'The docks aren't everything. People do have better jobs.'

'What do you know? Who does better than a docker?'

His friend smiled indulgently. 'I'll tell you in a couple of days time.'

In fact they did meet again, but this time not at a crowded bar, but in a quiet, empty corner. They chatted about trifles when suddenly the friend changed his tone of voice and asked quickly:

'How much do you earn a week?'

Hans gave a pretty high figure.

'Well, I make four times as much.'

'Are you mad? Who'll pay you that much?'

'Why should anyone have to pay me? I'm self-employed.'

In the course of a long conversation Hans found out that his friend had not been working for some time now, but had turned his hand to something rather more lucrative: burglary. So far he had only worked on private flats, but he had become bored and had decided to take up safebreaking. He had already gained some experience, but he needed a partner. This was where Hans came in. First of all he would have to get his hand in on flats before moving on to bigger things.

Hans's first reaction was to take offence and reject such a proposition. He was honest and felt that stealing from others was disgusting and unworthy of a working man.

He parted from his friend on rather cool terms. He continued to work on the docks, but his wages no longer delighted him. His tempter's words continued to ring in his ears: you could earn four times as much.

He finally allowed himself to be persuaded to go on a small job. They were to 'do' the flat of a wealthy businessman. His friend assured Hans that the businessman was insured and would never even feel it.

It went well and Hans got his 'cut', which was considerable. His friend had spoken the truth: it really was possible to earn very much more than labouring in the docks.

The first job led to another. Again it was a success. He had not yet officially handed in his notice, but was turning up less and less frequently at the docks. As his income rose, so did his scruples diminish. He finally left the docks, he was now earning more than enough and got on well with his friend. He became a burglar.

His scruples returned when he made his first slip and landed in the hands of the police and later in gaol. He swore fervently to himself that it would never happen again, but when he was released and tried to get a job, he found that every door was closed for him. That is every one, except for those he opened himself secretly at night.

Society had disowned him and Hans realized that a return to normal life would require years of hard and poorly-paid work, much humiliation and heroic determination. He had never been a hero and never considered himself one. He met his friend again.

The years passed and their fortunes were mixed. They learnt to use oxy-acetylene equipment to cut into safes and learned every secret of the trade. They made a number of famous raids, which brought them renown in the underworld, but they were well known to the police and went to prison many times. Things were getting hot for them in Latvia and they were on the point of taking themselves elsewhere when fate decreed that they were again caught for some minor offence and invited to spend some time at government expense.

One misfortune leads to another. While Hans, comfortably installed in his cell and lacking nothing, was calmly waiting for his sentence to end, there was a coup in Latvia which resulted in authoritarian government. The new leaders copied many things Nazi, among them their law on recidivism. Many faces suddenly lost their ironical and self-confident smile and no less Hans's.

The war came bringing with it Soviet occupation. Life in prison was tough, but experienced people somehow managed. Suddenly the frontier wavered and was broken by German tanks. A new occupation began.

At first not much changed, but after a time the Nazi authorities began to call upon the local population, which included a large number of Germans, to opt for citizenship of the *Reich*. They promised many advantages and held up German power and victories as bait. News of this travelled everywhere. Prison inmates were also informed of their right to choose and they were assured that they would go to Germany where they would become free people.

Hans yearned for freedom and anyway he was not very patriotic. His name sounded a bit German and so he signed on.

'Would you believe that that son of a bitch, Hitler, fooled us all? None of us was free a single hour. We were brought to Germany, sent off to various prisons and later camps. The only advantage for me is being an *Ehren-Häftling*, the devil take it.'

Capo Adam hated Hans from the outset, but this time he had to control his villainous temperament. Firstly, in case of any trouble Hans could simply strangle him and probably not suffer for it and secondly he was a safebreaker.

This second circumstance clinched matters and put Hans quite above Adam and even made him untouchable for the *Capo*.

The ill-informed outsider might well imagine that only normal life produces hierarchies, social distinctions, career structures and diplomatic protocol, while the underworld is uniform without distinctions. Not so. It is hard to find people more sensitive to status, social respect, fame and titles than common criminals. They are divided into many varied categories, doing many different things, they have their own code of ethics and all without exception respect one iron rule: the king of the underworld is the safebreaker. He runs the society in which he lives, he wants for nothing and enjoys the respect of every other criminal branch, while the young aspiring generation looks up to him as to God.

Hans was a safebreaker, while *Capo* Adam had begun his career as a pickpocket and had finished as a pimp. Self-respecting safebreakers, of whom there were a few in the camp, had no time at all for Adam, although he was the terror of the other prisoners. They were happy to exchange a polite word or two with a 'political', but talk to a pickpocket or petty thief? Never.

It must be admitted that their feeling of superiority and a certain sense of personal pride were justified.

In camp many lived off others, the strongest and most brutal terrorized the weakest, chased them to work, stole their food and beat them. Just such an adept was *Capo* Adam, and precisely because, in the underworld, he represented an inferior breed. No safebreaker would have demeaned himself in such a way. The thought of stealing bread from a friend or striking a human wreck produced only a shrug of the shoulders. But breaking in to the SS stores or carrying out a daring raid in the factory and smuggling a sack of potatoes back into the camp? Ah, that was something quite different.

My relations with Alyosha continued to be friendly and the boy sometimes shared my parcels, but we had to be careful for *Capo* Adam had begun to cast more than one glance in our direction and it was clear that some plan was hatching in his head. He came over to the boy several times and chatted about this and that and once, quite unexpectedly, brought him a bowl of soup and another day gave him an extra blanket. Alyosha feared Adam like the plague and so these sudden signs of interest chilled him even more. Yet what could he do? He looked at me enquiringly a couple of times, but I had no good advice to give him. All I could suggest was patience.

At the very same time Hans made friends with Alyosha. He met him at work, exchanged a couple of words and liked him. The usually unapproachable boy was not in the least frightened of him, for everyone was attracted to Hans. He was always in a cheerful mood and he was always friendly and generous to others. Alyosha felt secure and happy in the company of his broad-shouldered friend, but even his cheerful nature could not dispel the sadness and thoughtfulness from the young boy's face.

Adam continued to nose about Alyosha and do him little favours. He let him off sweeping and bringing coal and allocated him a better bunk, a single one on the top tier. The camp was dreadfully crowded and we usually slept two to a bunk. These moves reduced the boy to a state of constant fear. He relaxed only at work under Hans's eye.

Knowing that *Capo* Adam was interested in Alyosha and observing the boy's friendship with Hans, I expected trouble and feared that it might all fall on the luckless boy. There was no question of trying to influence the gangster, while Hans was no diplomat, had no time for Adam at all and so his response to all this might do more harm than good. I whispered to him in passing that *Capo* Adam was throwing his weight around a little too much in our hut.

'What's that to me? I don't sleep in your barrack.'

So ended my first attempt, but when Adam increased his attentions to Alyosha, I caught Hans again and again mentioned something about Adam. This time the giant's lazy mind moved a little faster.

'Just let that thief get in my way, I'll show him.'

Several days passed and suddenly Hans decided that he would move into our barrack. His rank of 'honourable prisoner' gave him the right to do this and even Adam's rage could not stop him. He arrived in the evening and sat down on a stool next to the lighted stove. A moment later the door opened again and the camp senior prisoner came in. He was a political, a German Communist, who had been inside for many years and was liked and respected by everyone. He went over to Adam and had a few words with him. The *Capo* yelled and curses fell from his lips. This had no effect. He had to give way and made one of his subordinates show Hans to a bunk. It was a single one, on the first tier and near to the stove. Hans clapped the junior trusty on the shoulder and clambered onto the bunk.

Night fell, the lights went out, the stove died down and men began to snore in the thick air of the crowded barrack.

I must have been sleeping quite soundly when the sharp creaking of a board awoke me. I pricked up my ears. Parcels had been handed out that evening and somebody might be trying to get at the treasure of someone more fortunate. The creaking was repeated and a muffled whisper came to me:

'Leave me alone, get off...'

'*Ruhe, ruhe Junge*' ('Be quiet, boy'.)

I woke completely. It was *Capo* Adam. He was launching his final attack. Poor Alyosha.

The noise on their bunk increased. Other prisoners also woke up and lay there in the darkness, not knowing what to do.

The boards creaked even more, there were now sounds of a struggle and suddenly we heard a quiet sob. I held my breath and unconsciously clenched my fists, when suddenly the bed-boards squeaked from another side, a great body moved and Hans said:

'Quiet there!'

The noises ceased as if cut by a knife. We waited for Adam's reaction, but he said not a word and after a moment the sounds of struggling again came from the direction of Alyosha's bunk.

Hans's bulk turned onto the other side. 'Shut up there, damn you!'

This time Adam apparently realized that he must react, for he screeched, 'Who's that with a lot to say? I'll show him a thing or two.'

'I want to sleep. Shut up, you.'

'I'm in charge here. Silence.'

'Silence yourself, Berlin pickpocket.'

'Who are you then, foreign tramp?'

Hans's bunk creaked violently. 'What did you say?'

'You heard. Verfluchte Russen-Polaken Mensch (damn Russian–Polish creature)'.

The huge body rose and hit the ground with a thud. Hans groped his way over to the bunk where Adam was sitting next to Alyosha on the top tier.

'Get down!'

His only answer was a string of German curses.

We heard a stifled cry of rage and the noise of breaking boards. Someone shrieked in fear and the whole bunk crashed to the floor. Alyosha at the last minute managed to jump onto the next bunk, but Adam was too late and went down with the bunk, landing amidst the wreckage. He instinctively clutched at a plank and struck Hans over the head. In the darkness he missed and only grazed him, but the blow had stunned him giving the German a momentary advantage.

The dying embers in the stove gave out a little light and by it Adam saw the door and made for it, but Hans had come round already and caught him by the jacket. A terrible blow to the back of the head knocked the gangster to the ground. The *Capo* was tough and strong, he struggled not allowing himself to be caught, the darkness made things more difficult and so they rolled around the floor upsetting stools and spilling coal. Eventually Hans caught his opponent in a corner, crushed him with his great mass, put his hands round his neck and began to throttle him.

Adam croaked desperately and it would certainly have been his last moment on earth if the sound of the fight had not woken others up. The door swung open and the camp senior prisoner rushed in with a torch followed by the Senior *Capo*.

They grasped Hans by the shoulders and began to drag him away, but he was in such a rage that they couldn't budge him. Other trusties appeared and eventually they somehow managed to separate the two. Someone put on the light.

Hans was more or less untouched, apart from a large bruise on his forehead. He was breathing heavily and continued to look round wildly. Adam on the other hand lay on the floor and appeared to be in a very bad way. Blood was trickling from his head, his face was blue and his eyes were black-rimmed and closed. He was lifted up carefully and taken off to our sick-bay. The trusties followed him out and for the time being peace returned to the barrack.

I looked down. Alyosha stood by the wall hunched up and sobbing quietly, while Hans, swaying on his widely placed legs, panted next to the stove amidst the scattered coal, broken boards and stools. He had calmed down and looked around normally, almost cheerfully. His gaze covered everything and he saw the sagging boy. The huge body moved and began to force a passage through the debris.

Hans went up to Alyosha, put his huge hand carefully on the boy's head and said in clear Russian, 'Don't cry.'

The huddled body stopped trembling for a moment. Hans repeated, 'Don't cry, Alyosha.'

He turned away, went over to his bunk, rummaged around for a moment in the paillasse, pulled out a piece of dry bread, returned to the boy and handed it to him.

'Here, take it.'

Alyosha trembled and looked up at his friend. He gazed at him for a moment through tear-filled eyes and his tight features began slowly to relax. Suddenly, for the first time in many years a trusting smile, bright as a spring day, spread across his sad face.

It was the smile of a child . . .

Chapter Eighteen

The Last Christmas

We were on the move again. Our motor truck with its trailer, both crammed full of striped passengers, still stood on the parade ground of Neuengamme concentration camp but was due to start at any moment. Every one of us had friends and a sizeable crowd stood around. Taking advantage of its being Sunday and of the SS men's indifference, they called out all the latest news and gossip.

The commander of the transport slouched out of the gate-house. The engine rattled and roared.

'Well, well, look after yourselves. There's no doubt about it. You've got it – couldn't be worse. That Wittenberge is a regular murder-shop.'

And yet, somehow, we arranged things when we got there.

It was a tiny camp, stuck on as an annexe to a system of factory buildings – like a swallow's nest on the verge of a precipice. There were at first fifty prisoners, then five hundred and, after a Latvian transport came, as many as 750 souls. With this figure, it was obvious no more prisoners could be crammed in. The Soviet prisoners predominated in terms of numbers, then came the numerous but sluggish Latvians, then German criminals, with about a hundred Poles at the bottom of the list apart from insignificant groups of other nationalities.

The Camp Commandant, an elderly non-commissioned officer with a fine drunkard's nose, was chiefly interested in pilfering, whisky and girls. The camp was therefore really run by the *Lager Altester*, the senior prisoner. He was called Ole and was a German Communist with twelve years of concentration camps behind him. He was still an idealist and, as most of the other

German prisoners were criminals and the level of the Russians was hopelessly low, he established closer relations with the Poles to secure support in his struggle against the camp authorities' systematic depraving and robbing of the prisoners.

The five score Poles in the camp mostly consisted of village youths who had been sent to Germany as slave workers and then imprisoned, often for the merest trifle. There were a few prisoners of war who had also failed to give satisfaction as forced workers, a small group of elderly craftsmen and a very few educated men who had been arrested in various parts of Poland, undoubtedly for underground activities though none of them ever admitted to this.

Some of the Poles even occupied exposed positions of trust in the camp, not always very honourably. One of them was, for example, Joe, a *Strohkommando** leader, who owed his rank to a brutality in no wise inferior to that of the Germans. He was, however, an exception among the Poles. Most of the others were men who maintained a kindly heart under a mask of unfeeling indifference; such were: Janek, the doctor; Bob, the camp clerk; Anthony, the cook and Henry of the laundry.

The Polish 'hundred' was a fairly harmonious group and its solidarity was even reinforced when the Allies landed in France and the war took a decided turn for the worse as far as the Germans were concerned. It became clear that the Polish prisoners should be very watchful and prepared for every eventuality. They began to organize in secret and with the greatest caution: small groups were formed, each knowing nothing of the composition of the others. They were all determined and ready to defend themselves should the Germans decide to massacre the prisoners, or in the event of anarchy breaking out during the 'finishing-up' confusion.

Quite a separate group were Germanized Poles, citizens of the Third Reich, bearing Germanized names. Though many of them spoke good Polish, they were Germans heart and soul, sworn enemies of all that was Polish. Their leader – for that matter the

---

*This working party had to move bales of straw (*Stroh*) into a factory where it was made into material for prisoners' clothing.

leader of the whole German group – was Bruno Konowski. He came of a family of miners in the Bochum district and was a habitual criminal, with a long experience of many prisons and penal camps. He was *Capo* for all the factory labour *Kommandos*.

Also in a class by himself was Lorenz, a German citizen, but, by his own admission originally a Pole. He was a very strange and cryptic fellow. We had first met him at Neuengamme towards the end of August 1943, right after our arrival from Auschwitz. In fact, he was the first to visit us – officially, as the interpreter of the camp's political department. This thin, long-nosed, partridge-faced type wrote down our personal particulars and at the same time told us in very broken Polish that he was with us heart and soul, that he had worked in the Polish consulate in Berlin, that he had been an agent of the Polish intelligence, that he had already been behind barbed wire seven years, that he would only be too glad to help in any way, and so on.

We were somewhat surprised by this frankness, so unusual in a German concentration camp. Further surprise was caused by the unexpected enthusiasm he developed for the few members of the aristocracy in our group. We all knew what to think of a political investigation department's interpreter but, be that as it may, he really interested us very little.

Then, suddenly, a surprise was sprung upon us. When we were taken to the bath before the medical examination which was to qualify us for the transport, this Lorenz – the leading trusty and the hidden mainspring of this camp – was found to be among us.

We landed in Wittenberge. Already in the lorry he had told us in a whisper that he was going there to reform camp relations – that his mission was a highly confidential and supremely important one. He did not explain who had sent him, whether the SS authorities or some mysterious camp executive. When we arrived at Wittenberge camp, he at once presented himself as the interpreter and later got a job as a *Kommando* leader. We could not even deduce what he was after. As a matter of precaution the principle was laid down: 'Careful with Lorenz'.

Rich in events, the year 1944 was nearing its end. Day after day the air raid sirens moaned and the clear sky was criss-crossed by the vapour trails of countless Allied planes. Page after page was torn off the calendar and winter was close at hand: yet nothing decisive happened on the fronts. 'Christmas in camp', a phrase most distasteful for every prisoner, became more and more of a certainty.

It was one of the traditions of concentration camp life that the striped community received a breathing space at Christmas time. Even during the worst years at Auschwitz efforts had been made to improvise something, to organize a party, and it was the same in the other camps. The SS men left us to our own devices on Christmas day and did not prowl about the barracks.

This year, the state of mind among the prisoners was particularly bad. It was worst with the Poles. Not only had their individual liberty not been restored, but their country was gradually passing from one alien occupant to another. Hopes of rejoining one's loved ones and of returning home became more and more remote, less and less likely. The Bolsheviks became increasingly insolent, whilst the German criminals simply ran amok at the mere thought of possible liberation in the near future. They revelled so noisily that it was difficult to stand it. Every evening, after work, late at night a several-piece 'orchestra' blazed out unharmoniously, wild yells took away sleep, whilst methylated spirits – lapped up in incredible quantities – deprived the rascals of the rest of their wits.

Regularly every Sunday a blasphemous 'service' was celebrated after which a clownish 'procession', with bells and mock priests in flowing robes marched around the quadrangle in a pandemonium of howls, yells, cat-calls and guffaws. The Russians simply reeled with laughter, the Germans roared with delight and we clenched our fists with the anger which we might not show.

Our secret organization functioned cautiously and stealthily. We quietly amassed some leather boots, cigarettes and warm underwear. Janek the doctor prepared a portable first aid outfit. God only knew what could happen on the next day.

Christmas, in the meantime, was coming on apace.

One day Bob, the camp clerk, said to me:

'Well, another Christmas in camp. It's the sixth time for me.'
'Yes. To hell with it all.'
'Listen! What about arranging something?'

At first sight, it seemed an absurd idea, but, after mature thought, I began to find much in favour of it. When the subject was broached to others in the group, they took it up very eagerly. The 'organizers' declared how much food they could contribute, and 'moslems'* licked their chops at the thought of at last filling their ever empty stomachs. After a short discussion it was decided to arrange a joint Christmas Eve party, to which we should invite – for the sake of peace and quiet – a few German functionaries and representatives from all the other national groups.

Ole was there no longer: he had quite unexpectedly been called to the colours to a first line SS formation! His place as senior prisoner was taken by his party and camp chum, Fide, who likewise despised the criminal prisoners and showed much liking for us Poles. Unfortunately, he was duller-witted, had less self control and was easily influenced. Bob, none the less, said our plan would be approved by him.

As a precaution, we found out what Bruno, the leader of the German group, and his gang thought of our idea. They had nothing against it whatsoever. In fact, the Germans were also arranging something, but he would make a special effort to drop in on us for a few minutes, because he always made a point of celebrating Christmas Eve.

We were now quite reassured and began the necessary preparations when opposition arose where it had been less expected. Lorenz suddenly informed Bob that he was withdrawing from the Christmas Eve party because he 'had to protect the rights of the poorest', whose interests were here being ostentatiously disregarded. We were astonished by this attitude: after all, the party had been planned for all whether they contributed to it or not. Moreover Lorenz's role as defender of equality was not only unexpected but even ridiculous.

The little Polish group hummed with indignation. Lorenz's

*See page 126.

opposition was roundly condemned and it was decided to carry on without him. But things did not remain quiet for long. Fide called me in and warned that if I did not immediately stop my 'Fascist' propaganda, he would report me to the SS.

We had a long discussion on the whole subject with the satisfactory outcome that this dangerous zeal was damped down somewhat and that we could identify the real culprit. It was, of course, Lorenz – the man who so recently had still admired the aristocracy but now felt the wind was blowing the other way and had decided to change his attitude to life. Hence his clichés about 'the wronged humble ones', hence his denunciation of me for my alleged political activities.

We put a spell on Fide but the whole plan of a Christmas Eve party had by now lost much of its attraction. In camps careful attention has to be paid even to details, and the situation now began to look very serious. There was provocation in the air and the danger of betrayal at the very threshold of liberation. We were furious with Lorenz, but there was nothing we could do about it.

Janek the doctor and Bob had another shot at winning over the newly converted 'Communist' but he stuck stubbornly to his dogmas and even added some more threadbare catchwords, as old as the hills and enough to make anyone sick.

Well, there was no help for it. With heavy hearts we gave up the planned party. We decided, however, that we should all assemble in our dormitory, where most of the Poles slept, and sing some Christmas carols.

The days passed uneventfully and 24 December came with its long tradition of rite and custom. We worked to noon as usual but were left in camp after dinner and told to clean up. The afternoon was well under way when the 'orchestra' in dormitory number 1 – where most of the Germans dossed under Bruno's eye – began its caterwauling and howling. Soon after, they began their yelling and kept it up until the noise became unbearable. We found out later that Lorenz was at the bottom of it all: he had smuggled in a pailful of methylated spirits and had bartered it to the Germans for cigarettes.

We got through our supper in this disturbing atmosphere and

each of us returned to his sleeping place to think of loved ones – to rejoin, at least in thought, those for whom our tired and desolate hearts longed. It was evening now and the first stars were shining in the cold, foreign sky. The noise in the German dormitory got worse and worse.

Suddenly one of the Poles hastily walked in and ran to our corner of the room.

'What's up?'

'There's going to be a row in a moment. Maybe they're fighting already.'

'But who and why?'

'Lorenz has got the Huns blind drunk and now he's egging them on us. He's howling that we wanted to have a Christmas Eve party only for the Poles and to chuck all the others out into the yard during it. He says the Germans have been insulted by us.'

'What a worm! Well, and ...?'

'They're coming over here. Bruno's roaring like a steer being slaughtered.'

'All of you come to us, right away! We've got to avoid a fight at all costs.'

We went out to dormitory number 1. The door was open as some Bolsheviks were pushing their way in. The 'orchestra' had given up its unequal struggle with the stentorian bawling and roaring of the Germans. The room had been cleared at one end, and a crowd of flushed and excited Germans were milling around Lorenz who was shouting and waving him arms about. At the other end, between the beds, Poles with a few Serbs and Czechs, had got together and were waiting for the outcome.

Just in the same moment Bruno leaped out of his gang. He had only his trousers and shirt on, his face was a fiery red, as if in a fever, and with wrinkled-up eyes he looked at his mates. For a moment he seemed to be listening to Lorenz's frantic yelling and then a sudden thought must have dawned upon his sodden wits. He dashed up to Lorenz and seized him by the lapel of his coat with his enormous fist.

'*Ja, gut – aber bist du Deutsche oder Pole?*' ('Yes, fine – but are you a German or a Pole?')

Lorenz tried to get away and began to stammer something. Bruno shook him like a dog and demanded again, still more urgently, '*Bist du Deutsche oder Pole?!*'

Lorenz tried to wriggle away, but in the same second Bruno slapped his face with all the strength of his powerful arm, leaving bright red marks standing out on Lorenz's livid pasty cheek.

The Germans laughed uproariously and then Bruno punched his victim in the stomach and himself leapt into the centre of the room. With one blow he swept all the pots off the hot stove and sprang at the crowd. Vitek the Serb fell on the floor with a battered head and the others began to defend themselves as well as they could. Confused fighting broke out, luckily, the Germans were all drunk whilst the others were sober, and in less than five minutes the German criminals were fighting each other with savage fury. We seized the opportunity to pull the others out and took them to our dormitory.

It was a frosty night but the iron stove heated the room very efficiently and we were soon resting in the pleasant warmth. We sat shoulder to shoulder around the tiny Christmas tree with lighted candle-ends on its twigs. Every now and again the door would open and a belated chum joined us. On one side, the Latvians stood in a compact group looking reverently at the tree. The Frenchmen, Dutchmen, Czechs and Serbs drew up closer and silence fell on the congregation.

The first carol was intoned – a plaintive, folk melody. In our hearts, as ancient tradition enjoins, God was being born, but the requirements of war are pitiless and so, as on the other evenings, the warning sirens moaned out and the cry of 'lights out'! rang out.

The light went out and the candle-ends gutted out one by one in the black-out.

Over us, in the cold December sky, innumerable flocks of Flying Fortresses with American boys were on their way to Berlin. They could not hear our voices, they could not even know of our existence – but none the less our singing soared with them and added its puny strength to the victorious thunder of their titanic engines.

Meanwhile, Lorenz stood alone by his sleeping place with swollen jaws painfully chewing the food he had amassed.

The 'orchestra' played with vigour and improvised unplanned variations while burglars and pickpockets, dressed up as girls, coquettishly swayed, clutched by the sweating, dirty fists of their unbridled partners.

Chapter Nineteen

Bread . . . Bread . . .

Yesterday I had a good day: I managed to get a place among the thirty going out to work and earned a litre of soup and a capful of vinegar-sour salad and, in addition, I 'organized' thirty-two potatoes and a few salted herrings. Such were the days that had come upon us. Not so very long ago, only a few days earlier, we had been driven to work with sticks and woe to anyone who was caught hiding in the barrack, and today ten thousand starving souls are breaking each other's heads to get into the groups going to work outside the barbed wire.

But this is the end of the war. The last days of April found us in a temporary camp near Ludwikslust where we had been driven during the crazy evacuation. Thus far and no farther – on the one side the Bolsheviks, on the other the Americans – so our escort had unloaded us into some unfinished airmen's barracks and allowed us to wander into every nook and corner. There is no more work but there is practically no food either.

Once a day about three o'clock in the afternoon bread is given out. A loaf is divided, sometimes into eight, sometimes into ten pieces. It works out at about 3–4 oz. each. With the bread: a scrap of margarine or artificial honey. Besides this there is soup but it is easier to get a blow from a stick in the crowd than a pint of swill. The trusties have completely lost their heads, the rest steal what they can and don't give a hang for anyone or anything.

When the shout is raised that the soup is being brought in, ten thousand ragamuffins crawl out of the barracks and move in a stream to the kitchen. Between the barracks and the wire is a broad patch of bare ground and there by rights the queue should be formed but there is no power on earth now which could bring about any order. The famished, weary, desperate crowd pays no attention to blows, and storms the barrels and cauldrons to the bitter end. There is not enough soup for all and besides there is a lack of bowls. In the queue we pair up anyhow, but it often happens that the fortunate possessor of a bowl gets two helpings in it and runs away from his weaker companion. Around the barrels there is a solid mass of bodies: on the one hand those who have not yet had their turn and on the attack, while from the other come madmen, dreaming of a second helping, and at the side lie beaten and trampled bodies.

It is no wonder that under the circumstances not everyone will risk an attempt at getting warm food, but what other hope have they? The camp is not large, surrounded by barbed wire, on it six, brick, unfinished barracks. Once upon a time grass grew around the barracks but the very first day the French grubbed it up and ate it and the rest has been worn down by the swarm of 'moslems'. So the square is bare, trodden down and emptier than the desert. No insect is to be seen there, no mouse runs across it, no passing bird rests there. Every living creature keeps far away from the infected place, where wallows a human mass maddened from hunger.

The only hope is to get work, get out beyond the wire and somewhere, by the trucks or in the woods, find some potato peelings, a rotten turnip or crust of bread.

Yesterday I was in luck. Someone shouted, '*Gemüse holen!*' ('Vegetable picking!') and in the same moment my legs carried me into the centre of the square. By a miracle I managed to keep my place in the first five. Surrounded by a tight ring of the disappointed we moved towards the gate. At the last moment we were in danger for a biggish group of Russians tried to force their way into our ranks and push out the weaker but finally we crossed the borderline of the camp and the gate shut behind the thirty of us.

'Vegetable picking' – can there be any sweeter sound to a man, who considers a rotten carrot to be a treasure and unattainable luxury? We turn to the left, towards the railway line. There stand our three trucks with vegetables, but unexpectedly we see beside them another, much longer, string of red horse-boxes. As we draw nearer it turns out to be a transport of women, also evacuated from some more westerly *Lager*. They are living in the trucks for want of room elsewhere. Our eyes, used as they are to anything, widen in unbelief and horror at the sight of these frightful human skeletons, swarming around the trucks.

'Well, where are your "Gemüse" ', I ask the foreman, a Silesian, who is looking after our group.

'When I tell you there's vegetable there is. And now shut up.'

We go through a glade beside the train. On the right rise some small hillocks, covered with blankets and branches. We approach the nearest.

'Now boys', says the foreman cheerily, 'get this done in a jiffy. *Ein, zwei* (one, two) there's a pot of soup waiting for you.'

We push aside the first branches and stand as if turned to stone. There lie the dead bodies of women, who had died during transport from hunger and lack of air. They are lying piled up like logs: silent, swollen, terrible. Our throats turn dry, our bodies involuntarily want to draw back, but the foreman is already shouting and organizing the work. The three first fives go to the trucks, get spades and go into the wood to dig a deep hole in the clearing. We stay behind to carry the bodies.

The first trips are unpleasant, but soon the disagreeable sensation wears off and our attention is turned to the one problem: food. Walking step by step, not for a moment do we take our eyes from the ground. Watchfully they run from blade to blade, from bush to bush, from trunk to trunk. People were here not long ago, perhaps they have left behind some remnants worthy of our splendid appetites. And at the same time our minds are working feverishly – how to get near to the trucks and snatch a few potatoes or turnips? And the tormenting question: are they going to do us down, will we get the promised soup?

The day however, as I have already mentioned, finished successfully and the return to camp was in the nature of a holiday among my closest friends. But that was yesterday and my memory does not go as far back. Today we are fasting and cold and there is no hope of any new success. We have got through the morning roll-call and are sitting wrapped in blankets in a row against the barrack with our faces turned towards the April sun.

All around wander the clumsy 'moslems', digging in the wet sand or lighting bonfires.

It's true that orders have been given that to light a fire is forbidden and that the penalty for disobedience is shooting without warning, but the times are such that life is stronger than orders – so no one shoots and round the numerous bonfires the wretches cluster, warming their limbs or boiling water with their treasures in it.

This is not so easy as it sounds. The camp is of brick and separated by barbed wire from the neighbouring woods, so after burning all the scraps and the scaffolding, the mob have started to pull out the bits of board which make up our three-storey bunks. There is literally nothing left to sleep on and the sand is damp and dull in the cloudy, spring nights. To get a bowl of water is not easy either for there is only one pump working in the whole camp. It is surrounded by a swarm of unfortunates, standing up to their ankles in mud and muttering plaintively, while a row of well-fed, arrogant youths ceaselessly pump water for their patrons, the various camp trusties.

But even if you've got wood, water and some wonderful treasure to cook, don't think, my lad, that you're well away. Before you start to make a fire, get round you as many friends as you can, promise them a share and organize a guard – because in the camp roam bands of Bolsheviks, who, taking advantage of the lack of discipline, quite simply plunder. Oh, there some wretch has 'organized' a few potatoes and is baking them in a fire. Suddenly he is surrounded by a band of hooligans. One grabs the poor fellow by the collar and with his fist reduces his nose to a bloody mess while the rest trample down the fire and grab the food from the ashes. Just so they saved themselves from dying of hunger, when as *bezprizorni** they covered the boundless distances of their fatherland. Here again these accomplishments have come in useful.

But every country has its own customs. There, from behind a wall, farther in the camp, comes a measured, ceaseless half

---

*Organized gangs of wild, abandoned children orphaned by the fighting in the USSR.

singing, half moaning. Those are the Dutch who have lain down inside a barrack on the sand and all day long sing hymns. One, obviously a clergyman, intones the next one, and the others repeat the refrain together. On unseen wings hovers victorious death and the curves of his flight are ever swifter, ever nearer. Only distance and time can beat him. In the rare intervals of the singing can be heard from beyond the noise of guns and above the woods, time and again, appear dark American fighters.

It is barely ten o'clock and not till three in the afternoon will they begin to dole out the food.

At nearly three. 'Do you know Frank that they haven't brought the bread yet.'

'Eh, don't be afraid, they will bring it. But, who knows?'

Suddenly our neighbour from the other side speaks:

'Hi, look, look!'

We follow his outstretched arm with our eyes. Behind the neighbouring barrack there is gathered a largish group of Russians. They are obviously lying in wait and watching intensely a point beyond the gate.

'Perhaps I don't see right but I fancy they are bringing the bread.'

A moment later it is quite clear that a cart is really approaching heaped high with loaves. We move uneasily. It is still not three, but it is always more agreeable to be sure that the provisions have come and that at any moment in the store room they will be starting to cut our titbits . . .

'What do you think – will a loaf be divided into ten today or perhaps into eight?'

'Quiet, be quiet! Look there.'

The cart with the bread had stopped just before the gate. An air force captain, the *Hauptmann* (commandant for the whole region) and apparently a decent German, is with it in person and is giving his assistants some final dispositions. He is standing in front, immediately behind him stands a small horse and cart with a German trusty on top, the procession being closed by SS men with rifles at the ready. I take another look at the lurking Russians. Their group has grown considerably. They are standing motionless, silent and ferocious. The gate creaks, the barbed wire opens and the procession moves. Involuntarily we make ourselves more comfortable on our bricks, like the audience in a theatre just before the curtain goes up. The cart rolls smartly into the camp.

Suddenly a wild yell bursts out: 'Ura'! The crowd of Russians leaps from behind the barrack and they throw themselves towards the bread. The orderly procession breaks up. The *Hauptmann* jumps to one side and, tearing its covering, tries to get out his pistol. The SS men begin to shoot into the air and the driver has whipped up the horse and races through the yard so that the wheels jump in the ruts.

But it is too late. The crowd of Bolsheviks have covered the cart in a living wave. The bullets begin to whistle louder and several bodies are already lying on the sandy ground, but the attackers pay no attention whatsoever. Anyone who has reached the bread, picks up what he can and makes to fly. The others after him. Frightful howls of *'Dierży! dierży!'* ('Hold on!') mingle with the shouts of the SS men and the noise of shots.

Just near us a young barefooted boy runs by with a loaf under his arm. Fleet as a deer he runs, yet the pursuing band are already on top of him. The boy trips, shrieks, falls, and in the twinkling of an eye the fighting mass has covered him. From underneath the pile of bodies comes a smothered lament: 'Puskaj! puskaj!' ('Let go!'). The heap of bodies rolls over, pants, yells. At last the lament dies down and the fighters get up slowly, leaving behind them on the sand a little blood, scraps of clothing and some trampled and muddy remains which in no way resemble bread.

From other corners of the square come the echoes of fighting, the trample of feet, shots and shouts. At last the noise dies down, the square empties, is deathly still. On the ground remain only the melancholy horse, the overturned cart, the swearing *Hauptmann*, the SS men and a few motionless bodies.

In silence we look on at this very eloquent scene. In one moment our breakfast, lunch and supper have been swept away. The hours of waiting anew seem like eternity and what will tomorrow bring?

Then other sounds attract our attention. Furtively, just above the trees, sneaks past a steel-grey German bomber, while just behind it, with a roar and a whistle, rush the rapacious American fighters.

And when the noise dies down, from beyond the wall, from inside, the monotonous, patient singing of the Dutch reaches us again.

In the intervals we can hear ever nearer, ever more distinct, the noise of guns.

Chapter Twenty

The Return

The first few days after my arrest were difficult for Eileen. Like everyone else she had been expecting it all along; but expectation is not the same as reality. She found it difficult to accept that evening and then night would fall, and there would be no one to wait for, no familiar footsteps on the pavement outside, no friendly voice in the doorway.

Fortunately we had friends who immediately took her under their wing. My good friend Kazio was full of understanding and tact, which prevented his commiserating too much or manifesting facile optimism. He was also deeply involved in our work in an area closely connected with mine, which gave him the possibility of establishing contact with me.

The first message that I had smuggled from prison made it instantly clear that danger was minimal: I had been arrested in place of someone else. If I had been arrested for my own activities, the situation would have been reversed, upside down, and Eileen would have had to go into hiding. As this was not however the case, she could afford to stay in Warsaw. She now had to start endeavours to get me released, although they were only illusory, without hope of success.

Activity is the best cure for depression, so after spending several days in a confused state, Eileen set to work with feverish energy. Kazio was in constant touch with my superiors, and together they decided what steps should be taken first. The target was twofold: to help me as best they could, and at the same time create the appearance of total innocence. Getting anyone out of the clutches of the Gestapo was a pretty hopeless enterprise at the best of times; but they might just succeed in lowering the heat of the investigation when the first thrust of the Germans missed its aim.

The two agents who searched our apartment the day after my arrest told Eileen that in the event of my not reappearing before Easter she should go round to the Gestapo. Caution demanded that she comply with this instruction.

The task was hardly a pleasant one. Everyone who possibly could steered clear of the headquarters of German terror. But Eileen had to go of her own free will, knowing that her husband was up to the neck in 'work' and even now steering a course between truth and fiction. She had to talk to Germans and act the role of injured innocence, though she hardly had what one might call a clean record herself; disguised as it was, her foreign-ness complicated the situation considerably.

Eileen was obviously afraid. But off she went all the same.

She chose an early hour, as she reckoned that Gestapo officers look more leniently on the world at the beginning of their day's work. It was towards the end of April, and the spring sun made the wet asphalt in Ujazdow Avenue glisten.

A short flight of stairs led into the Gestapo headquarters, past the guards on duty at the entrance. The sinister building was seldom visited by individuals unless escorted, so the guards blinked with startled eyes at the slight young woman in specta-cles coming towards them. Despite her fear, Eileen was determi-ned to get inside, so she walked swiftly and hardly even stopped for the armed soldiers.

'*Halt! was machen Sie hier?*' ('Stop! What are you doing here?')

She said she had been instructed to come to room number so and so.

The guard muttered something under his breath, but Eileen was already ascending the steps. She entered the dark hall. Inside was a glazed sentry box with numerous telephones. Some stairs ran downwards to the left, to the right was a black door and stairs leading upwards. Two NCO's were sitting inside the booth. One of them stood up and stepped outside.

'Who've you come to see?'

'I've been instructed to come to room X.'

'Who summoned you?'

'Two gentlemen who visited me before Easter.'

'Their names?'

'I don't know, they didn't tell me. One was tall and greying, the other shorter and dark-haired.'

The NCO's cheek muscles gave a slight twitch. 'Those two gentlemen ordered you to come here?'

'Yes.'

'Why?'

'My husband was arrested and hasn't returned, so I've come here. That's what I was told to do.'

'It's all a lot of nonsense. We don't arrest people. Please leave these premises.'

'But I was told to come and . . .'

'*Rrrauss!*' ('Get out!')

There was nothing to be done. Eileen turned round and began slowly to descend the stone steps. She was overcome with a feeling of stunned helplessness. What weird sort of institution was this, where some people were dragged by force, while others who come of their own free will are kicked out. As she passed the guards, one of them tried to make an overture and uttered a crude joke, but she quickened her pace and an instant later was back in the Avenue.

She sat down on a bench beneath the old, rustling trees, and tried to collect her thoughts. So her mission had failed. She had barely reached as far as the front vestibule, and had spoken to no one; and it had all cost so much nervous energy. Give up? No, start again from the beginning.

She rose from the bench and set off in the direction of the nearest tram. As she passed by she glanced again at the Gestapo building that was visible through the trees. She would have to come a second time, though probably when the fighting in the Ghetto was over. The Germans would calm down a bit by then, and it might be possible to talk to them according to plan.

The next few days were taken up with waiting for a smuggled message and preparing the two parcels she was allowed to send me at the Pawiak. The first, consisting of a few garments and underwear, could be sent once only. The second, containing food, was permitted only once a month and always posed considerable difficulties. Its weight was not to exceed five kilos, so all the foodstuffs had to be high in calories and easily preserved. One needed the advice of someone with practical experience; but that was no problem in occupied Warsaw, and the parcel was ready in a matter of days. It contained lots of slices of dark bread fried in fat, several onions, salt, sugar, bouillon cubes and two tins of condensed milk. The capital city was pretty well starving, but in cases of necessity it was still possible to track down high quality foodstuffs.

Around the tenth of May Eileen set off once more in the direction of Aleja Szucha. Her previous experience told her to walk swiftly past the two guards. She told them the room number and again found herself in the dark vestibule opposite the glazed sentry box. This time there was only one NCO on duty, and he was engaged on the telephone. When he finished, he replaced the receiver and gave Eileen a questioning look.

'I've been called to see one of the members of staff. He gave me his room number.'

The German stretched out his hand and without uttering a word took the card Eileen that handed him.

'Do you know this person?'

'Yes, he called on me several weeks ago.'

The officer looked again at the number, gave Eileen a wary lookover and reached for a pass-book. 'Your name and surname?'

He lifted the reciever, exchanged a few words in a soft voice and then filled in a small scrap of paper, stamped and signed it and, with a bored expression on his face, handed it to Eileen. 'The stairs are to the right, second floor, corridor to the left.'

Eileen slowly proceeded upstairs. The empty stairway glistened with cleanliness. Contrary to her expectations all was quiet and deserted throughout the building. It was hard to believe that this was the headquarters of the mighty Gestapo which already had so many victims on its conscience. The bright corridor was likewise empty. A long row of doors stretched ahead, each one was numbered. Eileen reached the door she was looking for and paused for a moment. After an instant's hesitation she overcame her fears and knocked.

'*Herein!*' ('Come in!')

She entered and took in the bright, spacious interior at a glance. A large portrait of Hitler in party uniform hung on the wall. Light flooded in through the two windows, where two men sat at their desks. She went up closer and then recognized their faces. They were the same two agents who had carried out the search the day after my arrest.

'*Gut Morgen.*'

The men rose, replied to her greeting; the elder of them pointed to a seat.

'Kindly be seated. What may we do for you, *gnädige Frau?*'

'You instructed me to come here. My husband was arrested and has not returned.'

'Aha. His name?'

Eileen replied, but the older, greying agent could not remember what it was all about. The younger one, who had dark curly hair, remained silent, but smiled imperceptibly and gave a slight nod of the head.

'And we ordered you to come here?'

'Yes, if my husband didn't return before Easter.'

The greying officer tapped his fingers on the desk, had a quick think, then finally stood up and went over to an iron safe. He pulled out a cardboard file and returned to his desk.

'That figures. Your husband's in prison.'

'But where was he arrested, and what for? In the street?'

'We never arrest in the street, please remember that. And we know exactly what he's in prison for. That file is full of evidence.'

'My husband is innocent, and you promised he would return.'

'We promised nothing, and as for his innocence, that file tells a different story.'

'So what am I to do?'

'Nothing, just wait. There's a war on. Whatever do you imagine?'

The conversation at the Gestapo ended the way she might have expected, but Eileen, though prepared for it, experienced a certain sense of disappointment. The nervous effort, which could not be measured in terms of her short visit to Aleja Szucha, had quite exhausted her, and the bulging file the agents had shown her caused her considerable alarm. For sure, my secret messages made it quite clear that the Germans knew nothing about me, but could she take that literally? I might after all have written just to cheer her up and prevent her getting upset. In moments of depression she sought consolation from Kazio, and he never once let her down. He had plenty of problems of his own, working hard from dawn till late into the night, but he always found a spare moment for Eileen and had the knack of keeping a discreet but affectionate eye on her.

'I feel so bad that I've got nowhere. Someone else would have done better.'

'Not at all. Another woman simply wouldn't have gone. You've done splendidly.'

'But what about that file? They said they've got lots of incriminating documents.'

'They're lying as usual. The messages tell quite a different story.'

'Is there anything more to be done?'

'Yes. Your husband was dealing in second-hand clothes, remember. You must trace as many contacts as possible who will if necessary confirm that they received goods from him. And you must look after your own alibi. The agents discovered that you're Irish and that you give English lessons. You must find a couple of people who'll admit to taking lessons and who have their own alibi. It's lucky they've left you in peace so far, but one never knows. Perhaps you ought to change your name and address?'

'No! That would instantly incriminate my husband, and then the Gestapo might really get down to business.'

Kazio screwed up his black eyes and gave a friendly smile.

'You're a loyal companion not only to your husband, but to all of us. When I talk to you I forget that you're not Polish.'

Eileen spent the next few days searching for the contacts Kazio had mentioned. The second-hand dealers were fairly easy to come by. Candidates for English lessons were more problematic; but some were found nonetheless. The solidarity of the fighting nation was quite exceptional at the time.

Eileen received another message from me in which I

informed her that a transport was being prepared at the Pawiak and was due to leave any day, presumably for Auschwitz. We prisoners often preferred to be moved, so as to leave the Gestapo and their interrogation behind; but people outside understood the situation differently and Eileen's heart sank when she heard the news. The Pawiak was after all in Warsaw. The thought that, though inaccessible, I was close at hand, that efforts could be made – that a miracle might happen – gave her the strength to carry on and concealed the real danger of the situation. Deportation to Auschwitz, by then a world famous mass extermination factory where thousands perished daily, shattered all her illusions and opened up the terrifying void of a cold, black, bottomless abyss.

Kazio did what he could to present the news in a positive way, but he made no attempt to conceal the truth. We were living in hard times, reality had to be stared boldly in the face. He had another meeting with Eileen and confirmed that the transport had set out and that I had been taken to the camp together with many others. That day Eileen was feeling particularly unwell, though she had not breathed a word of this to anybody. Some internal pains and giddiness, with a temperature and difficult breathing. Seeing how pale Eileen was, Kazio took her round to his house and entrusted her to his mother's care. His family had been exceedingly well off before the war. Not much was left of their former wealth, but it was still possible to eke out some sort of existence, and their spacious flat, which had by some miracle remained in their possession, gave them a basic backing.

Kazio's mother received Eileen like a member of the family. The bad news about the transport was known, it was late, Eileen felt ill, and was not allowed to leave. She had to spend the night there.

When she finally went to bed after supper at which the conversation had attempted to avoid the subject of present-day realities, she felt that her temperature was rising sharply. She did not wish to alarm anybody, the members of the household had already gone to bed. A dark night had settled over the town. She would have to pull through the long hours alone.

Her whole body was soon in the grips of fever. Her heart was beating faster and faster, her thoughts became confused. For some time she was still aware of being in Warsaw, far from her family and native land, she knew that a war was on, that some terrible people were destroying the land for which she had now developed a deep love. But after a while the images became muddled, entangled, and dissolved in a mist, and Eileen suddenly thought she was in Ireland in the parental home. She had just finished school and was riding along in a bus with her beloved brother Billy, who had died many years previously from a nasty spinal disease. The bus was going through vast green fields, over delightful hills, bridges and streams. Later they were sitting in a boat and rowing through the dark waters of Lake Glendalough. Billy was plying the oars and Eileen leaned back, touching the cool surface of the water with her fingers and splashing water at her brother. Suddenly a gale blew up and Billy lost the oar. He leaned far over the side, tried to grab it and lost his balance. Eileen leaped forward and seized her brother's hand, but a wave capsized the boat and it was too late for help. Billy fell into the water and vanished beneath the surface.

Eileen sat up in bed and cried desperately.

'No, no! Stop!'

Billy's body surfaced for an instant – but no, his face was completely altered. It was not Billy, it was someone else, someone equally dear, someone in the cold grips of danger.

Eileen caught her breath with difficulty and again called out into the void. 'Come back, come back! Stop!'

Eileen's breathing was accelerated, her pulse was pounding away, but providence was watching and summoned a new image.

A quiet summer evening in the Polish countryside. We are walking together through the fields, touching the drowsy ears of wheat, listening to the subtle music of the dying day.

Her breath subsides, the pulse slows down its lunatic pace, sleep falls like a mist . . .

The doctor who was called in next day was unable to give a precise diagnosis, but recognized that the state of the patient called for care and caution. He prescribed some medicines and gave an injection that had the desired effect. Her temperature dropped, and it remained down.

Eileen ought to have spent several weeks in bed. So as not to betray that she knew about the transport to Auschwitz, she had to deliver another parcel to the Pawiak. In the event of it being refused, she would have confirmation of the news. She had no alternative but to rise from her bed, track down some foodstuffs and set off for the distant office where ladies from the Patronage of Care for Prisoners took in parcels, women of exceptional kindness and self-sacrifice, whom the Germans for some reasons tolerated, and who would willingly have accepted any weight, had it not been for the Gestapo officer on duty who weighed all the parcels in his hands. Whenever he had the slightest doubts he ordered them to check the stipulated limit, and overweight parcels were ruthlessly rejected. Parcels could only be taken once a month, so the penalty was keenly felt.

Eileen somehow dragged herself to the office and took her place in the queue, but when her turn came up the parcel was refused. That meant Auschwitz for sure.

All that now remained to be done was to wait for my first letter from the concentration camp. There was no other source of information, as the Germans did not trouble themselves to inform the family of the whereabouts of an arrested man.

Eileen did not give up our small flat. She was still registered there, but she lived at Kazio's place together with his mother and two cousins, teenage boys under the care of a distant relative. It was a large flat, so there was plenty of room for everyone.

The atmosphere of a family home, the discreet care and kindness that Kazio's mother manifested at the least opportunity, and his own constant attention, meant that Eileen soon recovered her strength. The Home Army headquarters handed over my army pay regularly, and she eked it out by giving English lessons and even extended her contacts. She also devoted many hours to English translations on behalf of the authorities of underground Poland for the use of London.

My first letter from Auschwitz arrived at last. I reported that I was well and that we were allowed to receive food parcels in any number. The war was already in its second phase, and the Germans realized that they could not afford to destroy people mindlessly when their hands and brains could be put to use. As they had no food supplies to hand out, the families could chip in.

My letter caused great joy and set Eileen a task to which she devoted herself wholeheartedly. Three times a week she went round to our flat, kindled a fire, and baked cakes which she later packed carefully together with other foodstuffs and took round to the post office.

Who among us Auschwitz survivors will ever forget those evenings when, dead tired from work we returned to the gloomy blocks and, after receiving the miserable camp food, listened all ears for the guard to shout: *'Pakiete holen'* ('parcel collection') and a little later heard our own number called. We received the grubby cardboard with trembling hands and quickly returned to our corner so as to unpack the treasure among our closest friends. It was a solemn moment, celebrated like a ritual, like a sacrament. Hunger twisted our insides, as slowly and carefully we unwrapped the paper on which we could still feel the touch of beloved hands, the warmth of the family home, and the voice of the free world calling through barbed wires, sentry boxes and frontiers. With incredulity we examined the goods which starving Polish cities had not seen for a long time and which our dear ones had certainly not tasted. Each of us understood that our sisters, mothers and wives were working themselves to the bone, waiting in long queues, selling the remains of their wardrobes and suffering hunger so as to send us the choicest bits.

As well as Eileen's parcels I also received food from my mother (with what sacrifice on her part) and one of my aunts, so I was supplied in right royal style and, if I survived, it is certainly mainly thanks to their help. Although she was working extremely hard, Eileen was fortunately enjoying a tolerable standard of living. She lacked for nothing in Kazio's house. Kazio also gave her some money which was supposed to be the percentage from our joint business concern, but simply came from the remains of the capital he owned before the war.

The exchange of letters, which camp regulations allowed one to send twice a month, an endless stream of parcels to despatch, work from dawn till night – this life absorbed Eileen and sometimes enabled her to forget about the creeping pace of the days.

The days and months went by. At one point my letters stopped reaching her, and several parcels were even returned. My letter to the effect that I had been transported from Auschwitz to Neuengamme near Hamburg put an end to her worries. My letter gave no information whatsoever about the new camp, but our friends recognized that the change was to our advantage, as anything worse than Auschwitz was hard to imagine. After a period of depression Eileen felt much more cheerful.

The Germans were still arrogantly ruling the roost, but their situation was looking bad on all fronts. In Italy the Allies were forging ahead and a Polish corps was fighting there; a fact of which people in Warsaw were informed. Soviet divisions had already entered the eastern provinces of Poland, when the long awaited news struck with hurricane force from the West: on 6 June 1944, the invasion of France.

Warsaw, which had lived in a pitched state of excitement for years, now looked like a kettle full of boiling water waiting to explode. Eileen obviously sensed the general excitement and shared in the moods of the great city, but not for one moment did she alter her routine of many months' standing. Every week she sent off three parcels to me, every day she gave English lessons and translated difficult texts.

No one in Warsaw knew at the time that the letters addressed to barrack 'W' at the camp in Neuengamme were in fact delivered to me at a sub-camp in Wittenberge, where I was working with other Poles who had been deported to do forced labour. They were quartered in a special barrack and had little freedom of movement, but at least it was better than concentration camp.

I made friends with one of these Poles, a young farmer called Stanislaw Jeleń, and he agreed that I should avail myself of his right to send letters to Poland. To be on the safe side I would sign his name, but I did not doubt that Eileen would recognize my handwriting. I also decided to send the letter to the address of one of our friends, who was bound to be in touch with her. The issue was of paramount importance: if the contact succeeded, it would lead to an attempt to escape.

The letter reached its destination and Eileen, quivering with excitement, showed it to Kazio. It was phrased with great circumspection, resorting to figurative speech, but was fully comprehensible, and within a few days the ball started rolling. Kazio sprang immediately into action.

'I've obtained permission from my superiors, I'll see to this matter without delay. We have to organize his escape.'

'But what can be done? And what are the chances?'

Eileen was literally shaking with excitement.

'I can't say for sure. The most important is that we have the address in Wittenberge. The letter was written on the form used by Polish workmen in Germany. That speaks for itself. You must write back immediately and when you receive confirmation, one of my people will go to Wittenberge. But no one must know about this, not even my mother.'

When my second letter arrived, it was clear that an attempt at escape could be made. To get out of the heart of the *Reich* without papers was virtually impossible, so Eileen gave Kazio my photograph in officer cadet uniform from 1935, the only one she had. There was some trouble over this, but a couple of days later a *Volksdeutscher** identity card was ready. Additional documents were made out for a workman returning from Germany to Poland on leave, and Kazio's experienced courier, with a false-bottomed suitcase, set out for Wittenberge. Eileen was in such a state of excitement that she found it difficult to perform her daily duties.

Over a week went by, and a downcast Kazio brought the news that the courier had disappeared, having probably fallen into the hands of the Germans. Eileen lowered her head and shut her eyes for an instant. Bad luck again, and that terrible feeling of helplessness and debility.

Kazio gently touched her arm. 'Please don't worry, my man may return yet. And if he fails, we'll make new documents and then Karol, my deputy, will go, he's a hundred per cent reliable.'

It was by now the second half of July 1944 and the Polish roads were groaning under the caterpillars of Soviet tanks. The front was approaching and the Germans, first stealthily and then quite

*See page 76.

openly began to depart from Warsaw. Government offices fled, the number of police dwindled. What remained of once-proud front line troops dragged along the streets.

Eileen, together with other members of the household, was busily involved in collecting food and organizing the communal kitchen, but she did not give up teaching English or sending me parcels for one moment. The day came however when the post office refused to accept her parcel.

The postmaster handed back the last carton and said, 'I can take it if you like, but it's a waste of food. It won't get there.'

Eileen returned home, unwrapped the parcel and had a good think. What had happened to Karol? Had he reached his destination, and succeeded in establishing contact? What were the chances?

Kazio's mother asked her not to go back into the street, so they both busied themselves about the kitchen. There were plenty of provisions that had to be sorted out and packed separately.

Several days went by and suddenly, on the first of August, the door jangled and a breathless Kazio rushed in. He gave his mother a hug, then went up to Eileen and put a strong arm round her shoulders. 'Karol has returned, but he failed to establish contact.'

An instant later he added, 'It's too late now. The Uprising begins at five.'

The first days of the fighting in Wilanowska Street were fairly quiet. The Germans were shooting from Poniatowski Bridge, but intermittently and off the mark. One could move about quite freely, although in the gaps between the houses one had to run. A small Home Army detachment was located in the lower part of the street and Eileen went over one morning to see what was going on.

She was not far from the river when a man suddenly emerged from a doorway wearing an armband with the letters KB (*Korpus Bezpieczenstwa*, Security Corps). He stopped her and began to question her, and on hearing her foreign accent decided that she was *Volksdeutsche* and assumed a menacing tone. Eileen's explanation – that she was Irish, and had documents to prove it – was of no avail. That first week of freedom would no doubt have ended tragically had it not been for a young girl with a smattering of English who happened to be passing by. The girl confirmed that Eileen's accent was above reproach and the zealous patriots left her in peace. Eileen was thoroughly shaken when she reached home, and had tears of indignation in her eyes.

A few hundred yards away, by Czerniakowska Street, was a social security office that had been converted into a hospital. It had to be equipped, so the inhabitants of the neighbourhood availed themselves of the temporary lull and began to explore the abandoned German apartments and collect things that soon accumulated into a pretty substantial store. Care of the store was entrusted to Eileen. Fierce fighting had already begun in adjacent districts, but Wilanowska was not yet affected, and had not yet suffered any human losses.

More and more dark clouds of smoke were swirling above the fighting city. The fire of hand and machine weapons increased, deep and heavy cannon blasts were heard time and time again. German planes appeared above the houses with blasts of exploding bombs.

The fighting came closer and swept into Wilanowska Street. A communal kitchen began to operate, where soldiers and civilians lacking their own supplies could be fed. The Germans began firing with heavy mortar, the first victims fell, there were many wounded, and deep fissures appeared in the upper storeys of buildings. Eileen remained in charge of the stores and took care of the wounded. Several years previously she had done a year's practical in a hospital, so she had the necessary experience.

Information from other districts was meagre. The radio was listened to, but news was often conflicting. Help was expected from the West, operations on the other side of the river were monitored, while the general mood fluctuated between extreme optimism and a vision of total catastrophe.

A month went by and the situation began to deteriorate drastically. The insurgent detachments, ill-armed and without ammunition supplies, were unable to put up resistance to the superior equipment of the Germans. News got round that the

Old City had fallen, and this was confirmed a few days later by soldiers who had reached nearby Czerniakow from the ruins of the defeated district. The line of German fire was again approaching and the number of killed and wounded rose every day. A provisional hospital was set up in the cellars, where the civilian population not involved in the fighting had also taken refuge. There were no grounds whatsoever for optimism.

Suddenly, in the middle of September, hearts began to beat louder, as news spread among the fighters district that detachments of General Berling's Army* had crossed the Vistula and were coming to assist the insurgents. Some were euphoric at the news, expecting that victory would soon be theirs. Others gave it no credence, but changed their minds when several young boys in Polish uniforms appeared in Wilanowska Street. They were genuine soldiers who had crossed the river in a battalion but had lost contact with their commanders. They were given a heartfelt welcome, and further landings were expected, but the eastern bank of the Vistula fell silent and optimism began to peter out.

Almost the entire street was in ruins by now; but that was not enough for the Germans. Rapacious dive bombers began to appear in the azure and started plummeting down, filling the air with their screams and pulverizing the remains of walls. Hopes rose once more when the powerful American squadron of 107 Flying Fortresses hung high above Warsaw and containers swung on parachutes, but it was too late to alter the fate of the burning city.

In the evening of 20 September the last detachment of the Home Army came off the street; and next morning several men emerged from a cellar bearing a white sheet. There were many wounded underground, together with civilians, women and children. Help was needed for them, they had to be given the last possible shelter. Kazio's mother and Eileen were tending the wounded.

Many long minutes went by, when heavy footsteps thundered on the pavement. Someone gave a cry of despair, a volley of machine gun fire rattled, bodies fell with a dull thud. A few more instants passed, and a strong hand opened the door.

*The Polish Communist Army under Soviet command.

'*Raus, raus*! *Hände hoch*!'

The terrorized people slowly began to emerge into the courtyard. The stronger supported the wounded, women held the children close. As they emerged they were greeted by the grim, threatening faces of the SS men. The gashed concrete was covered in fragments of bricks, rubble and untidy heaps of sprawling bodies.

Eileen stood in a small group together with Kazio's mother and a couple of other women. The SS men looked their beggarly captives over with cold eyes and carried out a peculiar sort of selection. Anyone who looked like a soldier or was wearing an armband was dragged out against the wall opposite and was shot on the spot. Eileen's ten-year-old liaison boy Janek died in this manner only because he was wearing his scout's uniform; a nurse with a Red Cross armband was likewise killed. An SS man also went up to Eileen, looked her over and pushed her away. Only then did she realize that her armband was in her trouser pocket, where it must have slipped in the confusion of the last few hours.

The survivors were ordered to form a column. The soldiers walked round the ruins once more, peered into the cellar, climbed up what remained of the stairs and finally gave the signal to depart. A long snake of crippled and exhausted people slowly set off.

Thick, dark stacks of smoke covered the town. The sound of machine gun and cannon fire combined with the hiss of the flames that raged all around and devoured the remains of such buildings as were still standing.

The sun was hidden by the smoke, the wind struck up, the sky was blue, alien, distant . . .

Kazio's mother and Eileen were transported to a large camp for civilians near Warsaw, from which they managed to escape thanks to an acquaintance of theirs, a nurse, and a decent German doctor. They were helped by kind people and survived the next few months with some distant relatives of mine.

Winter came, and on 12 January, when no one was expecting it, the Soviet front suddenly launched its offensive.

It was by now Eileen's tenth year in Poland. In those years she had known it in a period of development, progress and freedom. She had lived through the German Occupation, and had come to love the people engaged with her in the fighting; and she was now the witness of a new invasion. She viewed the glum Soviet soldiers with alarm and incredulity, wondered at their primitive equipment and the chaos they created wherever they went. The local population greeted them stone-faced. Eileen understood full well what the Poles felt in their hearts. She was choked with shame and pain, and burning tears of humiliation and helplessness rolled down her face.

Eileen and I had realized from the start that a Soviet occupation of Poland was likely. In that case, we had agreed, if separated by the war, we would both try to head for the West, and would try to contact each other through her mother in Wexford, Ireland. This Eileen now hoped to do. Travelling westwards, she found herself in Czestochowa and there, quite by chance, came across some British prisoners of war who had been liberated by the Red Army.

In a few words she explained who she was and how she came to be here; she had her birth certificate concealed in her underclothes. She was informed that in a few days' time a large transport train would be setting out for Odessa, and decided to join the prisoners of war on it by hook or by crook. Captain Frewen, an Irishman, interceded; and a Soviet officer gave his approval.

Two thousand soldiers were taken in lorries to Katowice, where they were loaded onto freight trucks with bunks and iron stoves.

Seventeen officers of different ranks and from different parts of the empire were travelling in the truck. They installed themselves as best they could, and Eileen occupied the middle of the carriage and spread out her paillasse. She was in a perfectly exceptional situation. She had lived through the siege of Warsaw, the entire occupation and the uprising, and had thus witnessed things the existence of which she had never even suspected. But here, in the train, she came into contact with a reality that in spite of all her experience was a complete novelty.

She was surrounded by men who had been condemned for

years to male company in the isolation of prisoner of war camps. They had already told each other all their jokes, looked at every possible kind of photo a thousand times and more, analysed and dissected every hour of their previous lives, dreamed endless dreams of unexpected encounters, joyful returns and a rosy future. And now they were suddenly cooped up again in a confined space, but this time in the company of a woman. Admittedly she was dressed in rags, without a trace of make-up on her face, her hair had not seen the hairdresser for a long time; but the very sound of her voice, her every movement, and glance, seemed different, fascinating, enchanting.

Foolish male pride prevented their showing their feelings, they were ashamed in front of the others, but from the first instant each tried to come close to Eileen and help her in some small way. Every day someone cleaned her shoes and looked daggers at his neighbour, who was waiting for his turn. She was being constantly plied with cigarettes and chocolates on the quiet. While some with an indifferent expression showed her their faded photographs, the younger ones tried to deserve her smile with shy jokes. The situation was not easy for either side, yet a *modus vivendi* was somehow worked out thanks to the natural sense of comradeship that characterizes the British.

Near Cracow the train was involved in a collision and in one of the carriages eight NCOs were killed; afterwards it proceeded through Przemysl, Lwów, Koziatyn (where my family came from) and Zmerynka to Odessa without any further obstacles. It was the end of February–beginning of March; a hard winter was still holding good. From the small windows of the train the countryside seemed poor, deserted, gloomy. Railway stations were mainly in ruins, towns burned and dirty, the local inhabitants intimidated and dressed in rags. The effects of the war were everywhere to be seen.

The transport was delayed for several days in Odessa, though the vessel was ready to raise anchor. The city, where the Germans had put up a defence, lay partly in ruins, but even such houses as survived looked pitiful. They had not been restored for many years.

It transpired that some English soldiers had smuggled on

board the train six Russian women whom they had met and married during their spell of hard labour in Germany. The Soviet authorities discovered them among the throng of men, instantly isolated them and forbade them to proceed any further. The protests of their husbands and of the English transport commander were of no avail. For one moment it was touch and go for Eileen, as it was suggested that she should join the women's group, where she would enjoy far more comfortable travelling conditions, but she stoutly refused, and the officers whose compartment she was sharing lodged a protest. This would probably not have had much effect if the Soviet authorities had stuck to their decision, but the situation was saved. The vessels cruising between Odessa and Great Britain were delivering freed British prisoners of war in one direction, and Soviet ones in the other, so that a unilateral dictation of conditions was not in the interests of the latter.

Then at long last the transport was brought alongside the quay number 10 and embarkation orders were issued. Eileen quickly ran up the gangway and looked all round. As the daughter of a sailor, she felt quite at home.

The *Duchess of Richmond*, a large, handsome liner drawing 20,000 tonnes, had plied between England and Canada before the war, and for five years of insanity had carried soldiers over every sea and ocean. It possessed several cannons, sophisticated life-saving equipment, and its cabins had been adapted to mass transport.

The last soldier embarked, the gangway was raised, the siren hooted. It was a cool, cloudy day, a strong wind was blowing, a low heavy sky almost touched the water.

Eileen stood by the rails and silently observed the monotonous grey coastline.

A curtain was slowly descending over a great chapter of her life.

The most talented film producer could not succeed in conjuring up a more striking contrast. After the arrogance and brutality of the Germans, after the dirty Russian *tieplushka,** after the primi-

---

*Goods trucks with iron stoves used for carrying people.

tive chaos of the days spent in Odessa, and the Judas-like proposals on the part of Soviet officials – here suddenly was a great, handsome, modern liner. The deck had admittedly been painted grey, and the interior converted to hold a far larger number of travellers, but that in no way altered the character of the proud liner. The immaculate white of bedding and table linen, the stewards who circulated like ghosts, the great dining-rooms, reading-rooms and drawing-rooms, the pedantic cleanliness, peace, quiet, and self-control, all contributed to a picture that was unique in its way, and stimulating to the imagination, crowded as it was with the nightmares of bygone days. It was not only a question of comfort and luxury, but of being able to breathe freely at last. No one would scream 'Raus!', no one would stand you against a wall and shoot, no one would push and knock one over in the crush, or make a proposal that under the pretence of help could bring death.

The war was not yet over and German submarines were everywhere, so rigorous security measures were essential. Blackout was strictly in force, and each of the travellers on board was issued a life belt, survival rations, and a small red torch with a battery and a bulb. One had to keep this equipment on one's person at all times.

The liner crossed the Black Sea in one day, and dropped anchor for a while at Constantinople. It slipped past Crete, which was manned by the Germans, during the night, sailed round Greece and its innumerable, beautiful wild islands, circled round Italy and dropped anchor in Naples. The number of passengers on board was increased by an intake of several dozen officers sailing from Italy to England, among them over a dozen Polish soldiers of various ranks. When they found out that there was an Irish woman on board who had spent the entire war in Poland, they besieged her on all sides, and none of the Englishmen any longer had access to her. Eileen had to tell them about the German Occupation, about Warsaw, the Uprising. She had to recall the names and surnames of people they asked about with quivering lips, she had to paint for them many times over the picture of a country for which they had been heading for years through snows and sea and sand.

After a week's halt the liner set sail for Malta, thence to

Gibraltar, where it stopped for another few days to wait for a convoy. Sailing in the Atlantic was still very dangerous, as the Germans were sniping to the bitter end.

The convoy dragged slowly along, till the coastline of Great Britain finally appeared upon the horizon. The soldiers returning home from war were choked with emotion. Most of them had suffered from sea sickness; but now they all rushed onto the deck. They clung to the rails, fell silent and peered eagerly through the morning mist. Eileen was among them. Her eyes were moist, there was a tightness in her throat. After ten long years the familiar country loomed in the distance. What news would greet her here, what secrets would be revealed? Was her mother still alive? How were her father and brothers faring?

As it happened, the convoy had slipped across the Irish Sea in the night, and they were now approaching the coast of Scotland. The vessels sailed into the port of Glasgow. The movement of all transports was surrounded with great secrecy during the war, so there was no family waiting to welcome the passengers on the quay. Port officials obviously appeared, and representatives of the security forces. Everyone had to pass through their control. Eileen, together with other civilians, was then taken to a health centre where she spent the night. The next day she sent a letter to her mother, was given a free ticket and caught the train to London. She travelled in the company of a Canadian missionary, who had been a prisoner of war of the Germans.

Once in London she set straight off to the Polish Red Cross, whose address she had obtained while still on board from one of the Polish soldiers. She was carrying several letters that had been entrusted to her in Czestochowa, and had a number of verbal instructions. She also expected to find pre-war acquaintances from Poland.

In the first few minutes she was received indifferently and even with ill will. But when she told the officials where she had come from, the mood changed radically. Everyone wanted to talk to her and ask her questions. She asked for help and was given the telephone numbers of two women friends with whom she had parted in 1939. One of them was working in the Ministry of the Interior of the Polish Government and asked her to call round as soon as possible.

Eileen therefore went round to the Ministry and was immediately caught up in a vortex of Polish concerns. She was the first person to have arrived from Poland following the Soviet invasion, she had spent the entire war period in Warsaw, and had firsthand knowledge of the situation. Before she knew where she was, she was given a job as translator in the Ministry. That way she could be involved with problems that lay close to her heart, and at the same time earn some means of subsistence. A few days later she was put in touch with the Anglo-Polish Society and the League of European Freedom, which were planning a series of lectures in various towns and cities of Britain. Political decisions had been taken and there was no hope that the government of Great Britain would change its political course. But it was necessary to inform English society about Poland's situation and the tragedy that had befallen our country.

Though by nature shy and disliking public appearances, Eileen nevertheless accepted the proposal, as the bonds that tied her to Poland were no less strong than during the fighting in Warsaw. The first great meeting took place in London, followed by an arduous tour of the provinces. Several times a week, in crowded halls, she spoke about the horror of the German Occupation, about the nation that refused to surrender, about the Uprising, the new invasion, and about Poland. She also had meetings with members of Parliament who were opposed to the Yalta decisions.

In the meanwhile she received a letter from her mother, so she sorted out necessary formalities and set off for Ireland. Her mother, together with Eileen's youngest brother, was living in Dublin. Her father had returned to active service and was commanding a vessel, and three brothers were fighting on distant fronts. The eldest, Jack, had died at sea during a trip from Africa to Europe on duty. There was no news from me.

German resistance was on the ebb; and the day finally came when the Nazis asked for an end to war activities. The crowds came out onto the streets of London in their thousands, their joyous cries mixing with the clamour of military bands and the screech of sirens. The bells all rang loud and clear. Mingling with the crowd Eileen did not know whether to rejoice or be sad.

A new cycle of lectures was under way. Returning weary and depressed one evening to her room, she found a letter from her mother with an enclosure – an American field post form covered in my handwriting, in which I reported that I had come safe and sound out of camp and was serving as an interpreter in the American Army, in a tank of the Seventh Armoured Division. Eileen sat down on the bed and experienced at last a profound sense of relaxation and relief.

She immediately replied to the postal number given on the form, and returned to her daily tasks in a totally different frame of mind. We had both been incredibly lucky. Any day now she would receive a letter from me; and we would be able to plan a new life together.

However a week went by, then a second week, and no letter came. Eileen wrote to the sergeant who had lent me his form and postal number, but to no effect. Someone advised her to ask the chaplain of my division for help. The postman at long last delivered a square envelope from the American field post. The pastor reported that I had been taken ill with typhus and was in hospital in Halle; but that as a result of international agreements that region of Germany had been surrendered to the Soviet forces.

Chapter Twenty-one

City Lights

First there was voluntary service, working in the Seventh American Armoured Division and rounding up the last SS men in the woods, then a severe attack of typhus fever, the hospital in Halle and the nursing of the Polish nun, Sister Gerwasia; later there was the last transport from Leipzig, just before the entrance of the Russians, then another hospital in Heppenheim, and finally an ex-prisoner of war camp in Koefertal near Mannheim. For some months there I carried out the duties of interpreter and adjutant to the camp commander. Then, in Darmstadt, in a camp for women soldiers of the Home Army, I met a girl I knew, a friend of my wife's. From her I received confirmation that my wife, who had happily survived the Warsaw Uprising, was alive and living in London.

On the way to England I passed through Frankfurt and Heidelberg, before reaching Paris. Paris was bright with neon lights, full of gaiety and life, and my ill-fitting uniform, handed out from an American warehouse gave me the right of entry almost everywhere. While waiting for the necessary papers I went round the great city. I walked the length and breadth of the Louvre, visited famous churches, looked down onto the tomb of Napoleon in Les Invalides, went up the Eiffel Tower, looked through the plate glass windows of famous restaurants, saw the magnificent parade of the American Forces when they renamed one of the streets after President Roosevelt, searched the walls for marks of the recent fighting and listened to Marlene Dietrich singing for the soldiers.

It all seemed to me unreal. Every few moments I looked behind me, searching the crowd for thugs chasing me with sticks in their hands. Standing before famous paintings I found myself listening for the sudden snorted '*Rrraus!*' At night, in my shabby hotel, I ate dry bread and the remains of American hot dogs with a constant fear that I would be thrown out the next day.

At last there was the train to Dieppe, the stormy channel and the dark railway station at Victoria. I stood on the platform, waiting. Perhaps my telegram had not arrived. I was alone again. The underground railway took me to West Kensington, where I wandered around for a long time before I found the address that Eileen had given me in her letter telling me that she was safe. The lift took me to the sixth floor. I stood in front of the door, on which I had only to knock. I was still ill and felt weak and deathly tired. My breath came in gasps, my heart thumped.

And then I remembered my wife's words, spoken in Warsaw, back in September of 1939:

'I will wait for you . . .'

Waves of memories washed over me. How many of us, how many of the millions of nameless castaways had lived to see this moment, when they only needed to knock at a door?

Had Jurek ever felt the warmth of his mother's hands, had Marian met Halinka, had Staszek found the sister, who had been deported with him, had Jaszka felt the embrace of his son's small arms in the distant Ukrainian village, had Willy stood before the gate of the house where his old mother had waited for him for so long?

And where are all of you, who in those never-to-be-forgotten years, walked beside me on the pavements of our underground city?

My joy faded. What had I done to deserve the happiness of being alive, of being free? What price had I still to pay for the smile of providence, which had allowed me to survive?

I walked down the corridor and looked out of the window. Down below, covered by the autumn mist, great London was spread out, bright with the lights of countless street lamps, whispering to the sound of thousands of vehicles, boisterously alive. Above, in the dark sky, driven by the wind, ragged wraiths of clouds glided towards the East. Over Poland, over Warsaw . . .

It is worthwhile, it is necessary to live.

I turned back to the door and knocked hard.

Epigraph

Dr Garliński now lives in West London. Sadly, Eileen died in March 1990. They have one son who lives in Minnesota, USA, with his wife and two children.